Chinese Painting

Traditional Chinese painting was fundamental
not seek to produce direct copies of the natural
paintings sought to portray the harmony between the natural world and human emotion, evoking ancient Chinese philosophy. From ancient scroll paintings to Buddhist grottoes to modern art, Lin Ci explores the history, theory, and development of distinctive styles of Chinese painting, illustrated throughout with full-color examples of these unique, treasured works of art.

Introductions to Chinese Culture

The thirty volumes in the Introductions to Chinese Culture series provide accessible overviews of particular aspects of Chinese culture written by a noted expert in the field concerned. The topics covered range from architecture to archaeology, from mythology and music to martial arts. Each volume is lavishly illustrated in full color and will appeal to students requiring an introductory survey of the subject, as well as to more general readers.

Lin Ci

Chinese Painting

Cambridge
University Press

CAMBRIDGE UNIVERSITY PRESS
Cambridge, New York, Melbourne, Madrid, Cape Town,
Singapore, São Paulo, Delhi, Tokyo, Mexico City

Cambridge University Press
The Edinburgh Building, Cambridge CB2 8RU, UK

Published in the United States of America by Cambridge University Press,
New York

www.cambridge.org
Information on this title: www.cambridge.org/9780521186636

Originally published by China Intercontinental Press as
The Art of *Chinese Painting* (9787508516691) in 2010

This updated edition is published by Cambridge University Press
with the permission of China Intercontinental Press under
the China Book International programme .

For more information on the China Book International programme, please visit
http://www.cbi.gov.cn/wisework/content/10005.html

First published 2011

Printed and bound in China by C&C Offset Printing Co., Ltd

A catalogue record for this publication is available from the British Library

ISBN 978-0-521-18663-6 Paperback

NOT FOR SALE IN THE PEOPLE'S REPUBLIC OF CHINA (EXCLUDING
HONG KONG SAR, MACAU SAR AND TAIWAN)

Contents

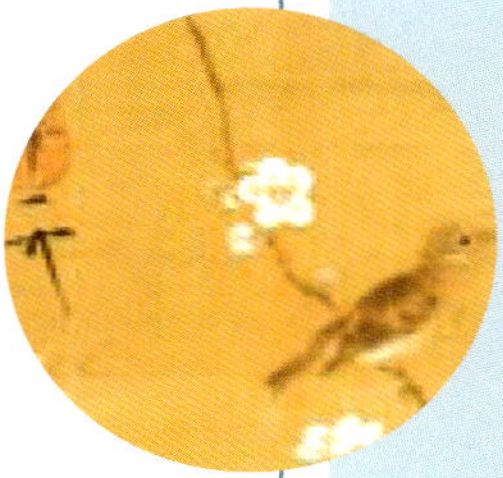

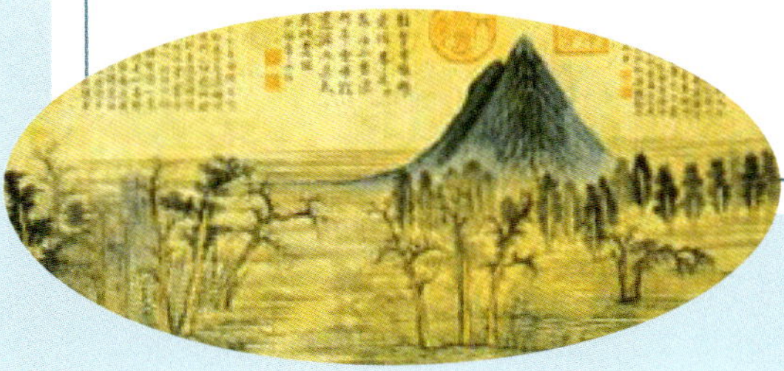

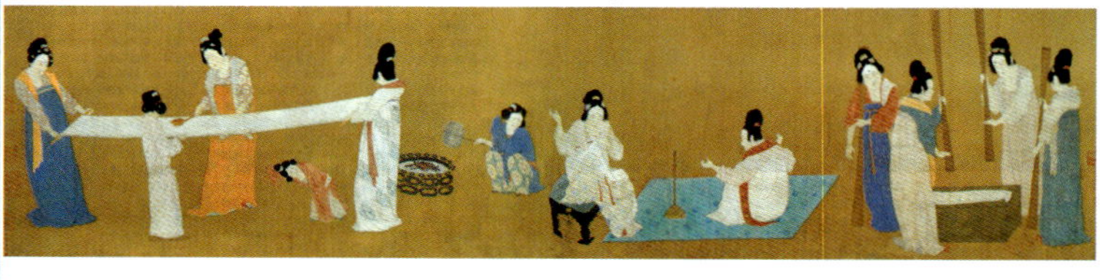

Preface

The Yellow River is the cradle of Chinese civilization. On the fertile lands along this mother river, tribes settled, clans formed, civilization developed, and art emerged. Chinese painting can be dated back to prehistoric times. The earliest such art was found on pottery made by several early civilizations, unearthed in the Yellow River Valley. For example, the Yangshao civilization around 5000–3000 BC was a great and influential society, its geographic area reaching from today's Hubei Province in the south to Mongolia in the north, and it existed in a transitional period from matriarchal to patriarchal society. Cultivation and agriculture were already extensively utilized by this civilization. Fine pottery pieces that survive demonstrate identifying characteristics of their own. The colorful pottery of the Majiayao civilization in the upper region of the river from early Neolithic times, around 3000–2000 BC, is considered to be the finest of that period and achieved an unprecedented level of sophistication. Also important was the Dawenkou civilization in the lower region of the river, around 2300–500 BC, a typical society of the late Neolithic

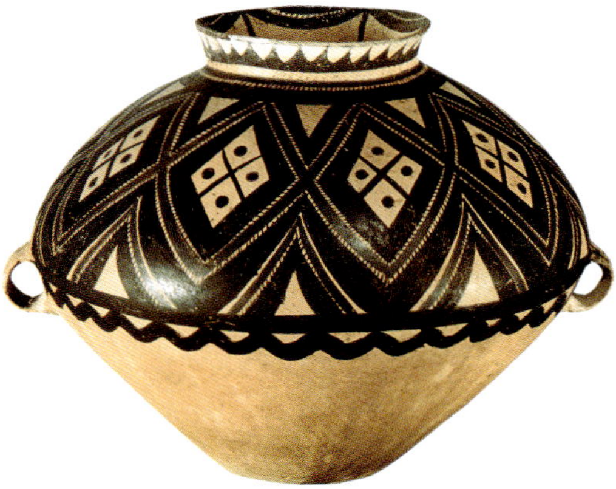

A colored pottery pot, Majiayao civilization, found in Lintao in Gansu Province.

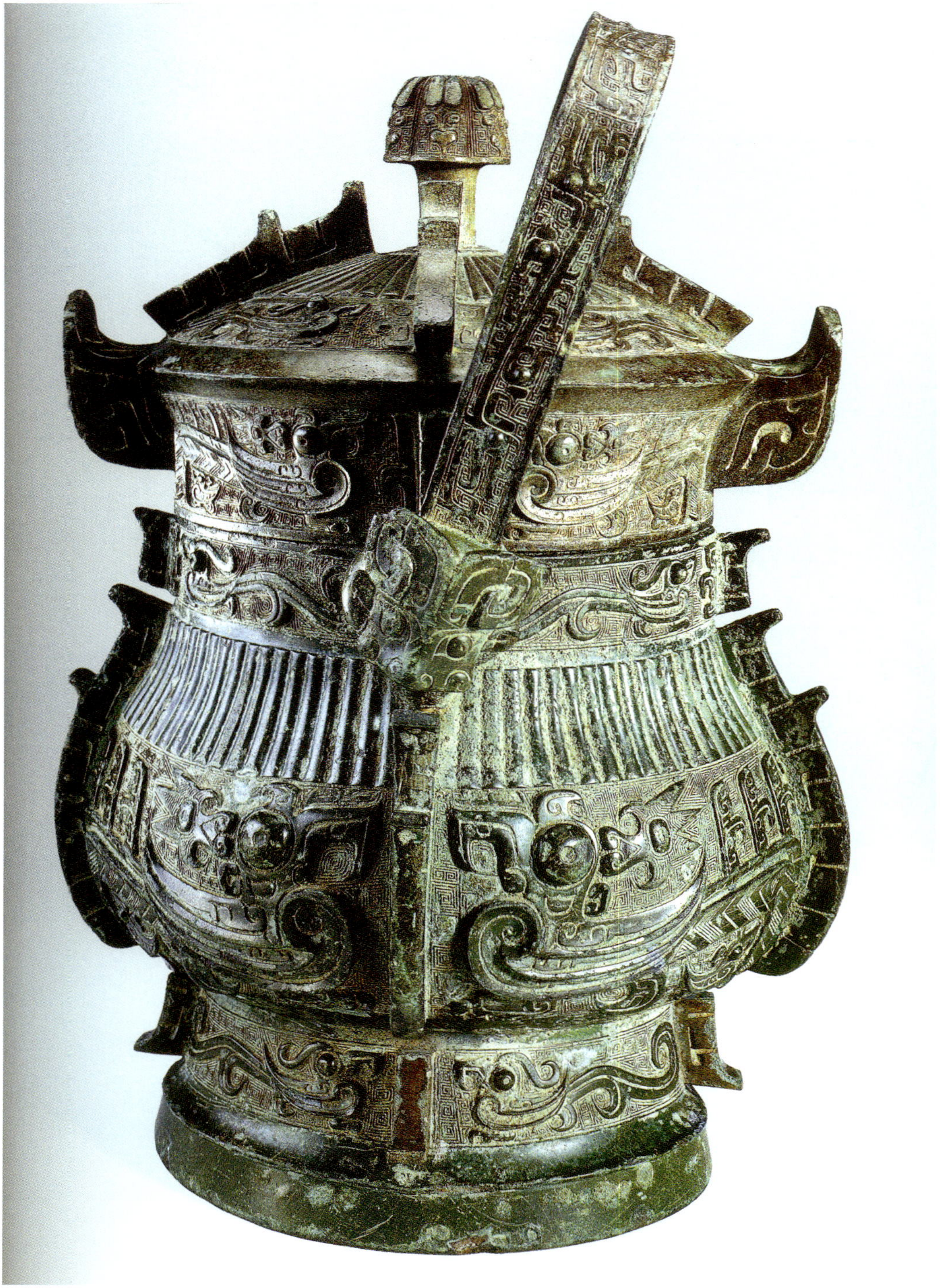

Fuding you (wine cup), late Shang period, (thirteenth to eleventh century BC), height 35.5 cm, internal diameter 26.6 cm, Shanghai Museum.

period. Collectively these groups are called color pottery civilizations, and many pieces unearthed from the sites associated with them have remarkable, colorful painting and patterns. The composition of the paintings includes human figures, fish and insects, birds and animals, flowers and plants, and abstract patterns. The advancement of this ceramic pottery laid the foundation for the development of the Bronze Age, and perhaps foreshadowed porcelain pottery. Ceramics, bronze, and porcelain were all important carriers of the new art form of painting. The artists were anonymous, many of them tribe women who had just settled on the Yellow River and were still considered to be following a craft, so they had a low social rank. Even those with the finest skills and those who served in the imperial court found it difficult to achieve a personal reputation.

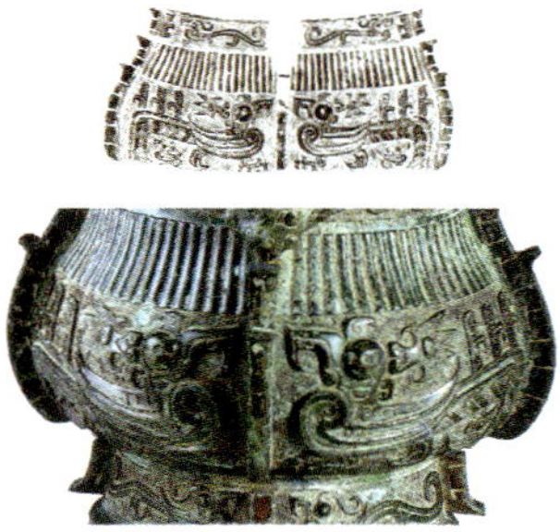

Fuding you (detail).

During the Sui (AD 581–618) and the Tang (AD 618–907) Dynasties, a system of official examinations was developed to select mandarins (scholar-officials) to serve the court. Therefore, an elite cultural class was formed in the early stages of Chinese imperial history. The aim of scholars was to do well in the examination, so they would be selected to become mandarins and achieve their political ambitions. To reach this ultimate goal they first had to read and practice calligraphy thoroughly and extensively in order to become a cultured person and "gentleman." Painting and writing poetry were very important in this endeavor. The greatest Chinese philosopher and scholar, Confucius, said to his fellow students: "ambition must come from truth (The Way); be based on integrity, exercised through kindness, and expressed through the arts." This suggested that integrity, kindness, and art were integral to true greatness. He also said: "A scholar can not be without truth," and "Artistic skill is the nearest equivalent to the truth." This demonstrates a logical, underlying similarity between seeking the truth in a spiritual world and practicing a skill in an artistic field. Thus, the practice of art was elevated to be part of the spiritual process of seeking the truth. For scholars and mandarins, art training was not a simple task just to master a skill but a method to approach The Way (truth).

Consequently, there were two types of paintings: those done by craft painters (usually uneducated) for the sake of art and those by scholars as a part of their training. The latter were part of the ruling class and so spoke for society. Their paintings and books promoted their understanding of painting theory and proper technique. Therefore, they effectively created the criteria by which paintings were judged, but more importantly, because they were more interested in the meaning or theory of painting, they used it as an analogy for seeking the truth. Painting was a means not an end; it was the process not the end product. They judged a painter not only on his technique with pen and brush but also his ability to illustrate he was a great philosopher. From the Song Dynasty (960–1279), gradually scholars came to use the calligraphy of a poem to decorate a painting in order to illustrate its philosophical meaning. The modern artist Huang Binhong (1865–1955) has said that calligraphy and drawing follow the same principle: the key is at the tip of the writing brush. The methods of Han-character calligraphy are fundamental to the techniques of Chinese drawing.

The craft or career painters, even with the very finest painting technique, found that their ability and freedom to express their understanding of painting was limited and controlled by their patrons. They normally painted scenes of real life and religious teaching, including figures, landscapes (mountains and rivers, or *shanshui*), flowers, fish, or insects, primarily for decorative purposes. In contrast, the scholars did not paint to imitate nature but as a way to express their philosophical feelings; mind came before nature. Therefore, their landscapes were not mechanical copies of beautiful scenery, rather the spiritual combination of their mind and nature.

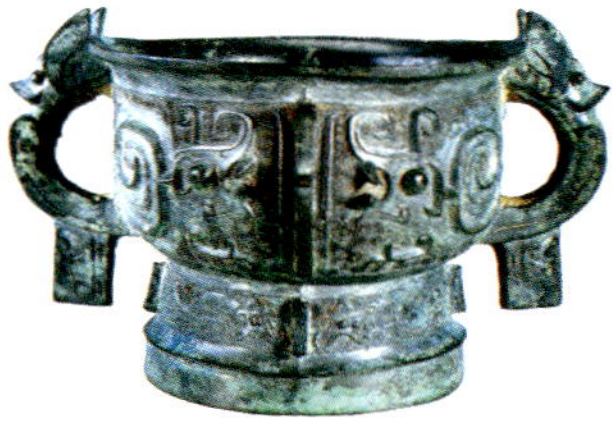

Food vessel with snail shape and beast skin pattern, early Western Zhou Dynasty (11th century BC), height 14.7 cm, diameter 18.4 cm, Shanghai Museum.

Confucius said in the *Analects*: "The mountain fulfils the wise and water gratifies the learned." While not a direct comment on paintings, this did link the beauty of nature to wisdom and knowledge. It had a profound effect on painting aesthetics, and his followers further developed it: "Those who appreciate the beauty of nature are the wise and the learned." This provided a new philosophical meaning to living in seclusion, which was admired by the cultured elite.

Another important system of thought in China is Taoism, and *Dao De Jing* (*The Book of the Way*) is a philosophical work by the founder of Taoism, Laozi. It is also contains important, concise views on painting: "A strong voice appears gentle," "a grand shape looks vague," and "great skill seems easy."

During the Warring States Period (475–221 BC), the king of the Song kingdom invited a group of painters to his palace. Almost all of them were overwhelmed in his presence, stood idle and shaking in the court. Only one was very relaxed and even arrived late, he painted without any hesitation and went home after a routine show of courtesy. The king was very impressed and sent a servant to visit him immediately, who saw him sitting naked at home without any worry or expectation. The king said he was a true artist.

Another sage applauded as a spiritual leader of Chinese artists is Zhuangzi (ca. 369–286 BC), who wrote in *Knowledge Wandering North*: "Nature possesses the best beauty," and he promoted the ideal to "go with nature," "inner tranquility," and "concentrate without distraction." In *An Essay about Tianzi*, Zhuangzi stated that a true painter should not feel constrained by tiny details. He should act according to what he felt in his mind and paint freely. Taoists promoted the philosophy that simplicity was best. Laozi had said: "What you see is not what you learn. That is the way of the world." Zhuangzi had a very similar view: he said in *Heaven and Earth* that "Only five colors dazzle the eyes." According to him (*Constrained in Will*), "Simplicity is essence without disguise." He strongly believed that "nothing could compete with the beauty of simplicity" (*The Way of Heaven*). Both Laozi and Zhuangzi promoted the philosophy of simplicity without the unnecessary "five colors." So "sitting naked" was an illustration of inner tranquility and free spirit. This view inspired freehand painting with ink-and-wash to become the ultimate style of Chinese paintings.

The invention of photography in 1839 caused a panic among many painters in the West, where the primary purpose of painting was to imitate nature rather than express it. They saw an apparatus that could do the job better than they could. Paul Klee (1879–1940) said that art started to express the spiritual world rather than the material from the moment photography was discovered. From the mid-nineteenth century, Western painting started to embark on a new trend of Modernism. Photography arrived in China ten years later but never had the same impact on Chinese painters, although the cultural elite and the ruling class in China admired Western painters for their ability to copy natural objects and use perspective. The royal family of the time, including the grandmother of the emperor, Cixi, had a tremendous curiosity about the newly arrived technology, but they never viewed it as alternative to painting. Traditional Chinese painting was fundamentally an abstract art form: a combination or harmony between the world of nature and human emotion, a product of "heaven (nature) and man." Chinese painters did not try to illustrate the visual effect of colors and patterns as their Western counterparts did. Few were concerned with colors, perspective, anatomy, surface feel, and relative size. They did not want to make a true copy of the natural world, but took elements from it to build their own world.

Chinese artists considered nature to be a subject that they worshiped. They created images to demonstrate the multiplicity of nature, such as remote mountains and running streams. The seventeenth-century German philosopher Leibniz used *Naturliche Theologie* (nature theology) to describe this unique Chinese attitude towards nature. In his *Dao De Jing*, Laozi saw nature as the ultimate force: "Humans are governed by earth; earth is governed by heaven; heaven is governed by *Dao* (The Way); *Dao* is ultimately governed by nature."

This logic of Taoism from humans through *Dao* to nature was clearly demonstrated when artists painted landscapes. They were touching the *Dao* through which they ultimately immersed into nature. Nature was not only great and worthy of respect but also appealing and inspirational: it should be respected and eulogized. But that the rules of nature could be understood and acted upon changed how nature functioned. In the ordinary world, nature was often hidden behind the chores of daily life, so a painter needed to see through to nature clearly and access its true form in order for his mind to resonate with it. The talent of a good painter was also a force of nature, through which true nature would appear clearly, and people could feel the vigor of life and the warmth of the spiritual world in paintings.

Although scholars had political and, in many cases, administrative responsibilities, they could not forget the lure of nature, and painting a landscape provided a way for them to enjoy what they missed. Guo Xi (1020–1109), a painter in the Song Dynasty, indicated in his *Spirituality by the Stream in the Forest* (*Linquan Gaozhi*) that intellectuals admired the forests and streams simply because they were the places to which they would like to belong and could not reach. He stipulated that if a landscape was "walkable," "visible," "accessible," and "livable," it would

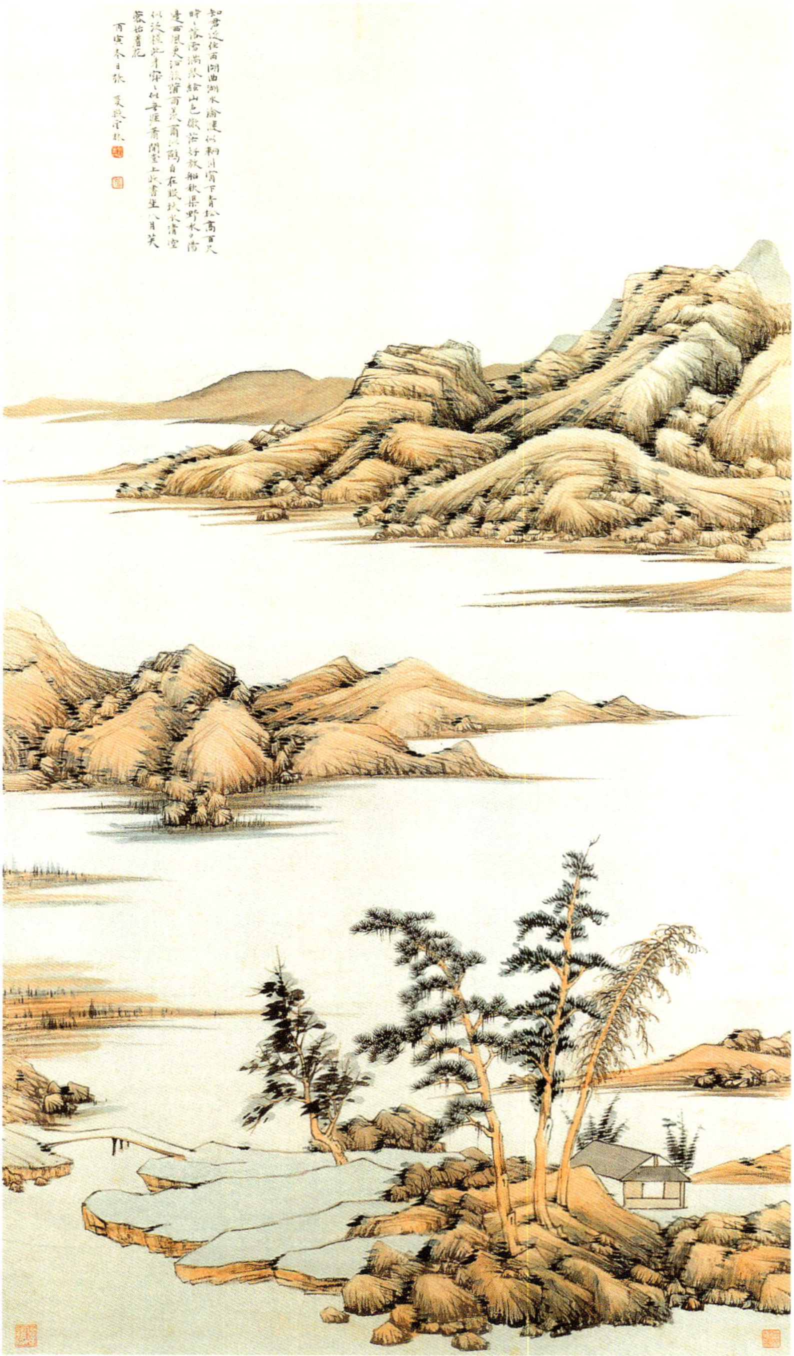

Imitating Ni Yunlin's Autumn Water and Lucid Sky by Zhang Daqian (182 cm × 79.5 cm).

be a masterpiece. He wrote: "All the painters should bear this in mind when they paint and all the art critics should remember this when they judge." It was very rare for an ancient Chinese painter to concentrate on the details or on a small part of landscape; but from the Tang and Song Dynasties onwards, painters included mountains and streams and also roads leading to the top of the mountains, streams by a road that intersected with another road, buildings on mountain ridges, people on roads, and boats on water. The Chinese like to say they "read" a painting: they appreciate both its content and its spiritual meanings.

Guo Xi also discussed in detail the composition of a painting. He wrote, "A thousand miles of mountains couldn't tell the complete wonder; ten thousand miles of rivers still leave out the beauty. A simple outline on paper is no different from a map." In his view, landscapes should display the overall view in essence, the "great shape" and the "grand view." This was a further development of the Taoist theory that "a grand shape looks vague." He also compared a painting with a human body:

"To a mountain water is the artery; grass and plants are hair; mist and clouds are colors of life. A mountain becomes alive when it has water; it becomes vivid when it has grasses and plants; and it becomes dainty and charming when it has mist and clouds. To water, the mountain is the face; the buildings on ridges are the eyes; fishermen by the river are the soul. Water becomes charming when it has mountains to decorate; it becomes pure when it has buildings; it becomes spacious when there are fishermen. This is the essence of composition for *shanshui* [landscape]."

When humanity and moral values were applied to a painting, it would obviously affect the way a painter viewed the world. Guo Xi illustrated this: "There are three types of remoteness for a mountain. Viewing from bottom to top, it is remoteness in height; viewing from front to back, it is remoteness in depth; viewing from nearby to faraway, it is remoteness in horizon." Remoteness in height, in depth, and in horizon directs our view from a point in

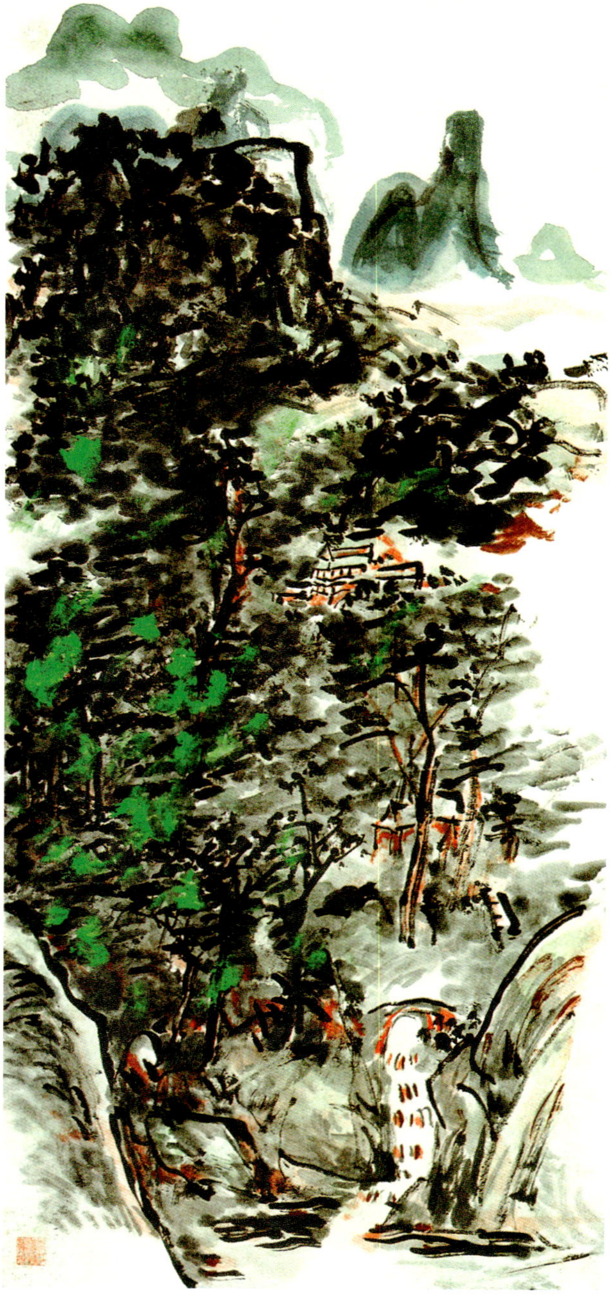

Ink and Colored Shanshui by Huang Binhong (102 cm x 39 cm). Many art critics consider Huang Binhong to have had a very similar influence on Chinese painting as that of Impressionists on Western painting. He completed the transition of the traditional *shanshui* to the modern.

the painting to beyond the whole of it to the "grand view" and to an infinite universe. This provided a symbolic meaning for "in the world" and "out of the world." The cultural elite would endeavor for most of their life to become mandarins in a material world: this was being "in the world." But at the same time they did not like their spirit being spoilt by the temptations of the material world and hoped that landscapes would give them a sense of being pure and lofty. The artistic conception of landscape was closely related with "remoteness," and that "remoteness" symbolized their being "out of the world." This philosophy of painting composition satisfied the spiritual gratification of the cultural elite. If a painter lost his admiration for "remoteness," his work would become merely a painting of a landscape.

Chinese artists often say that the whole horse is in the heart, the ripe bamboo is in the heart, the valley is in the heart. This means artists need first to command a thorough and deep understanding of nature and a vivid memory of natural scenery, and only then should they prepare paint and paper. With the brush at hand, white paper and bright sky express emotion free from the disturbance of the world. The silk and paper were viewed as representing a vague world and an infinite universe. The brush and pen are the means. The artist would like the brush and pen to travel freely on silk and paper to reflect their freedom in an infinite universe. Landscape painters always left much blank space on their compositions, space for the imagination. For example, they had empty space around fish in the water and around birds in the sky, which give a sense of being in the presence of an expansive universe.

"Soundless Poems"
Chinese painting is done on rice paper or silk with a brush dipped in black or colored ink. The finished work is then mounted on scrolls, which can be hung or rolled up. Chinese painting features multi-focus perspective, depends on lines and ink color to represent forms and texture, and is often complemented by poems, verses, calligraphy, or carving. Major subjects include human figures, landscapes, flowers, birds, and animals. There are two main techniques in Chinese painting: meticulous and freehand. Since the rise of scholarly painting in the Song and Yuan Dynasties, painting became increasingly integrated with poetry, calligraphy, and seal carving, and contains inscriptions of varying lengths. Chinese paintings often reflect the painter's emotions and feelings, and are representational and philosophical, and are therefore called "Soundless Poems."

From Gu Kaizhi to Wu Daozi

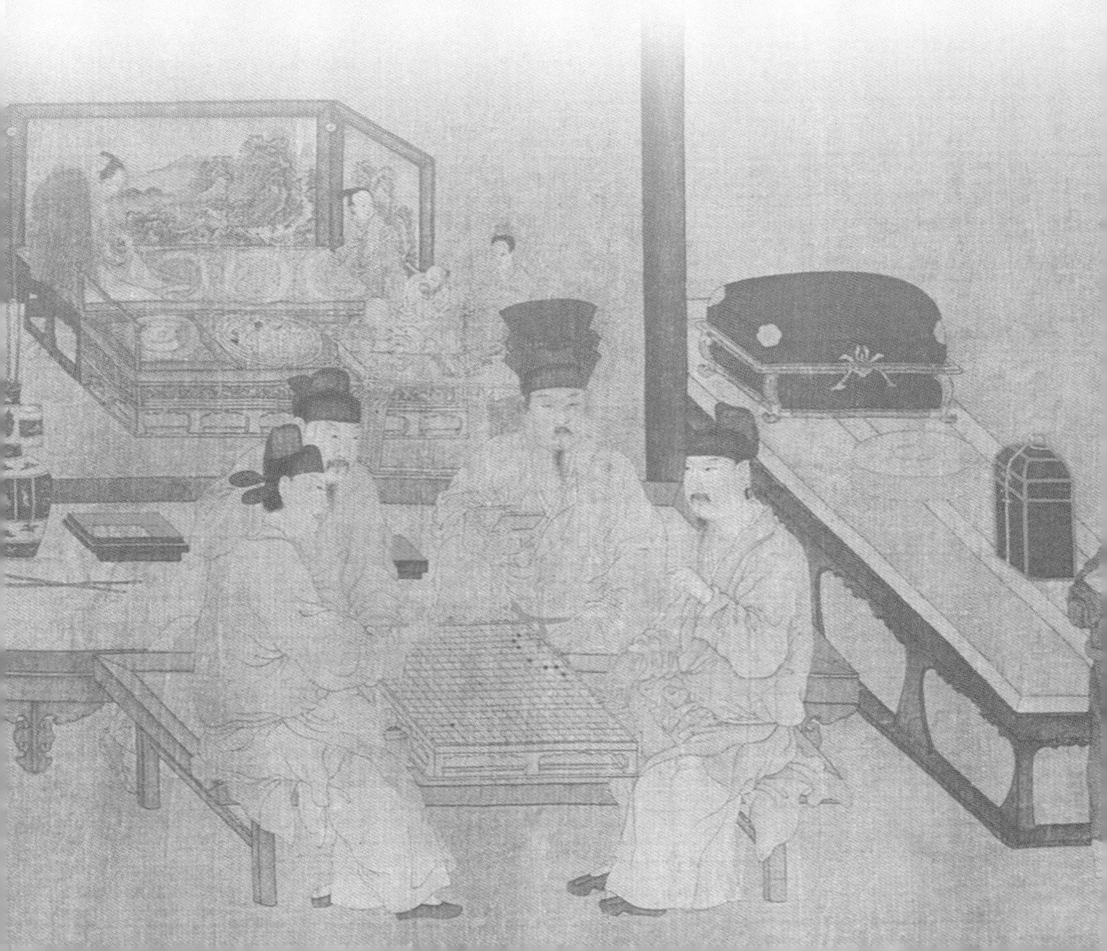

Tomb Chamber Paintings

The Chinese historian Qian Mu once said that, apart from calligraphy, the most important form of Chinese art was paintings. Although the earliest paintings can be dated back to prehistoric times, most art in the Qin (221–206 BC) and Han (206 BC–AD 220) Dynasties was murals and stone carvings in palaces and tomb chambers. It was not until the Wei (AD 220–265) and Jin Dynasties (AD 265–420) that paintings had developed into a more popular art form as silk and paper became more affordable and were gradually used for paintings. The earliest Chinese paintings were made almost exclusively for the aristocracy and for religious purposes. From the Jin to the Sui and Tang Dynasties, paintings gradually became more accessible to relatively ordinary people. Since the early works were mainly drawn or carved on the walls and floors of religious buildings, tomb chambers, and palaces, most paintings of Qing and Han Dynasties disappeared when these places were destroyed. A few are preserved in tomb chambers where the murals were relatively difficult to destroy and so survived for us to study.

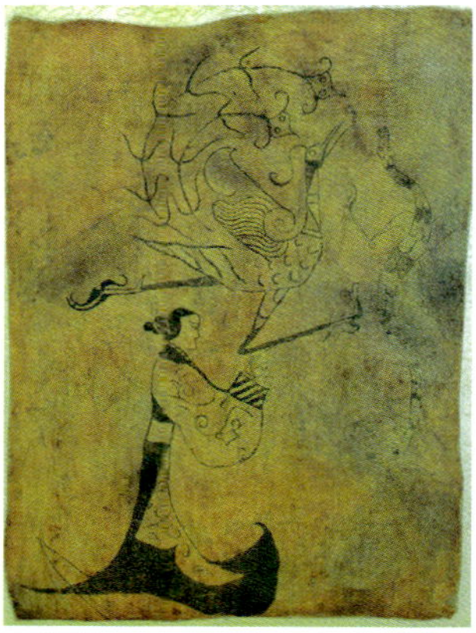

Dragon, Phoenix, and Beauties, silk painting, one of the earliest known Chinese paintings.

But perhaps the paintings that have most caught the imagination of art historians are those painted on silk and buried with emperors and aristocrats. *Dragon, Phoenix, and Beauties*, discovered in 1949 in a grave in Chenjia Mountain in Hunan Province, is one of the earliest known and is dated to 475–221 BC. After the Xia, Shang, and Zhou Dynasties, China entered the Spring and Autumn and the Warring States Periods when Confucius lived and during which many kingdoms fought for dominance in China. The

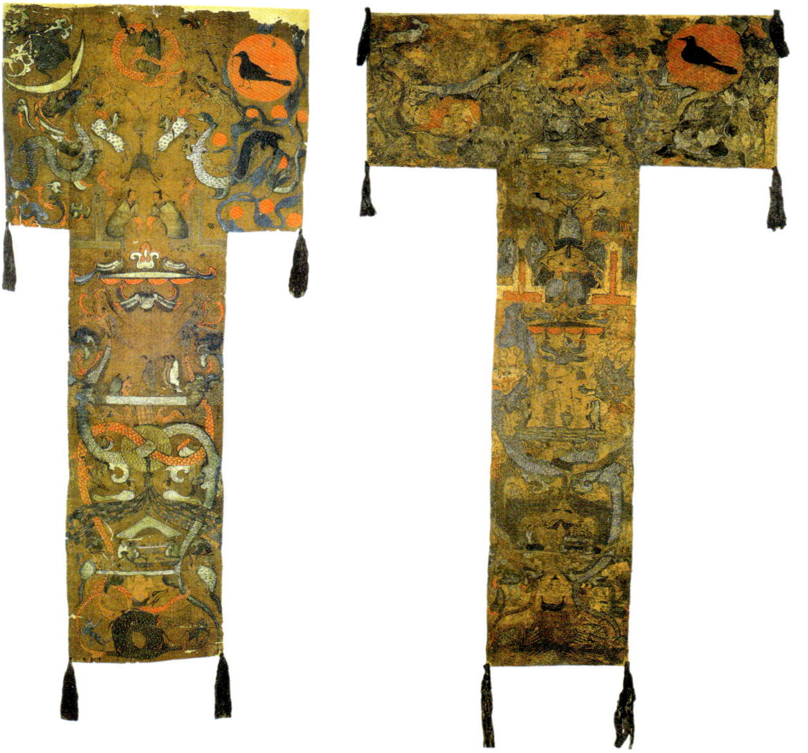

"Non-dress," silk painting.

site where *Dragon, Phoenix, and Beauties* was buried was in the middle of the kingdom of Chu. Like clay figures buried in graves, paintings accompanied the dead to protect them. Painting was not yet seen as an art. In the middle of *Dragon, Phoenix, and Beauties* is a lady, but it is difficult to tell whether she is a shamen praying for the deceased or the deceased herself. Above her are a dragon and a phoenix; both were mythical creatures in ancient China and auspicious signs. Like angels in some Christian teaching, they were believed to be able to guide the dead to heaven.

Another important silk painting was unearthed from the Mawangdui Tomb near Chanshan, dated to around 165 BC. It is in a T-shape, so archaeologists have called it a *feiyi,* which literally translates as "non-coat" painting, as it is in the shape of a coat but could not be worn. The painting depicts a soul going to heaven: the top section clearly represents heaven, the middle is the earth, and the bottom is an underground scene. Reality is mixed with fantasy. The middle section tells the story of the dead woman, the wife of Licang, an aristocrat. She is dressed in very colorful, lavish silk. Judging from her composure, she looks like a mature woman. She is walking through a large hall with servants kneeling in front of her and maids following behind. Slightly below this, there is a banqueting scene with tables packed with luxury dishes, plates with delicious foods, and glasses full of wines. There is no master present, so no one is eating or drinking, all are standing and bowing forward as if they are seeing Licang off. Symbolically, the wife is being sent off to heaven by all her servants and maids. The top section is an imaginative and romantic fantasy. The traditional belief in the Han period was that when a person died his or her soul would go to heaven and become a celestial being. In the painting this celestial world has the Sun, the Moon, and stars above. There is a golden horse on the Sun and a jade rabbit on the Moon, two auspicious animals. Also included is a large mulberry tree shining in the moonlight and a dragon flying through the sky. A young woman looks as if she has escaped the chores of earthly life and is totally rejuvenated, dancing with the dragon in a celestial world.

This Han painting carries on the traditions which we first see in *Dragon, Phoenix, and Beauties* of the Warring States period. All the characters shown are in profile. Our Chinese ancestors believed that a person's profile could show more of their character. The Han silk painting is the more sophisticated of the two. The earlier painting only has simple lines for symbolic meanings, while the later has more elegant lines and fine composition to depict an imaginative and romantic story on earth and in heaven. It has adopted the "non-dress" format to show the direction of painting, from top to bottom, from heaven to the underworld. In the middle earth section, we can also see the direction of time from present to the past. The Han painting also demonstrates a more elegant and sophisticated drawing technique. It uses black ink for outlines and added colors afterwards. The mineral pigments of cinnabar red, malachite green, azurite blue, and chalk white retain much of their original color more than two thousand years later.

The Most Romantic Painting

The Han Dynasty began to employ royal painters to serve solely in the imperial court, and the emperors built special pavilions to store the collections of paintings, which mainly illustrated the contributions and achievements of the emperors during their reigns. All the dynasties kept this tradition. One important task for the royal painters was to draw portraits of an emperor's many wives and concubines so he could use them to select which lady would spend the night with him. As a consequence, many court ladies would bribe the painters to make their portrait look more beautiful than they actually were. But there is a famous story of the Han Dynasty about the royal painter Mao Yanshou. When he was serving at court, he met one of the most beautiful women in Chinese history, Wang Zhaojun. She did not bribe Mao and so the Emperor never asked her to accompany him during her entire stay at the court. Even worse, the Emperor married her to the King of Xiongnu when he came to the Han capital to seek peace with the empire. When the Emperor saw her just before her departure, he found Wang Zhaojun was absolutely beautiful. The Emperor was furious and investigating why he had not asked for her, he found her portrait. One legend says Mao Yanshou was executed. This incident illustrates that painters still had very low social status and that painting was only a way to earn a living. Even royal painters were slaves and their destiny was completely in the hands of their master.

During the rise of the Wei and Jin Dynasties, many social changes began. Two of the most significant were the arrival of Buddhism and foreign cultures, and the emergence of an active scholarly class. During the Wei, Jin, Southern and Northern

Dynasties, China was divided into small states, and there were many political upheavals. However, Buddhism prospered tremendously and reached an unprecedented level of acceptance. Thus, caves of religious importance were carved and temples were built, and this required many painters to decorate them with murals. Consequently, painting technique developed rapidly. At the same time, because of social and political upheavals intellectuals sought refuge in Buddhism and seclusion metaphysics, and many scholars established their place in the cultural history of China. For example, Ji Kang (224–263) was, like other scholars, good at poetry, painting, music, and chess. Wang Xizhi (321–379 or 303–361) was the most important of all, and today he is considered the Calligraphy Sage. Other famous scholar painters include Cao Buxing, Cao Zhongda, Dai Kui, Gu Kaizhi, and Lu Tanwei. Unfortunately few of their works have survived.

One exception is Gu Kaizhi. Although none of his original work is known, he has still acquired a legendary status, both as a painter and as a writer on Chinese painting. His paintings were copied by many artists generations after his death in order to learn his technique, and today his work is known mainly through Tang period copies. Gu Kaizhi was given extensive coverage in the dynastic histories and the seminal text on painting, *Famous Paintings Record of Past Dynasties* (*Li-dai ming-hua ji*) by Zhang Yanyuan (ca. 815–875).

Gu Kaizhi (346–407) was born in Wuxi Jiangsu Province and first painted in Nanjing, the capital of the Eastern Jin. Legend says he was devoted but shrewd, humorous and boastful but honest and direct. He was a man of contradictions, typical of scholars of the Wei and Jin Dynasties. He was born into the nobility and had been appointed to various official positions but had little responsibility. During his early years, he never shied away from friends who were skillful craft painters and stayed away as much as possible from pursuing political ambitions, he devoted much of his time to painting. When he was only twenty years old, he started to paint murals for Buddhist temples and become well known. Many of his paintings are recorded in imperial archives of the Tang and Song Dynasties, but copies of only four paintings survive. They are still very important, and *The Admonitions of the Instructress to the Court Ladies* and *Nymph of the Luo River* are the best known.

The Admonitions of the Instructress to the Court Ladies was completed in the Western Jin period (209–306) to illustrate a political parody written by Zhang Hua (c. 232–300). The *Admonition* was written to promote the values of Confucianism and Zhang Hua takes a moralizing tone, attacking the excessive behavior of Empress Jia to teach court ladies the proper moral virtues. Gu Kaizhi illustrated all the characters in the story; emperor, empress, and court ladies. The protagonist is the court instructress who provides guidance for the ladies of the imperial harem. Two copies have survived, one from the Tang Dynasty at the British Museum (acquired 1903) and the other from the Song Dynasty at the Beijing Palace Museum. *The Admonitions Scroll*, a copy from the Tang period, has nine scenes, but the first two are missing, as well as the text of the first scene. Each has the original story written on the painting, and the painting has been executed in a fine linear style that is typical of fourth-century figure work. There are texts that describe Gu Kaizhi as having painted in this manner, and similar pictorial motifs have been discovered in contemporary tombs. The inscriptions and seals on this scroll date back to the eighth century, when this copy was probably painted.

Nymph of the Luo River illustrates a romantic poem of this title by Cao Zhi, the younger brother of the Wendi Emperor of the Wei Dynasty. In the painting, Gu Kaizhi transformed the feeling of the poet into a touching visual display. Standing by the Luo River, Cao Zhi stares at the Nymph on the other side. He could see but not touch: he watches her lingering and feels despair. The nymph seems to walk slowly over clouds and ripples towards him, elegant and romantic. The wind blows gently across the scene and the river flows vigorously along, vivid and dramatic. The painting

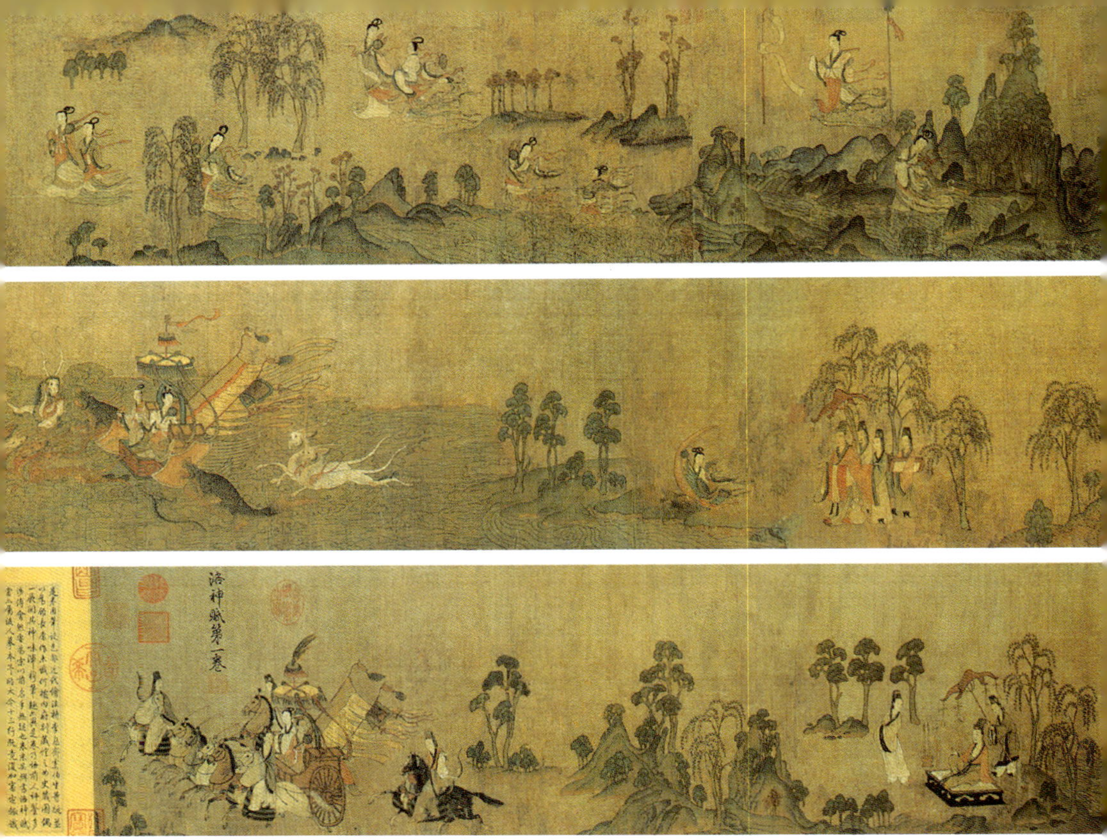

Nymph of the Luo River, scroll (27.1 cm×572.8 cm), ink and color on silk (sections), attributed to Gu Kaizhi, Beijing Palace Museum.

has created a perfect visual, poetic story, combining reality with imagination, and mixing a fairy tale with earthly life.

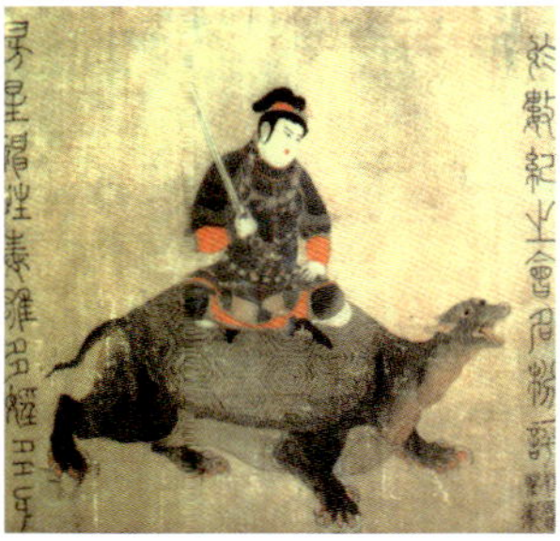

18 Mansion Gods, scroll (28 cm×491 cm) (detail), attributed to Zhang Cengyao of the Southern Dynasty, Osaka Municipal Museum of Art.

The silk paintings discussed above illustrate the basic traditional Chinese painting technique, which outlines in black ink and fills in with color afterwards. The paintings of Gu Kaizhi show an extension of these early techniques and perfect the format. Zhang Yanyuan, described Gu Kaizhi's paintings as "compact without interruption, repetitive with transcendence, stylish with variety, and swift as thunder." Like the calligraphy of Wang Xizhi, the lines drawn by the painter not only illustrate figures and subjects but themselves have a rigorous structure and rich rhythm,

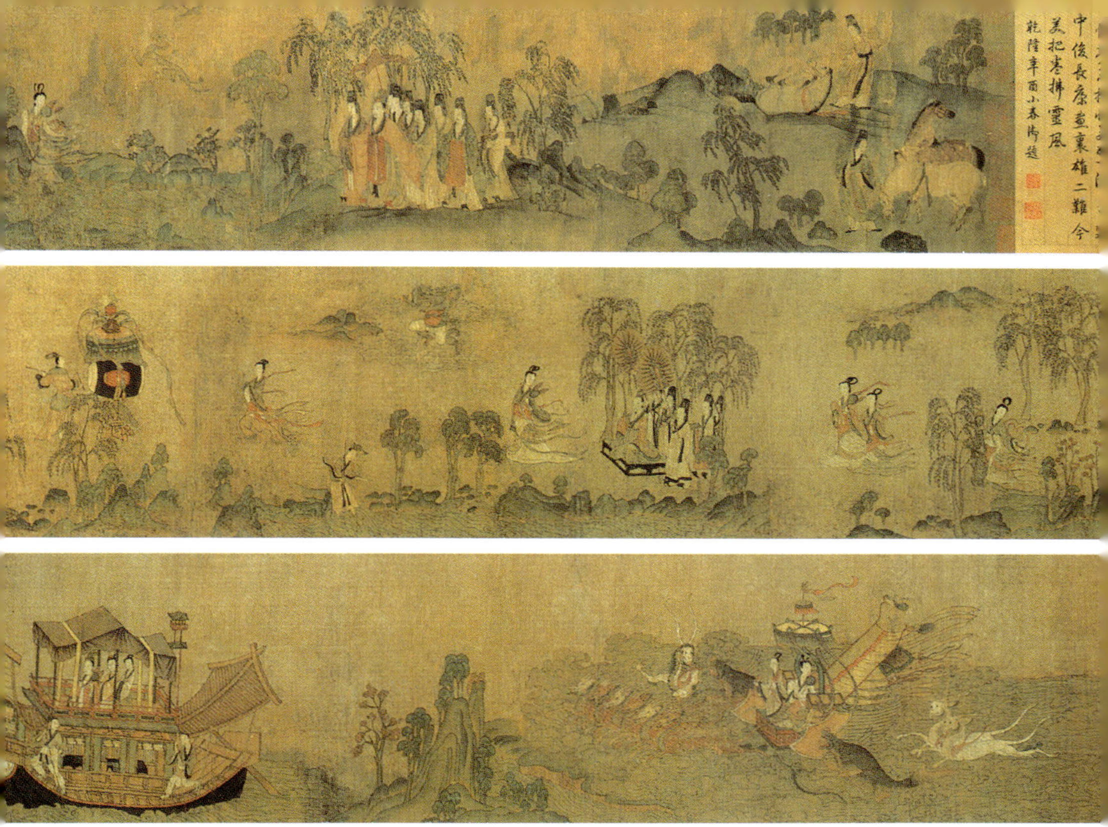

showing the beauty of structure and composition. The court ladies, the mountains, and the shooting scene of his paintings are almost a direct copy of conceptual techniques used in Han silk paintings. This does not suggest that Gu Kaizhi was not an imaginative and creative painter, but rather that the conceptual formula had already become habitual and compulsory. Like calligraphy has its own rules of writing, the command of conceptual formula in painting is a symbol of accomplishment in training. However, because mountains, stones, trees, and other large subjects are drawn with a single line in this traditional technique, the sizes of figures and other natural subjects have no visual perspective, and this generally indicates that the technique of the Wei and Jin periods was still in its infancy as far as an overall view was concerned. As a great artist of that generation, Gu Kaizhi analyzed and refined the good elements of painting of that period and used them creatively. This makes his work an example of exceptional excellence, and many painters in the generations that followed copied his paintings to learn these refined techniques. His style and technique can be found in the paintings by artists Zhan Ziqian and Wu Daozi of the Sui and Tang periods.

"Communication of the Soul"

Until the later years of the Han dynasty, scholars were not involved with paintings, but by the Wei and Jin periods, it was relatively common for the cultural elite to paint, share the art form with professional craft painters, and start a discussion of the theory of painting. Gu Kaizhi was a pioneering theorist and wrote three books: *On Painting, Introduction to the Famous Paintings of the Wei and Jin Dynasties*, and *Painting Yuntai Mountain*. In these works, he proposed the theory of "communication of the soul": that the deciding factor of good painting was whether it communicated the soul. In *On Painting* he said:

"The soul belongs to the other world and it is the entirety of endeavor."

"The beauty of shape, the dimension of body, the shade of *yin* and *yang*, the line of the sketch; all are common features of the natural world. The spirit and rhythm, however, are in the mind. If the hands can represent the eyes of a painter, the reward of communication is beyond comprehension."

The Wei and Jin periods were a time when Buddhist metaphysics were the fashion of cultured society. However, Gu Kaizhi was a painter of simplicity. Although communication of soul or creation of rhythm was the goal of painting, he insisted this could only be achieved by copying nature and working on shapes and contents. Therefore, he considered it necessary to study "the beauty of shape, the dimensions of body, the shade of *yin* and *yang*, and the line of the sketch." The communication of soul and rhythm could only be achieved by means of shape and subject. He considered that achieving this harmony in entirety once or twice in thousands of paintings was a reward from heaven. He wrote: "In figure paintings the clothes and the belongings are not very important. The spirit, composure, and poise are more essential. The eyes are the spirit and the decisive factor." He also mentioned "bone structure method," in which the composition of painting is likened to the structure of the human body, and "balance of composition" in *On Painting*. He believed that the former was a reflection of the inner spirit of rhythm. Composition balance meant the choice of subjects and their relationship in a painting.

The Six Dynasties (220–589) were a period when the fundamental Chinese painting aesthetic standards were developed and when painting critics were active. The painting philosophy of Gu Kaizhi was summarized by one critic, Xie He (479–502) in the six principles: "give life to the body"; "ink sketch the bone structure"; "apply rhythm to shape"; "paint color by type"; "balance composition by relationship"; and "copy by transcendence." "Give life to the body" was the primary rule. These principles were first applied to figure painting and were universally adopted, and thereafter extended to the paintings of landscape, birds, and flowers. Communication of soul and rhythm had become the ultimate criteria by which to judge a painting.

Spring Outing (You-Chun Tu)

The painting style of the Sui Dynasty was transitional from the old to the new, and it showed refinement and beauty. Many painters assembled in the capital, and most were good at religious subjects, and the other popular topic, the life of the aristocracy. Landscape developed into an independent style of painting during this period after the relative positions and the ratios of landscape objects were finally addressed.

Zhan Ziqian (550–604) lived through the North Qi and North Zhou Dynasties, and after the Sui reunited China, he served as an

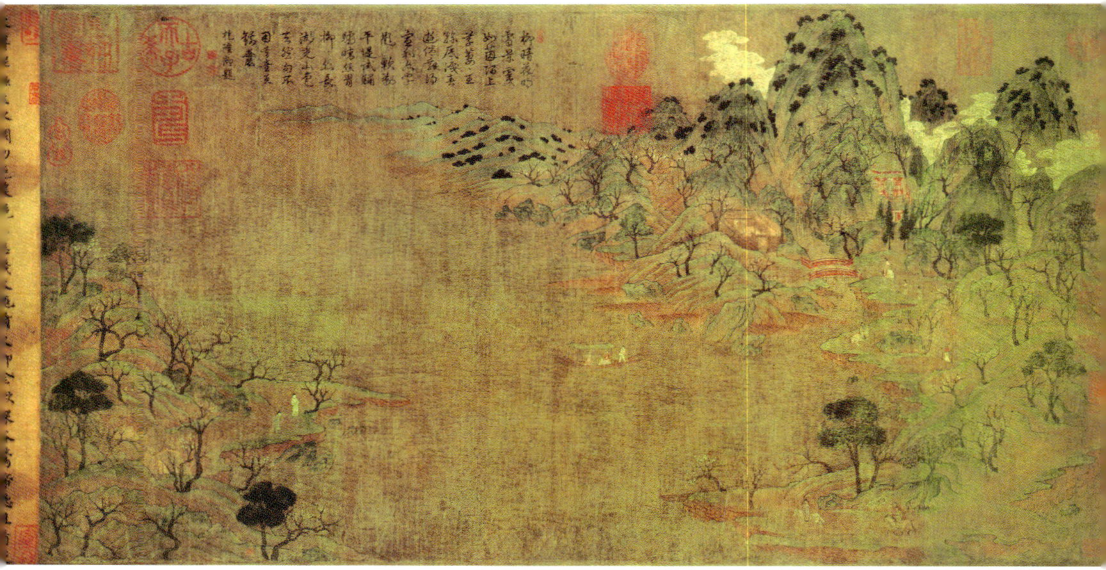

Spring Outing, scroll (43 cm×80.5 cm), ink and color on silk, attributed to Zhan Ziqian, Beijing Palace Museum.

adviser and administrator to the imperial court. Historians have commented that his paintings have fine details and are colorful. He was a natural successor to Gu Kaizhi. In *The Admonitions of the Instructress to the Court Ladies* and *Nymph of the Luo River*, Gu employed sketch lines that looked like silk threads coming out of silkworms, and this technique was imitated by Zhan Ziqian in *Spring Outing*, which helped him to create a magnificent landscape with crisp, lucid lines as smooth as silk, and he developed landscape into an independent style of painting. The *Xuanhe Collection of Paintings* says he had "a special talent of creating distance and space in a drawing of a few inches." He was a master in using space to express the beauty and rhythm of landscape. He is the first person to paint in the true style of *shanshui*, and his landscape style had an especially profound effect on painting in the Tang and Song Dynasties. A critic in the Yuan Dynasty, Tang Hou, said that he was the father of painting for the Tang Dynasty.

After passing through many hands, the original *Spring Outing* is the only surviving work by Zhan Ziqian; it is the earliest Chinese painted scroll on silk, and also the first true landscape painting known to us. On the front is written "*Spring Outing by Zhan Ziqian*." The painting was in the collections of well-known connoisseurs who added their own seals and inscriptions; for example, the imperial seal of the Huizong Emperor of the Song Dynasty, the inscriptions of the Qianlong Emperor of the Qing Dynasty, and the seals of imperial courtiers and other collectors. The painting, mainly using green and dark blue, shows a spring outing by a group of aristocrats. The outlines are fine, smooth, and strong with bright and pure color. Although the people and horses are tiny, they are detailed. While the original use of landscape was to show the people, this emphasizes the natural world.

There are green fields and flowering trees in full spring sunshine, with mountains in the background. Ripples of water reflect the light. Clouds fly smoothly and lazily between the mountains. An embankment extends into the distance, with an arched bridge in the background. The gentlemen are riding horses and walking, and the ladies are boating on the lake, moving towards the waterfall. It is drawn from a bird's eye view, with the front and back sections focused towards the middle; this creates a rhythm of harmony and depth. Composition is constructed along a diagonal line from the bottom right to the top left, and this is also the direction of the running water. The green and blue emphasizes the spring colors of the plants and trees, and so the two colors together came to be called the "blue and green style." Since there is a third dominant color, golden yellow, this is a further development and is called a "golden green landscape" (*jin bi shanshui*). The mountains, plants, and stones are outlined by fine lines and then filled in with color. Zhan used many mineral pigments.

Most art historians agree that *Spring Outing* marks a new era of Chinese painting, which ended the traditional view that "characters should be larger than the mountain, and water can not cover the major part of a painting." During the Han Dynasty and the period of Gu Kaizhi, landscape painting was mostly an abstract form. In Zhan Ziqian, we can see his efforts to try to upgrade the place of

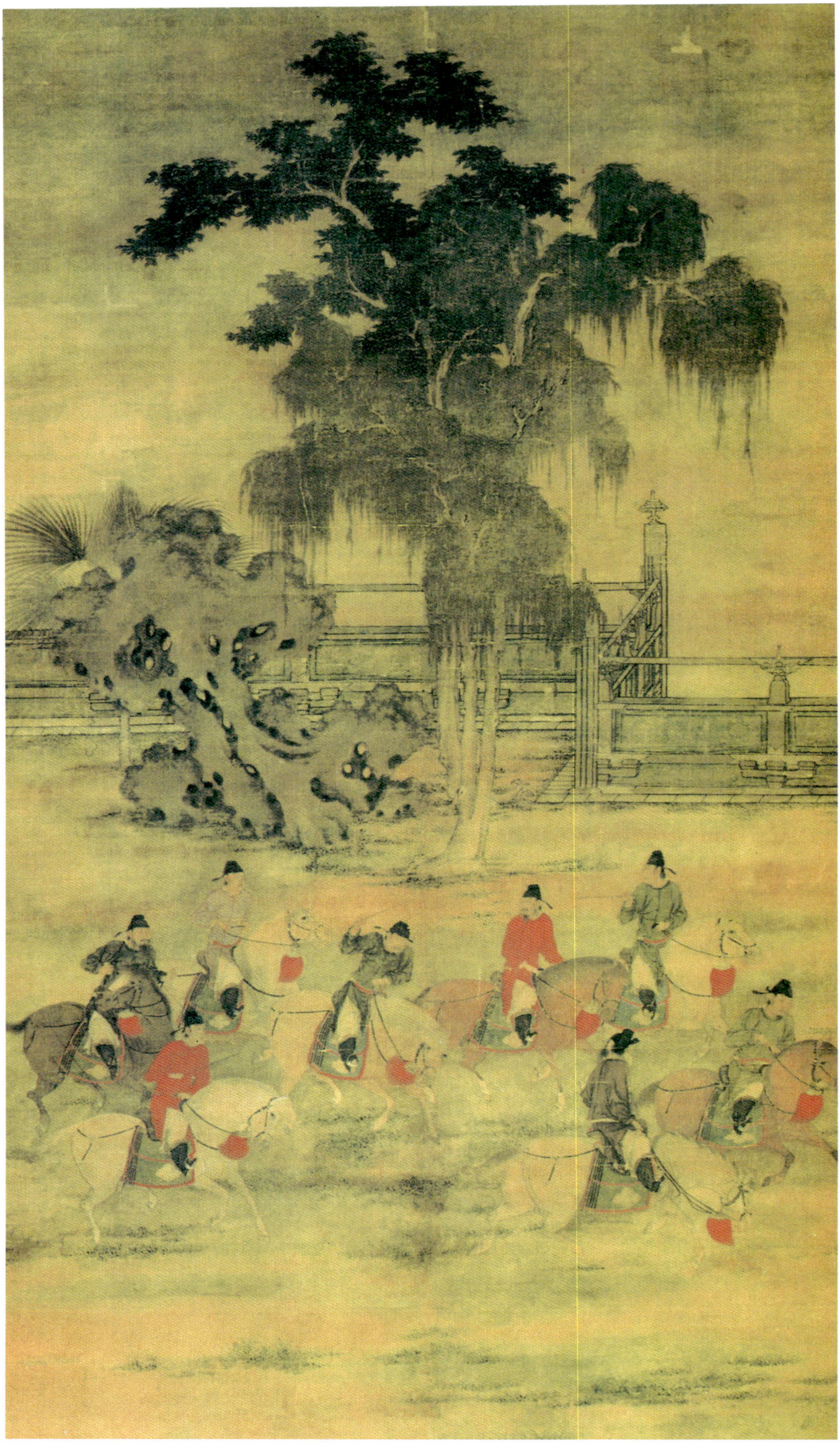

nature and reduce human beings and indicate their relationship to the natural world. Zhan also used rather realistic spot coloring to show the distance between different subjects, and used the traditional abstract technique of level brushing only for the clouds. The balance of the two techniques created a realistic, vivid world with a dreamy sensation.

Spring Outing is a textbook painting, following all the rules of landscape set by Guo Xi in *Spirituality by a Forest Stream*. As an early painter of simplicity, Zhan Ziqian clearly demonstrated realism in contrast to the artists in the Yuan period, who would emphasize the subjective painting of nature. He had perhaps wanted to portray an actual experience through painting; for example, the ripples that give a sense of gentle breezes, the highlighted spots on green stones, and the bright flowers to announce the arrival of spring. His landscape has elements both of so-called "blue and green *shanshui*" and "ink-and-wash *shanshui*," but not very clearly, which indicates that his generation had not yet found a perfect harmony of realism and expressionism.

Emperors of Great Prosperity

The Tang Dynasty (618–917) continued many of the painting traditions of the Sui Dynasty, but made major advances in key areas of paintings, such as showing people on horses, maturity in the blue-and-green ink-and-wash landscapes by improving the Sui period compact style (although landscape was less important), the creation of a new genre of painting flowers and birds, and, most importantly portrait painting. Several painters established themselves as specialists in flower and bird paintings. Another significant trend was using religious paintings to depict ordinary life. During the period of great prosperity of the Tang Dynasty, the emperors still viewed painting as a way to enhance their control of the country and to maintain their superiority in the arts. So portrait and figure paintings of royal, religious, and historical

< *Eight Gentlemen on a Spring Outing*, (161 cm×103 cm), attributed to Zhao Yan of the Five Dynasties period, Taipei Palace Museum.

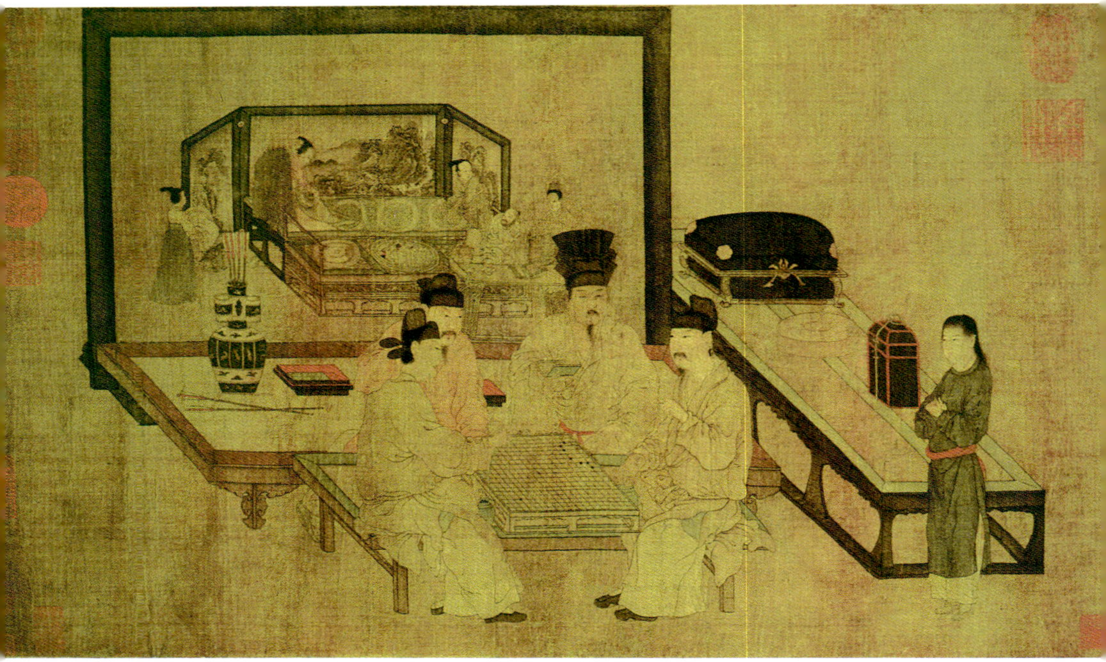

Playing Chess Behind a Screen, scroll (40.3 cm×70.5 cm), ink and color on silk, attributed to Zhou Wenju, Beijing Palace Museum.

subjects rose to an unprecedented importance. Yan Liben, a noble man by birth, was one of the most famous of these painters of portraits, figures, characters from history books, and he was also a royal architect and engineer. He had been the chief engineer for the imperial court, in charge of building and manufacture, but despite such achievements, he still felt inadequate and inferior socially. He told his descendants that when he was young he read extensively, as much as those who became mandarins; but he chose painting and was treated like a servant even after he became famous, so he advised them not to follow his career.

Under the instruction of the Taizong Emperor of the Tang Dynasty, Yan Liben completed *Thirteen Emperors from Han to Sui*, *Eighteen Scholars of the Qin Household*, *Twenty-four Heroes in the Linyan Pavilion*, *The Imperial Palanquin*, and *Court Officials* (*zhi gong tu*); *Thirteen Emperors* and *The Imperial Palanquin* have survived.

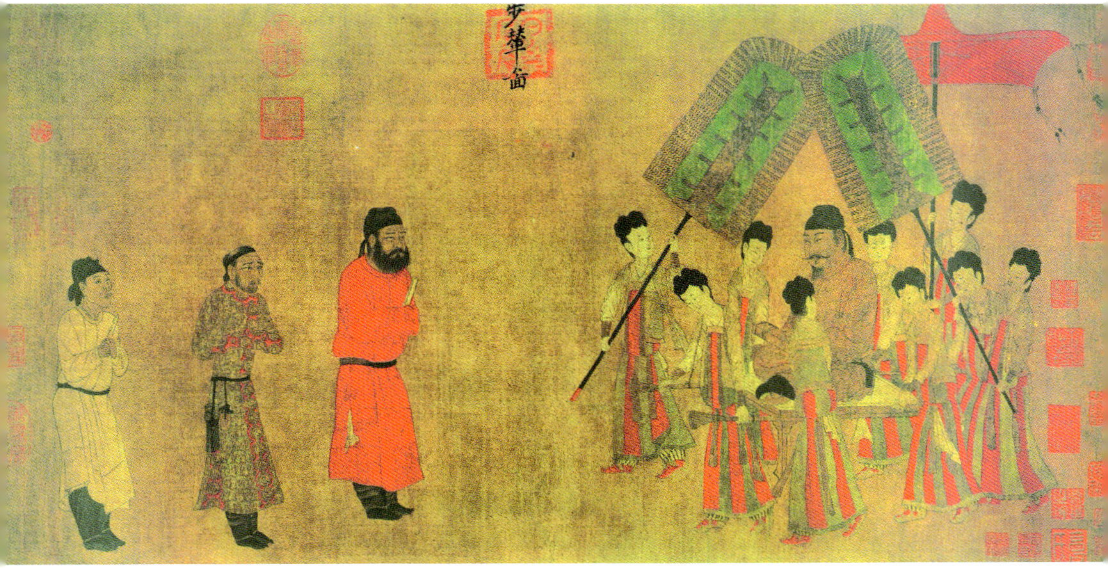

The Imperial Palanquin, scroll (38.5 cm×129 cm) (detail), ink and color on silk, attributed to Yan Liben, Beijing Palace Museum.

The *Thirteen Emperors* are portraits of emperors from the Han to Sui Dynasties with their attendants, including the Guangwudi Liu Xiu of the Han Dynasty (reigned AD 25–57), the Wendi Cao Pei of the Wei Dynasty (220–226), King Sun Quan of the Kingdom of Wu (222–252), Wudi Sima Yan of the Jin Dynasty (265–290), who were all founders of dynasties, and the last king of the Chen Kingdom (583–587), and Yandi of the Sui Dynasty (605–616), who lost an empire. All the empire founders look solemn, benevolent, and graceful, while the losers are dejected and apathetic. The rulers of the Tang Dynasty wanted to teach their descendants how an empire was built and lost. Yan Liben was appointed as a royal painter by the Taizong Emperor (627–649). Although each portrait is individualized, the formulas used since the Han Dynasty are followed, for example, the posture of the emperors can be traced back to *Nymph of the Luo River* and the murals from the Tang Dynasty in Dunhuang.

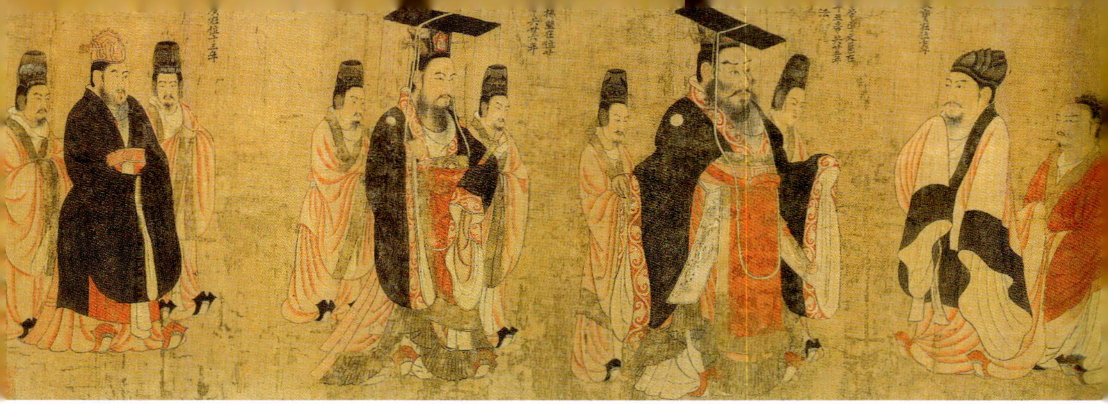

Thirteen Emperors from Han to Sui, scroll (detail), attributed to Yan Liben, ink and color on silk, Boston Museum of Fine Arts.

The Imperial Palanquin, records the grand occasion when envoys from Tubo (in the present-day Tibet) came to Chang'an (present-day Xi'an), the Tang capital, to ask for permission to marry Princess Wencheng in 490. Since this was an actual event which provided an abundance of people and details for inclusion, the painting is vivid and realistic without abstract conceptual elements and shows a true artistic creativity. At the bottom right is the imperial sedan carried by court ladies, on which sits the Taizong Emperor. On the far left are three ceremony masters and in the middle, the emissary Lu Dong Zan and at his back a court attendant. The emperor, the focus of the painting, looks solemn with perfect composure and grace, with a sense of deep vision: a ruler in a time of great prosperity. There are nine court ladies, six carrying the sedan, and two holding large fans overhead and one a round red parasol of silk, adding color and beauty to a very political scene. Their tenderness, gaits, and postures are in contrast to the majesty and determination of the Taizong Emperor. The Tubo envoys are smaller, and look submissive and eager. The painting has no background scenery. The composition is compact and moves from right to left, with clear focus, distinct rhythm, bright colors with large areas of red and green. The painting has a strong visual impact: it is a perfect combination of highly decorative dimensional geometry and realistic representation of unique and distinctive persons. The court ladies are gracefully balanced by the symmetric column of ceremony masters, giving the sense of an important official event and balancing and contrasting the Taizong Emperor.

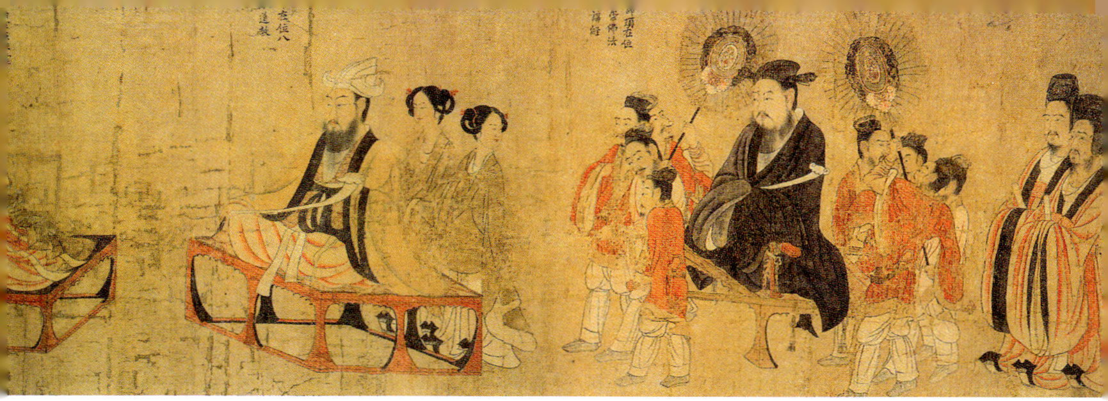

The Imperial Palanquin is included in the *Xuanhe Collection of Paintings*, which was compiled under the supervision of the Huizong Emperor of the Song Dynasty, by the painter Mi Fu (1050–1107), who wrote *Painting History* and numerous art works. The painting has remained a favorite in the imperial collection and for art collectors, and represents the highest level of excellence achieved in the early Tang period. *The Imperial Palanquin* in the Beijing Palace Museum is a copy from the Song Dynasty. Yan Liben used more solid, simplistic lines, which art critics call "the iron lines," than his predecessors but was more representative and responsive to the subjects painted. He used cinnabar red and malachite green extensively to give balance and symmetry to the composition and to illustrate royal status.

Other Figure Painters

Aesthetic standards of beauty in the Tang Dynasty were very different from those of today. They appreciated the beauty of rich and luxurious living and admired the full, plump bodies of court ladies, as surviving sculptures and paintings show. The so-called "*Qiluo* Characters" have the characteristics of this aesthetic standard: plump bodies, chubby cheeks, curved eyebrows, thin eyes, relaxed postures, and happy, fulfilled facial expressions. Historians think these figures reflect the opulent living of the imperial and noble houses, and that the fashion was imitated by the general public.

The most famous painters associated with the *Qiluo* Characters are Zhang Xuan (active 713–755) and Zhou Fang (active 766–799,

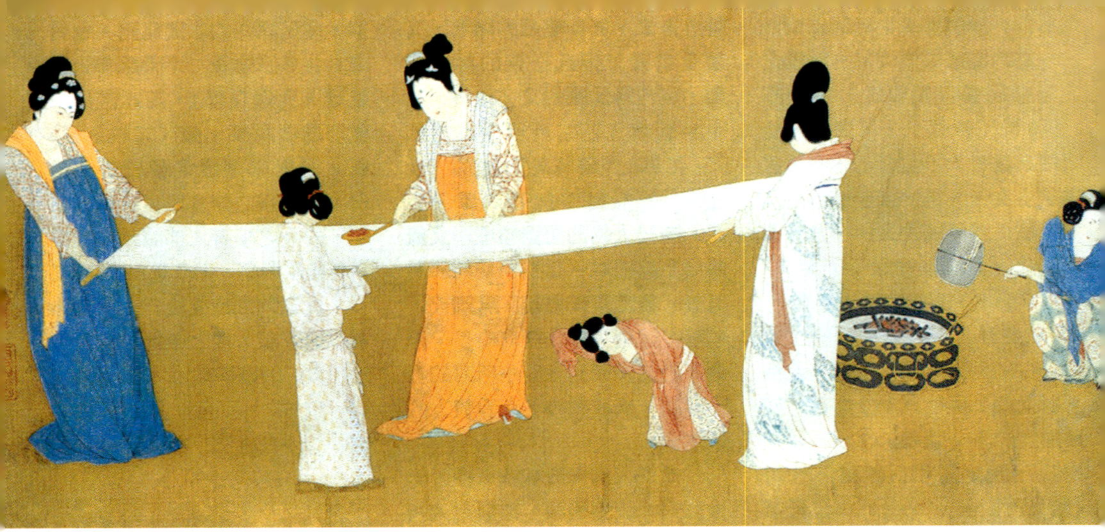

Court Ladies Preparing Newly Woven Silk, scroll (37 cm×145.3 cm), by Zhang Xuan. Copy attributed to Emperor Huizong, Boston Museum of Fine Arts.

785–804). During the reign of the Xuanzong Emperor (712–755), Zhang Xuan served as a royal painter, and he was famous for his skill with figures. The records indicate he also explored ways to paint other subjects, such as pavilions, forests, birds, and flowers. But he mostly painted court ladies in opulent and rich social scenes, such as spring outings, snow sightseeing, dressing up, playing hide and seek, and using musical instruments. Zhou Fang was born into an aristocratic family. *Xuanhe Collection of Paintings* states: "He often visited the rich and beautiful and was good at painting nobles and their opulent living, and depicting the beauty of plumpness." Both artists' works have been among the favorites collected by emperors, especially the Huizong Emperor of the Song Dynasty, who was himself an artist, and owned *Guo State Queen Spring Outing* and *Court Ladies Preparing Newly Woven Silk*.

Guo State Queen Spring Outing is a magnificent scroll, completed when it was fashionable to use new trends and styles to depict the newly found confidence and prosperity of the Tang Dynasty. However, Zhang Xuan adopted a more realistic approach for the painting, resonating with the epic poem of Du Fu "The Beauty." The Guo State Queen went on a sightseeing tour, with a column of riders on saddled horses strolling in small groups. The painting uses strong but slender lines and balanced colors, rich, bright but

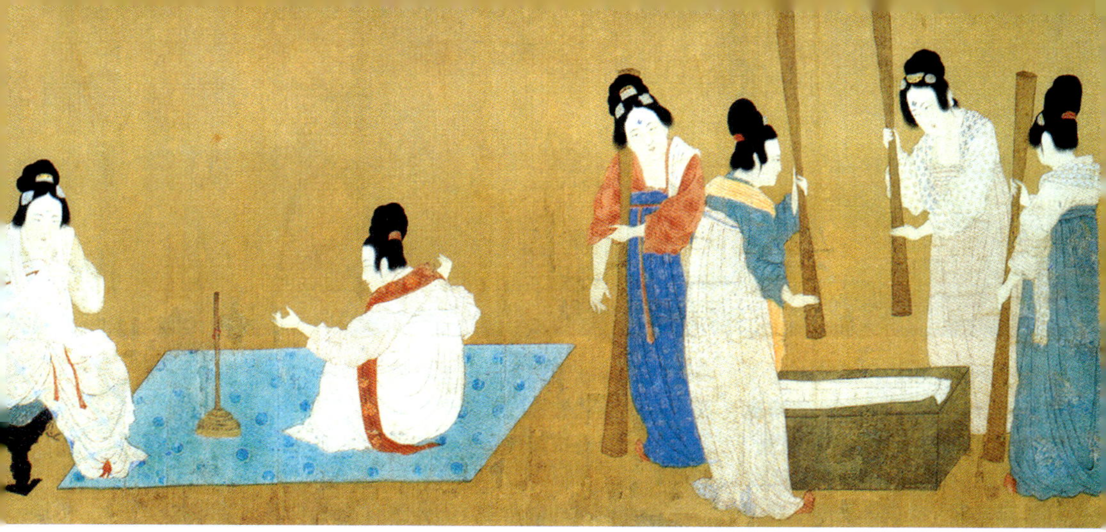

fresh and elegant, meticulous but without dullness. The Guo State Queen is grandly dressed and accompanied by servants and court ladies, enjoying the sights of a spring day. There are nine characters in the painting, plus eight horses and a baby carried by a court lady. The Tang Dynasty loved saddle horses, and Zhang Xuan was skilled in painting them. The red horse of the queen is vividly portrayed and is given a name, Hualiu, by historians. Like his mistress, he radiates grace and elegance.

In comparison *Court Ladies Preparing Newly Woven Silk* depicts a more ordinary court scene, but all the ladies are plump and dressed with elegance and grace so it is also representative of *Qiluo* Characters. The court ladies are grouped according to the tasks they are performing with the silk: spinning, weaving, and ironing. There are twelve court ladies, old and young, sitting and standing, all with distinctive characteristics. Some have their sleeves pushed up and are holding pestles, the lady who is weaving is totally focused on her task, while others are pulling and leaning back to straighten the silk fabric, a young girl is fanning a burning fire, and another is watching the ironing of the silk. All are vividly portrayed. On the front of the scroll the Zhangzong Emperor of the Jin Kingdom has written *A Copy of Zhang Xuan's Court Ladies Preparing Newly Woven Silk* and has

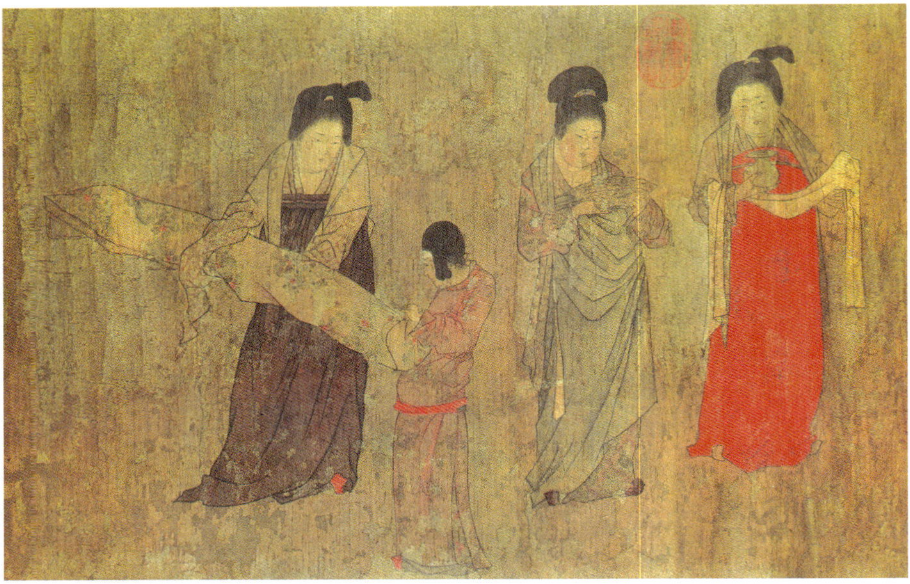

Court Ladies with Fans, scroll (33.7 cm×204.8 cm) (detail), ink and color on silk, attributed to Zhou Fang, Beijing Palace Museum.

added his "Mingchang Seven seal." Zhan has portrayed spiritual elegance in ordinary life.

According to the *Famous Paintings Record of Past Dynasties* and the *Xuanhe Collection of Paintings*, Zhou Fang was particularly good at painting *Qiluo* Characters and portraits and was also accomplished at religious subjects, of which his *Relaxed Mother Bodhisattva of Water and Moon* is a fine example. The Huizong Emperor of the Song Dynasty was a keen collector of his works, particularly those of court ladies, and today we only know many of his paintings through the copies made by this emperor. The aesthetic conception of the *Court Ladies with Fans* is very similar to *Court Ladies Preparing for the Newly Woven Silk*, but Zhou has a contrasting story of bored court ladies. There are sixteen of them and depicted vividly is their sense of loneliness and melancholy in the imperial court: they are more luxurious, dispirited, and plump than is usual. He was criticized in his lifetime and since as being too extreme in his depictions, distorting the *Qiluo* Characters and

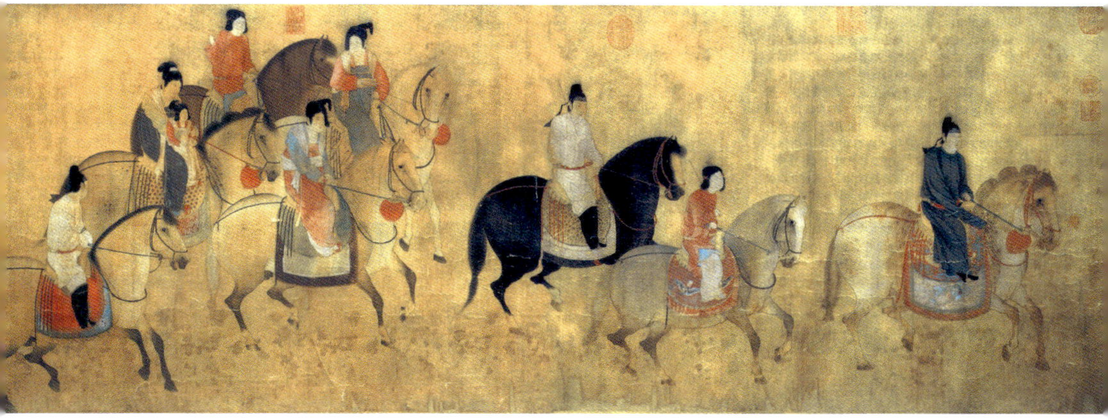

Guo State Queen Spring Outing, scroll (52 cm×148 cm), ink and color on paper, by Zhang Xuan, copy attributed to Emperor Huizong, Liaoning Museum.

ignoring the contemporary aesthetic standard. However, such standards are influenced by the social values and perceptions of the time, and his paintings are a reflection of the fashion and luxurious living of a dynasty at its peak. With the fall of the empire, this aesthetic standard and the fashion associated with it were gone for ever.

The meticulous, rich, and luxurious characteristics of court paintings were gradually extended to the other types, for example, *shanshui*, flowers and birds, and religious paintings during the Tang Dynasty. Chinese paintings are classified into categories by their subject, and each painter would devote himself to one particular branch in order to excel. For example, *Famous Paintings Record of Past Dynasties* alone collected paintings of more than seventy flower and bird specialists. Because of their love for horses, "Saddle Horse Characters" were another important subject for paintings during the Tang Dynasty, for example Cao Ba (active 713–741). Du Fu, wrote in his poem to General Cao Ba, "Jade Flower Piebald Horse," that Cao's painting was like a dragon dancing in the celestial heaven and his skill drove all the horses on other paintings to want to vanish. Han Gan, a student of Cao Ba, was born in Chang'an and lived during the reign of the Xuanzong Emperor,

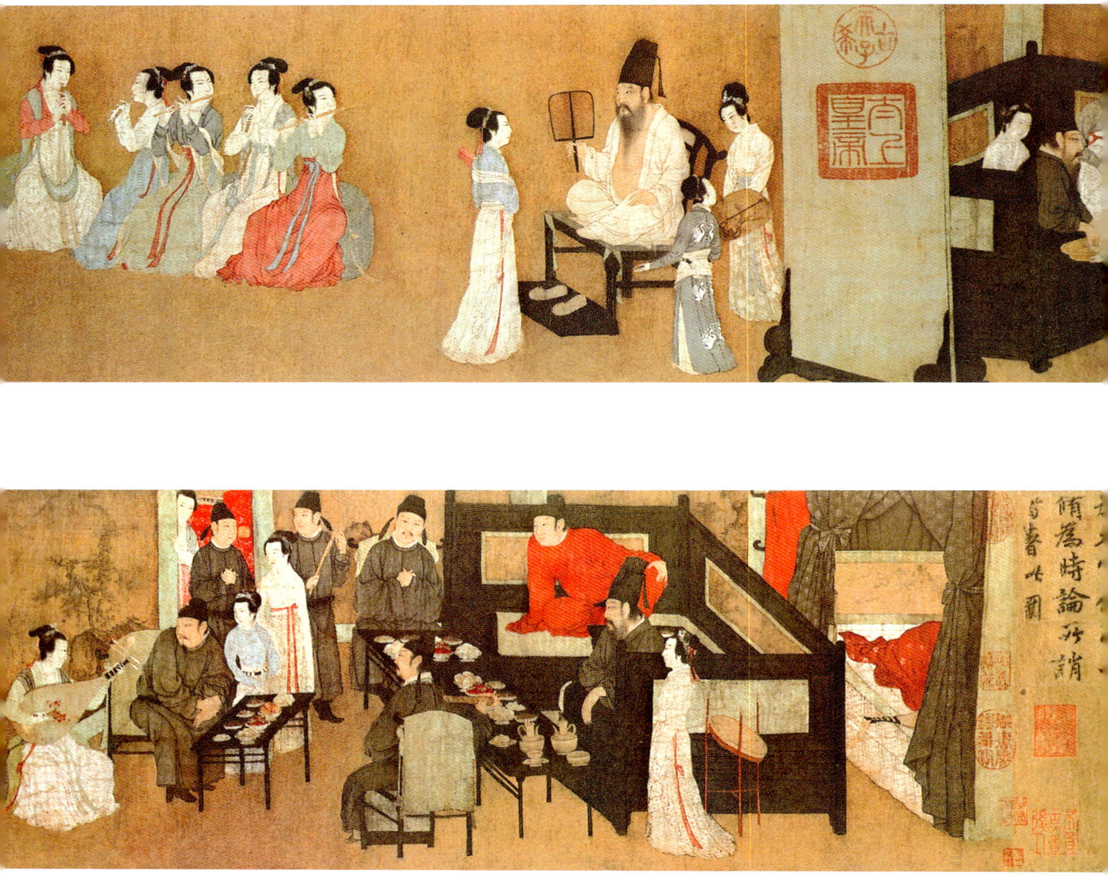

The Night Revels of Han Xizai, scroll (28.7 cm×335.5 cm), ink and color on silk by Gu Hongzhong of the Five Dynasties period, Beijing Palace Museum.

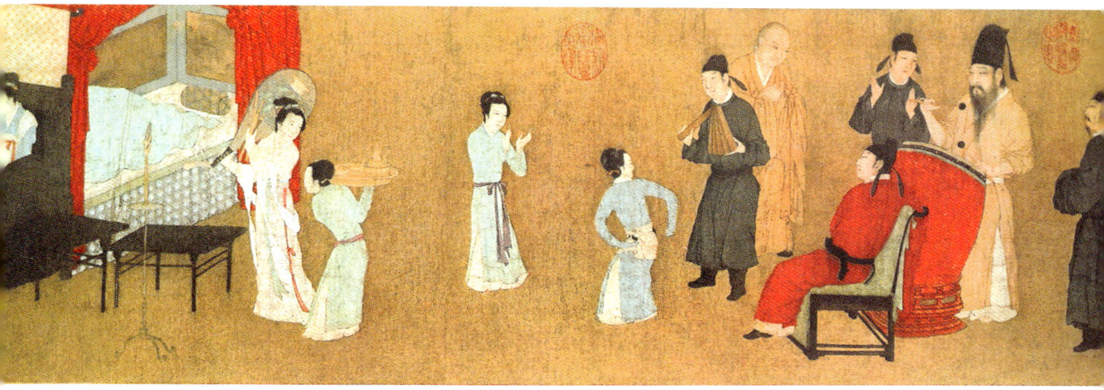

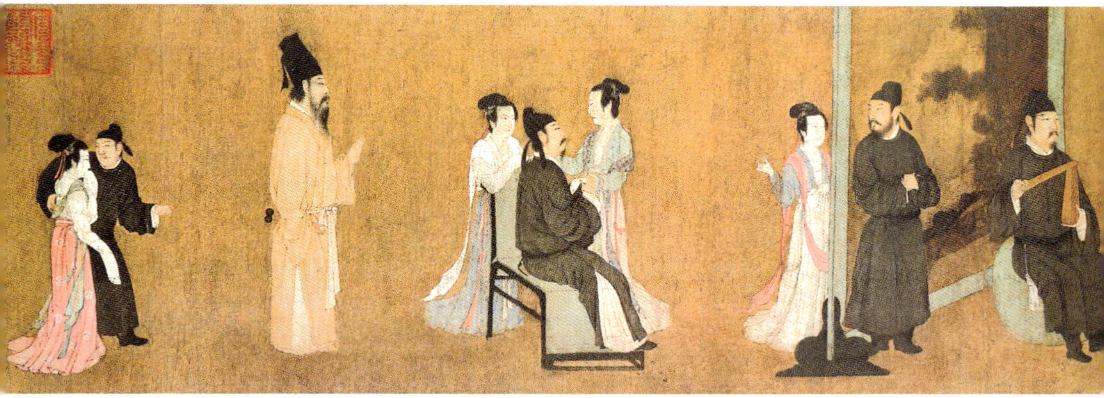

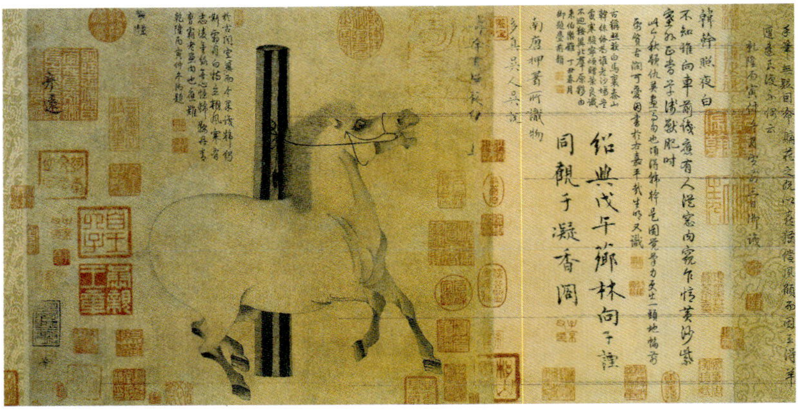

Night-Shining White, scroll (30.8 cm×33.5 cm), ink on paper, by Han Gan, Metropolitan Museum of Art, New York.

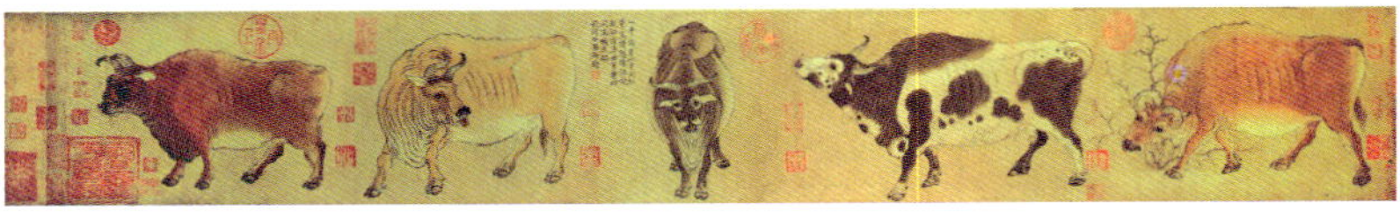

Five Buffalos, scroll (20.8 cm×139.8 cm), by Han Huang, Beijing Palace Museum.

and worked in a winery during his youth and met the famous poet and painter Wang Wei (701–761), who helped him financially so he could learn to paint. After ten years of hard training he was good at portraits, figures, ghosts, and celestial beings, but it was as a leading horse painter of the Tang Dynasty that he was most celebrated for drawing not only an animal's physical likeness but also its spirit. Du Fu in another poem said: "Han Gan painting horses with love on the tip of his brush." Jade Flower Piebald and Night-Shining White were the names of the favourite chargers of Emperor Xuanzong. In *Night-Shining White*, the fiery-tempered steed, with its burning eye, flaring nostrils, and dancing hooves, epitomizes Chinese myths about imported "celestial steeds" that "sweat blood" and were really dragons in disguise. This sensitive, precise drawing, with delicate ink shading, is an example of *baihua* (white painting), a term used in Tang texts to describe monochrome painting with ink shading. The horses in Han Gan's paintings are strong, sturdy, and beautiful, and depicted with meticulous care. They also inherited the fashion of the period, looking plump, almost fat, but muscular. To some extent, they resemble a lovely image of a family pet. Han Gan's other important painting is *Shepherd Horses*, depicting a knight riding a strolling white horse, with a black horse on his right. It is a typical painting of "Saddle Horse Characters" with strong, fine, meticulous sketch lines, and contrasting but complementary colors. The painting was in the imperial households during the South Tang Dynasty and the Xuanhe period, and during the reign of the Huizong Emperor, he wrote on it: "The original copy by Zhou Fang."

Han Huang (723–787) painted *Five Buffalos*, a masterpiece considered as one of the "rare treasure of all periods" by artists and critics during the Yuan Dynasty. Han was an amateur, whose main occupations were agriculturist, and a court official. His speciality was countryside scenes, and farmers and farming animals. *Five Buffalos* is painted on a long paper scroll, and all are contented; each animal has a distinct positioning: grazing quietly, running with head up, facing head-on with a leg stretched from its post, licking at its back, and strolling along. The composition is balanced, with accurate ratios and perspective. The outlines are simple and solid; the color is light but gives a strong sense of heaviness.

The emperor portraits by Yan Liben and the fashionable *Qiluo* and Saddle Horse Characters displayed the newly found generosity and confidence of the Tang Dynasty. From the grace, solemnity, and elegance of the imperial court to the affluent and opulent living standards of aristocracy, we find depicted a golden age of economic prosperity and artistic creativity.

The "Painting Sage"

The outstanding painter of the Tang Dynasty is Wu Daozi, who is considered by many collectors to have the greatest talent ever known. The great poet, Du Fu called him the Painting Sage. *Famous*

Paintings Record of Past Dynasties states: "Wu was walking on the timeline of artistic achievement but he could not see Gu Kaizhi and Lu Tanwei in front of him and turning his head back nobody was following." The poet and painter of the Song Dynasty Su Shi said, "For poets, you could not go beyond Du Zimei (Du Fu); for writers Han Yu; for calligraphers Yan Zhengqing; and for painters Wu Daozi. All the development from the past to the present were completed without exception." Almost all books on painting and its history have admired Wu's achievement and call him the "Painting Sage for a hundred generations."

Wu Daozi (685–785) was born to a poor family in Yu Xian in Henan Province. He started learning calligraphy from a young age and later turned his attention to craft painting, and at the age of twenty his talent started to shine. He went to the capital Luoyang as an amateur painter, and soon the Xuanzong Emperor learned of his reputation and appointed him a court scholar. This was when the Tang Dynasty was at the peak of its prosperity, and the empire enjoyed an unprecedented economic power and sponsored artistic freedom and creativity. In the two capitals, Luoyang, the eastern capital, and Chang'an, the western capital, were assembled the cultural elites and the best, like stars, lit each other up. *Famous Paintings Record of Past Dynasties* notes: "Till now, the Tang Empire had enjoyed its prosperity for nearly two hundred and thirty years, and all the talents assembled and enriched each other, and the most active were during the Kaiyuan and Tianbao periods of Xuanzong's reign," when the important Tang painters, Wu Daozi, Wang Wei, Zhang Zao, Li Sixun, Cao Ba, Han Gan, Chen Hong, Xiang Rong, Liang Lingzan, Zhang Xuan, and Yang Huizhi lived. Together with numerous craft painters, they all competed in artistic creativity, enriched each other, and created a tremendous period of artistic variety and prosperity. Into this environment arrived Wu Daozi, and he grew rapidly to prominence. *Famous Paintings Record of Past Dynasties* presented the Painting Sage as having a near mythical dimension: "He was good at depicting characters of Taoism and

Buddhism but he also showed great talent with other subjects such as *shanshui*, birds and animals, grasses and plants, pavilions and pagodas – almost everything was his specialty."

He painted about four hundred murals of Buddhist subjects in temples around Luoyang and Chang'an, each with its own characteristics and emphasis. The circle of light above Buddha, pillars and beams, arches and frames were all drawn with a single stroke and without the aid of ruler or compass. His unique orchid branches and Brasenia leaves, which look like wrinkled dresses, appear to show gentle breezes, and this style of painting was given a special name, "wind of Wu." He often painted spontaneously in public at Xing Shan Temple in Chang'an, and the people of Chang'an would swarm there, to see the master in action, practicing his one-stroke spontaneous technique, and to cheer the creation of masterpieces in front of their eyes. Wu Daozi also often used a meticulous method to decorate palaces and temples like the craft painters did and became a master of the artistic principle of "following the rhythm and perfecting each one." Consequently, he was not only admired by the cultural elite as the Painting Sage but also considered by the craft painters and decorators as their founding grand master.

Wu Daozi had worked enthusiastically in art, very much like Michelangelo during the Renaissance. *Famous Paintings Record of Past Dynasties* says: "When Wu Daozi was painting, his arches were like blades, his lines like pillars and beams – all without the help of rulers and compasses." When he was doing a figure, whatever the size, he could start with hands and arms or legs and feet and keep the balance of the

"Fluttering Sleeves" and "Wet Clothing"
Tang Dynasty painter Wu Daozi is renowned for his Buddha paintings using smooth strokes. His long sleeves flutter as if blown by the wind, so "Fluttering Sleeves" has become the term used for superb painting techniques and graceful styles, as well as for a representational technique for sleeves. "Wet Clothing" is a style of figure painting in which the clothing appears to be sticking to the bodies of the figures as if they have just come out of water, and was originated by Cao Zhongda in the Northern Qi Dynasty.

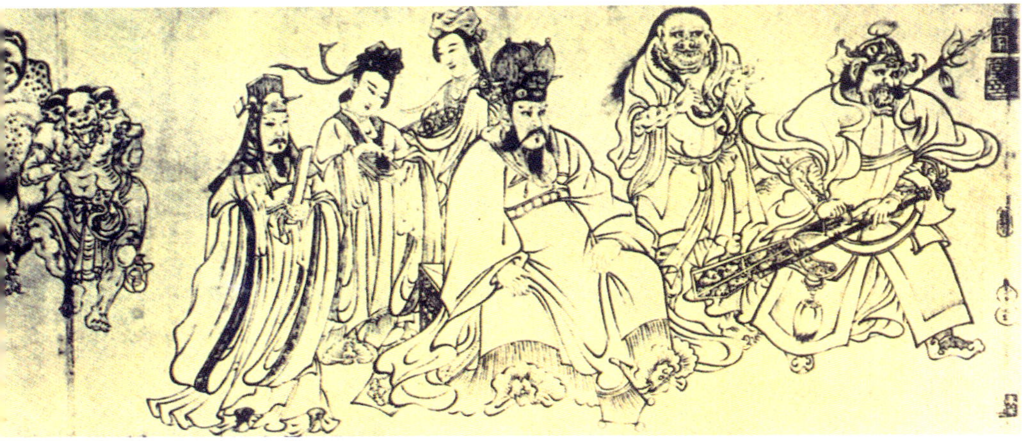

Wu Daozi's painting (copy).

overall composition. With the combination of the meticulousness of calligraphy and the creativity of a great imagination, he painted vivid pictures beyond comparison, full of rhythm, color, and magic. His paintings did not deliberately exaggerate the wonders of heaven or the horrors of hell, and his inspiration mainly came from his thorough observation of earthly reality. His bold and unconstrained style of painting formed a remarkable contrast to the grace and elegant style of his predecessor Gu Kaizhi. However a common feature linked them: they both followed the principles of calligraphy, in particular, the exquisite use of pen and attention to the whole composition. Wu Daozi was a student of the great Tang calligraphers, Zhang Xu (most active during the reign of Xuangzong) and He Zhizhang (ca. 659–744). He was especially fond of the *caoshu* style (a rapid cursive writing style of calligraphy), and his paintings radiated with the vibrant *caoshu* rhythm of "writing."

Wu Daozi spent almost his entire life on religious murals, including paintings depicting Buddhism and Taoism teachings. For example, on the north corridor of the western pagoda at Qianfu Temple, he created a Bodhisattva in his own image. Thereafter,

Han Gan did the same in his religious murals, *Prostitute Xiao Xiao Writing on Chastity* and *A Column of Masters*. They tried symbolically to break the restraints of strict religious teachings and to be creative in a divine world. Wu would not act like a guardian of religion, but as an ordinary painter enjoying free artistic expression. He even brought the aristocrats into the *Hell: A Teaching Illustration*. Wu was also a very successful landscape painter. Once the Xuanzong Emperor sent him to Sichuan to study the sights and views of local importance and specifically asked Wu to bring back sketches of places he visited so he could paint them properly on his return. He returned without a single sketch, and the emperor was very annoyed. However, Wu came to the court, calmly and without any concern, and painted without hesitation. Before the eyes of the emperor and his court officials, a hundred miles of the roaring Jialin River and the vast land of Sichuan appeared at lightning speed. Wu finished the whole painting in one day. The court was astonished.

The religious paintings during the Tang Dynasty followed the traditions of earlier eras, among which the "Cao Family Style" was the most popular. It was started by Cao Zhongda (active 550–577) and was a local version of the original Buddhist painting formula. It depicted figures with their clothes closely sticking to their bodies and was called "Cao dress out of water" or "Wet Clothing." Wu Daozi also distanced himself from the "Cao Family Style" of religious painting, and used a local method. During his early years, Wu Daozi often used delicate lines and a compact and concise style to paint, but in his middle age he adopted a more muscular and free way of expression, often using stronger but mellow lines alternating fine and heavy strokes, and full of life, especially in his signature Brasenia leaves. There were often small spaces between his strokes, giving a sense of broken lines but continuous rhythm. Together with another painter Zhang Sengyao, they collectively created the so-called "Shuti" (the loose style), in contrast to the "Miti" (the tight style) of Gu Kaizhi and Lu Tangwei. During the Six Dynasties, Sui Dynasty, and early Tang period, the Cao Family style

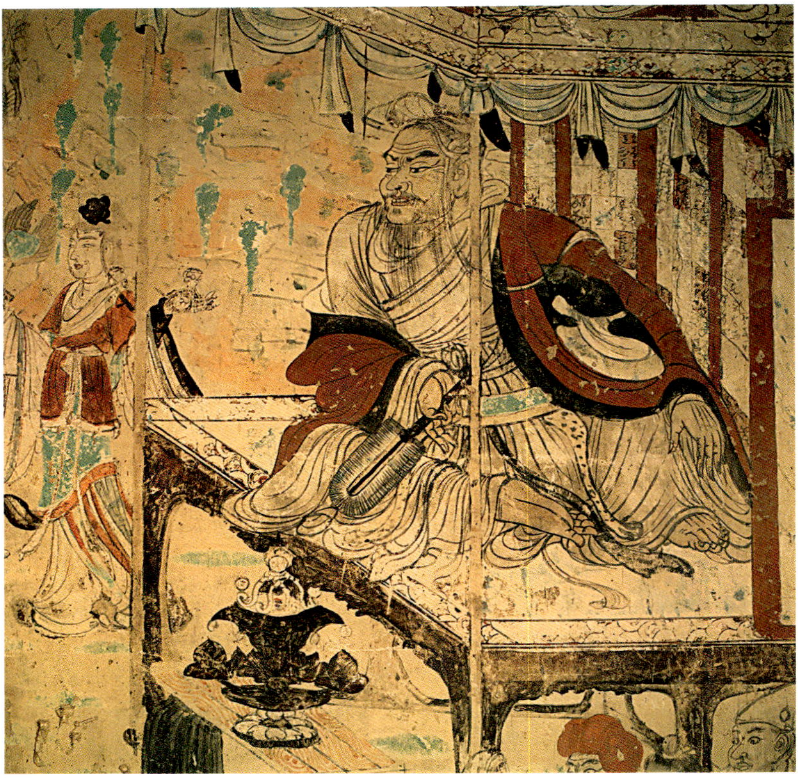

Mural, cave 103 of Mogao Caves, carved in the heyday of the Tang Dynasty, painting of Vimalakirti.

dominated the field while after the Tang Dynasty reached its peak, the local religious painting style of Wu assumed its dominance.

Wu Daozi was a very prolific painter and there are ninety-three paintings in *Xuanhe Collection of Paintings*, including *Presentation of Seal to the Emperor*, *Zhong Kui with Ten Fingers*, *Peacock and Ming Emperor*, *Celestial King with Pagoda*, and *The God Guardian of Buddhism Scripts*. *Celestial King Delivering a Son* is his most important painting, in the Osaka Municipal Museum of Art, and the portrait of Buddha, in Toufuku Temple, Kyoto, Japan; both are considered to be copies. His other important work, *Daozi Book of Scroll Paintings*, is a collection of ink-and-brush sketches painted on

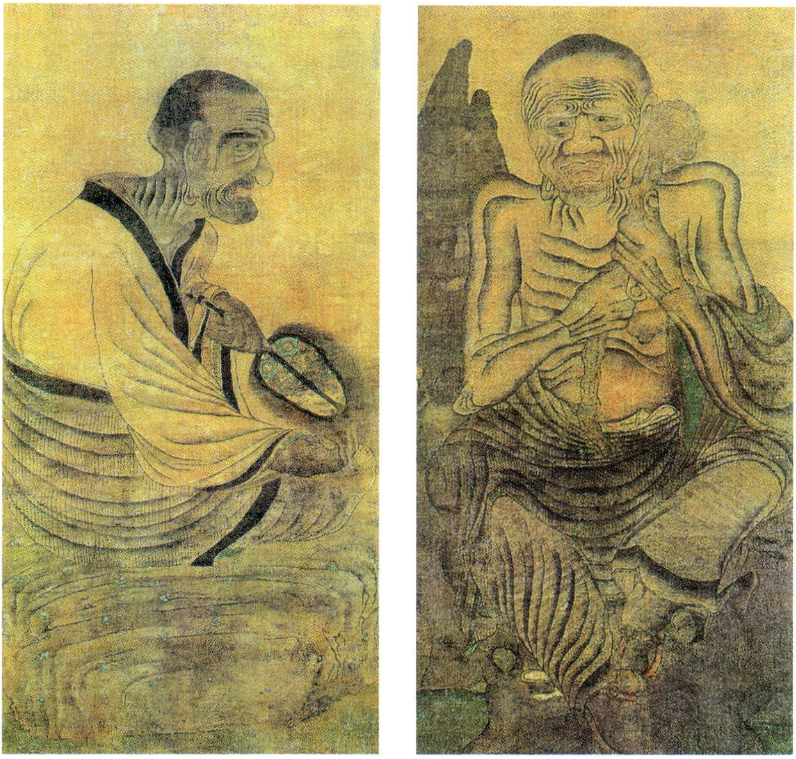

Sixteen Arhats (details), by Guan Xiu of the Tang Dynasties.

paper. It is believed that fifty pieces survived but were smuggled out of China in 1911 and their location is unknown; today we only have copies. Many of the so-called "original" paintings by Wu Daozi are actually copies done by later generations of painters, and although they are much less valuable than his originals, they allow us to study his style and technique. They are the only testimonial to the Painting Sage.

Celestial King Delivering a Son, also called *The Birth of Shakyamuni Buddha*, has been a favorite of connoisseurs for many generations. This masterpiece was based on the Buddhist teaching of the story of the birth of Shakyamuni, the son of King Shuddhadana. The foreground depicts a celestial being riding on an auspicious animal and delivering a baby, while the celestial king, sitting upright, has a happy and anxious expression for he has just completed a very important task. All the court ladies and servants around him express a very similar anxiety. The background illustrates King Shuddhadana carrying the baby Buddha gently, walking slowly forward, with respectfulness and gracefulness. *Daozi Book of Scroll Paintings* depicts many Taoist gods of the earth and their associate celestial beings. They are walking above clouds, and the celestial court provides a heavenly atmosphere. However, all the celestial beings are images of ordinary people of the Tang period, and many of them describe the ghastly tragedy and punishment of hell in the format of a Buddhist teaching illustration, by coincidence very similar to the scenes of Satan and Purgatory in epic poems of the Renaissance in Europe.

Famous Paintings Record of Past Dynasties (Li-dai ming-hua ji)

The Tang Dynasty presided for more than several hundred years, during which time China enjoyed great prosperity, and its artistic world experienced tremendous progress. Many paintings of this period achieved a significance never seen before or afterwards, and many works were published studying them. The earliest such book, *Famous Paintings Record of Past Dynasties*, was written and published by Zhang Yanyuan during the late Tang Dynasty. Zhang Yanyuan's great-grandfather, grandfather, and father all served as high ministers in the Tang Dynasty. His household collected many paintings of the Six Dynasties, Sui Dynasty, and Tang Dynasty.

Other important works on painting and its history during the Tang Dynasty include *Famous Paintings Records of the Tang Dynasty* by Zhu Jingxuan (active 806–835), and *On Shangshui* and *On the Methods of Shanshui* by Wang Wei. *Famous Paintings Record of Past Dynasties* is a comprehensive review and record of paintings in ten volumes divided into three sections: the history of painting, biographies of painters, and collections of paintings. The book deals with all the important issues associated with Chinese painting, from its origin and its social functions. The second section lists 372 important painters, from Xuan Yuan to the Tang Huichang Dynasty period. It also collects comments of critics, noting previous works on painting history and theory. It is essential reading for all those who are interested in Chinese painting.

Desert Treasures

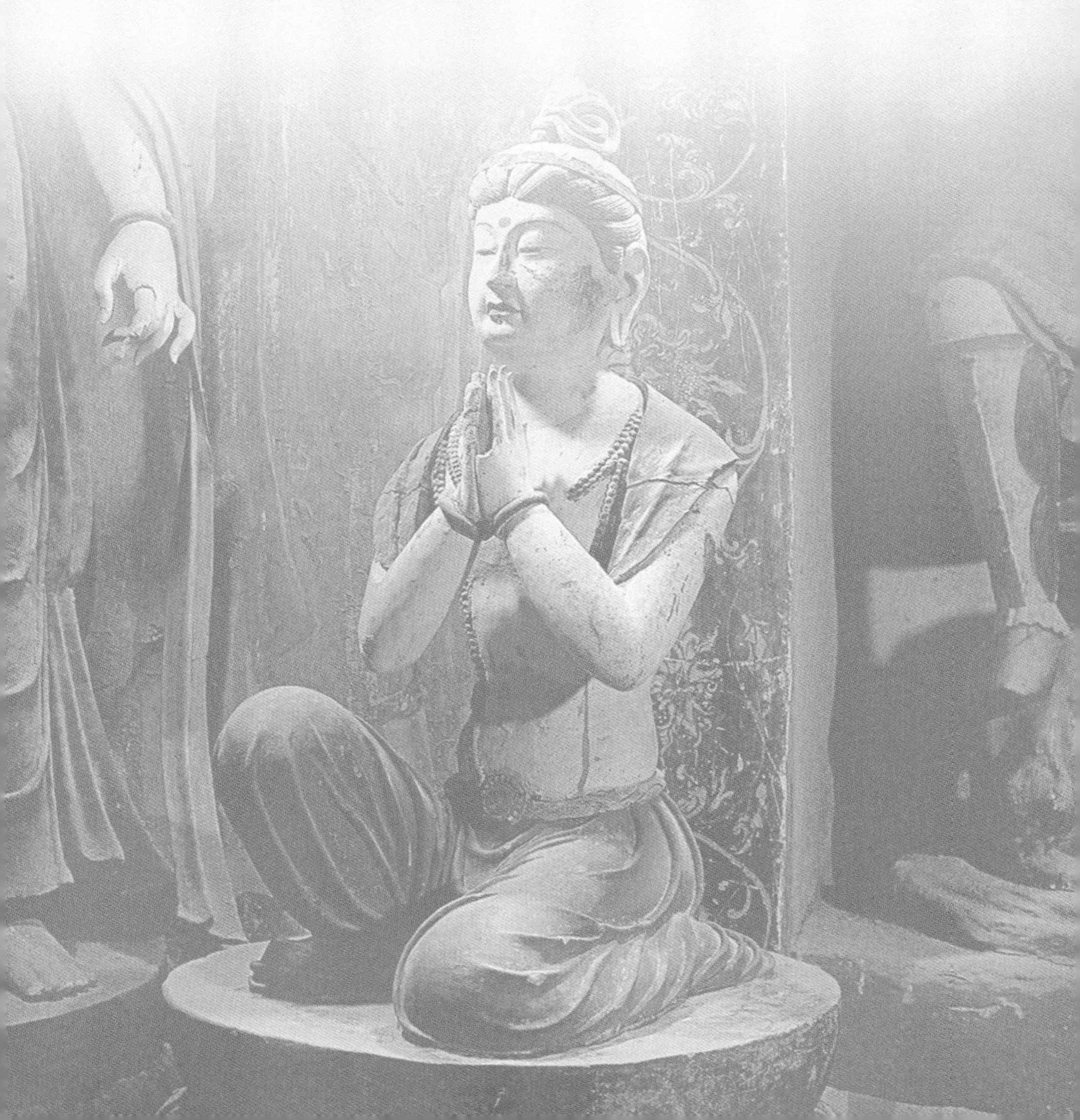

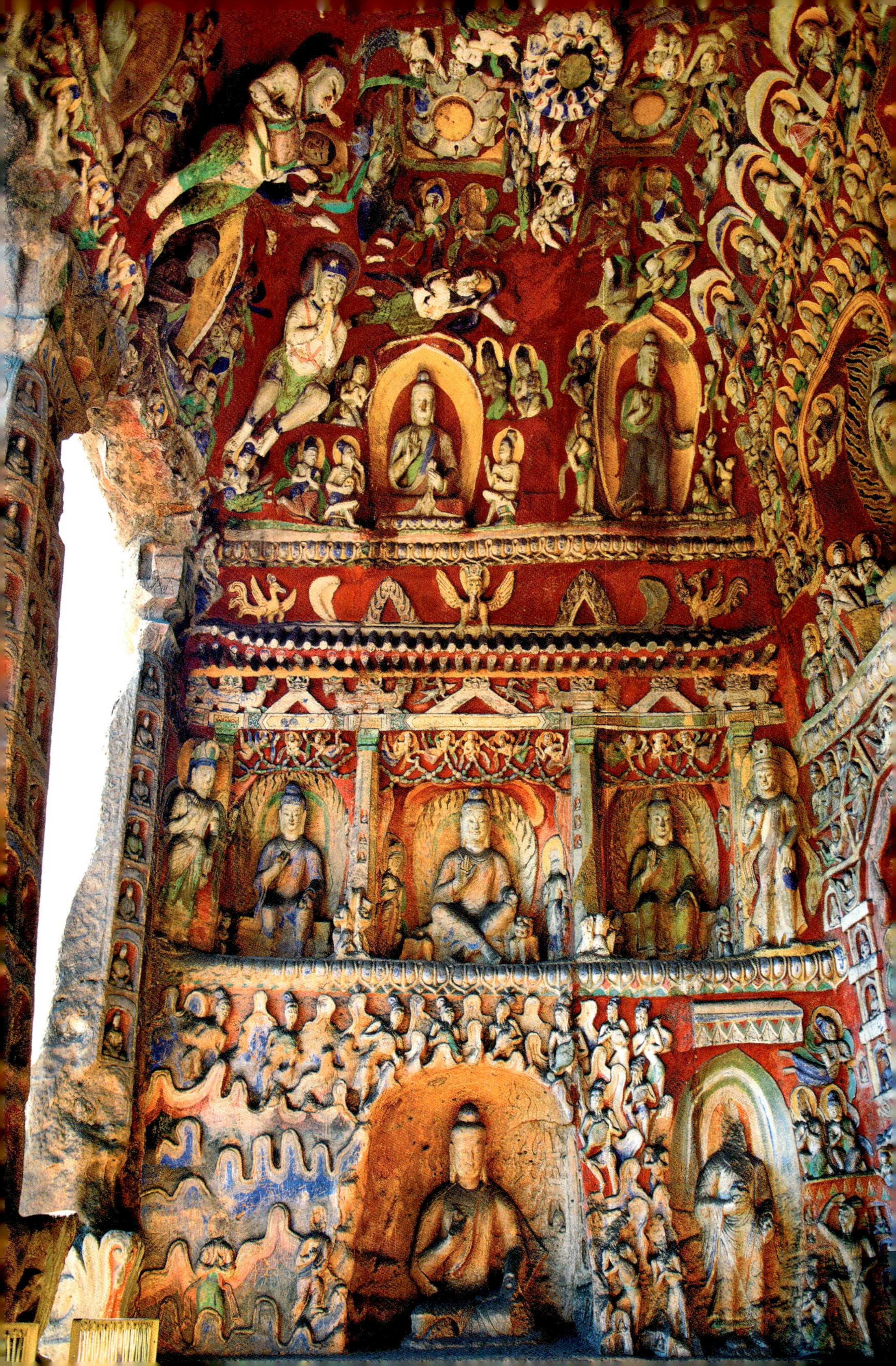

Buddhism Moving Eastwards

Buddhism and the art associated with it originated in India and was spread mainly by two routes, north through central Asia, China, Korea, and Japan, and south to Southeast Asia, and it syncretized local practices and beliefs during its journey. It arrived in China during the reign of the Eastern Han Dynasty in the second century AD, as the "Monograph on Buddhism and Taoism" in *The History of the Wei* states: "As the White Horse Temple built in Luoyang was decorated with plenty of Buddhist drawings that were painted meticulously, the temple became the model for building Buddhist temples in China." The Mingdi of the Han Dynasty ordered portraits of Buddha painted and displayed in the Qingliang Pagoda and the Xianjie Imperial Tomb, which demonstrated that Buddhist art had as long a history in China as Buddhism itself. Both Buddhism and its associated art

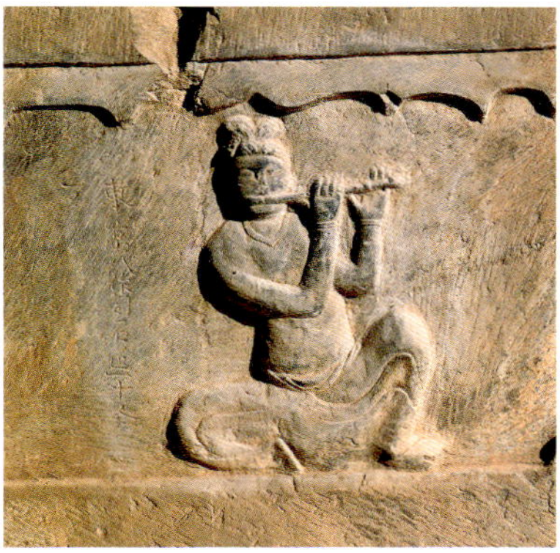

Statue, Longmen Caves, musician.

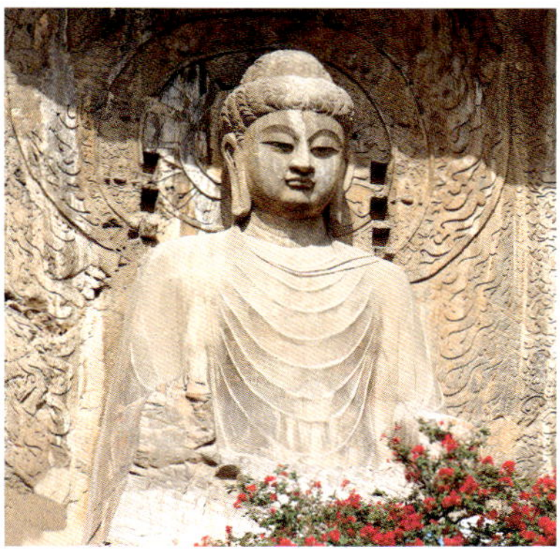

Feng Xian Temple, Longmen Caves, statue of *Lushena* Buddha, height 17.14 m.

are very important and influential sources for the development of art in China, second only to the traditional Chinese philosophical wisdom (Confucianism) and teachings.

The development and progression of Buddhist art were primarily subject to its religious beliefs, and two of the most

< Cave 12 of Yungang Caves, the "Music Cave," with scenes from a music festival celebrating the enlightenment of Sakymuni.

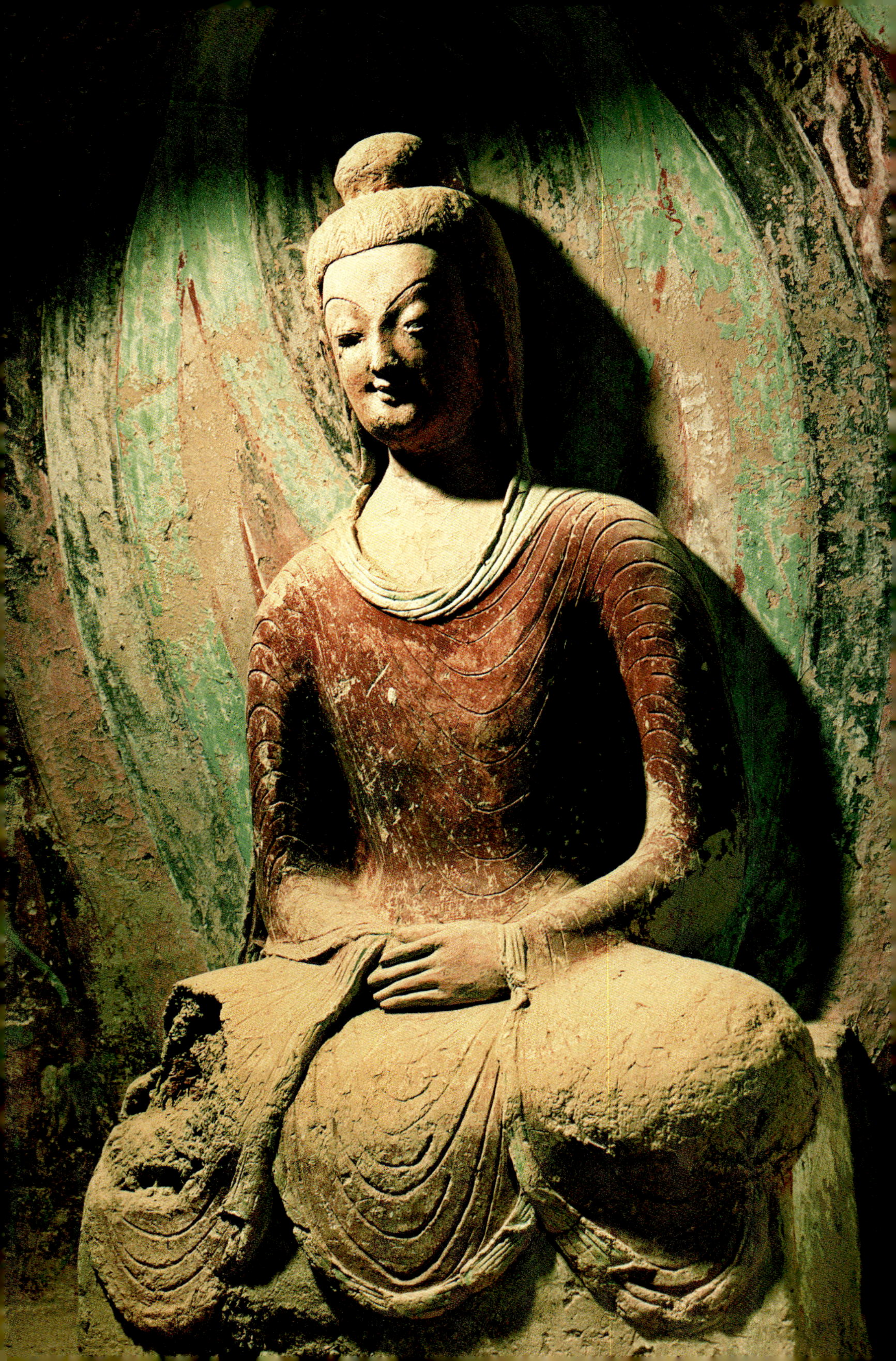

important characteristics of Buddhism are worship of Buddha's image and the confirmation of protocols. Buddhist art developed in line with these traditions in order to help the teaching of the sutras and to assist the monks living in groups: the Buddha's Sculptures were so important to Buddhism that in China it was often called the religion of Buddha's Sculptures. Their paintings mainly displayed the image of Buddha and illustrated their teachings, such as the birth of Buddha, the legend of reincarnation, and penance and enlightenment. In the very beginning, Buddhism was a practical religion, but after the death of Buddha Shakyamuni, believers started to worship his relics and possessions after his cremation. They began to build pagodas to store these relics and painted murals and created sculptures to worship him and his teachings.

The Chinese cave murals by and large illustrated Buddhist arts. The Shanxian Caves and Kizil Caves in Xinjiang are perhaps the earliest and were carved in the third century AD. The Mogao Caves, or the caves of the thousand Buddhas, in Dunhuang are the most representative of a large-scale group of caves to have survived. They played an important role in transforming Buddhist art from that of its birthplace to that of the religion as it became in China. The Mogao Caves influenced both the Buddhism that was spread to the west of China and the Buddhist cave art in other parts of China itself. Other important sites of mural caves in China include: Bingling Temple Caves and Maijishan Caves in Gansu Province, Yungang Caves and Tianlong Mountain Caves in Shanxi Province, Longmen Caves and Gongxian Caves in Henan Province, Xiangtangshan Caves in Hebei Province,

Bian Xiang

"Bian Xiang," or just "Bian," refers to illustrations in pictures or carvings from the sutras. They primarily depict three types of scenes: the activities of the supreme Being and its attendants in their Pure Land, often known as "Configuration," for example, "The Configuration of the Pure Land of the West"; one or a series of paintings recounting the life of the Buddha, from the biography of Sakyamuni, often known as "The Legend of the Buddha"; and one or a series of paintings themed around the classics in the tale of Jataka (prior to the birth of Prince Sakya), often known as "Jataka."

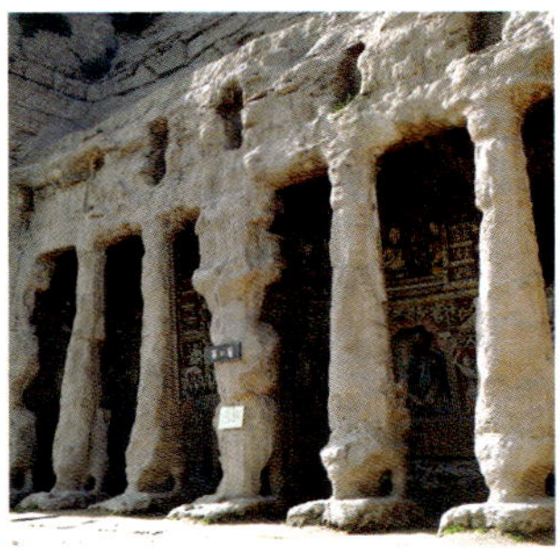

Murals on the top of cave 10 of Yungang Caves, *Fairies Going to Heaven.*

< Cave 259 of Dunhuang Mogao Caves, carved between 384 and 534. Most statues in these cases are colored images of Buddha, of which this is a fine example of the early period.

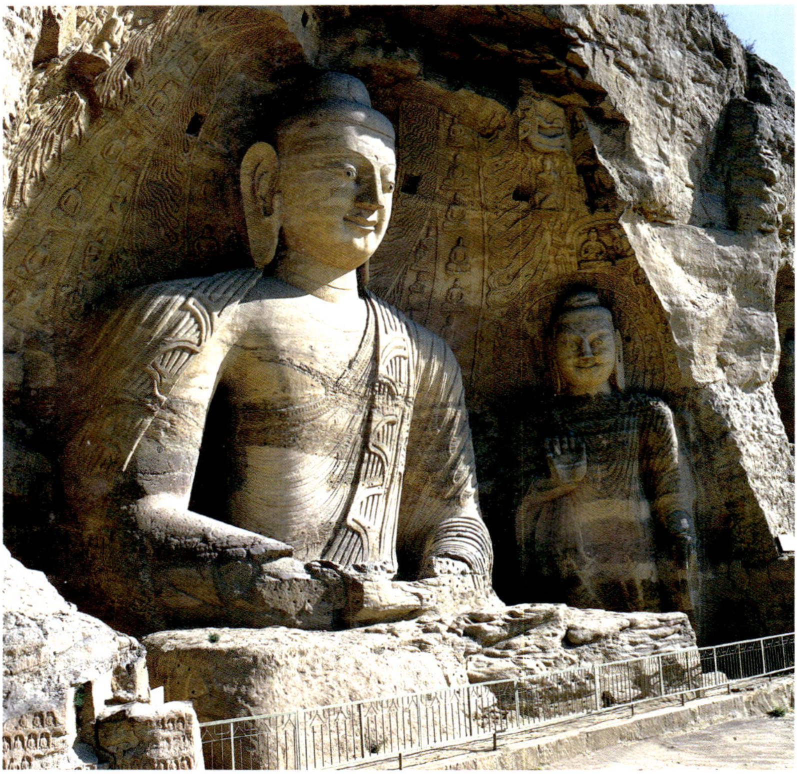

Cave 20 of Yungang Caves, statue of sitting Sakymuni, height 13.7 m.

Dazu Caves in Sichuan Province, and Jianchuan Caves in Yunnan Province.

Zhang Yanyuan writes in *Famous Paintings Record of Past Dynasties*, that many important painters in the Wei and Jin Dynasties and the Tang Dynasty, including Cao Zhongda, Gu Kaizhi, Lu Tangwei (ca. 485), Zhang Sengyao (active 502–549), and Wu Daozi were also known for their achievements in painting Buddhist subjects, which broadened their appeal and their renown. During the late Wei and Jin Dynasties, Zhang Sengyao was the most influential, as *Famous Paintings Record of Past Dynasties* comments on his technique: "One or two strokes, and an image appeared; from what was available he created what was almost impossible;

his were accurate portraits and an unprecedented achievement; his art had precise features and communicated rhythms." Before the Sui and Tang Dynasties, he was one of the most important pioneers and promoters of the newly arrived Buddhist art form. Cao Zhongda, however, had created his own style of religious painting, the "Cao Family Style," one of the four important schools of religious painting techniques. Earlier paintings and sculptures during the Wei and Jin Dynasties had a very similar artistic style to that of Indian Gupta Dynasty, with figures in closely fitting clothes showing the body beneath ("Wet Clothing" style). This and the "Wu Family Style" ("Fluttering Sleeves" style) of Wu Daozi were the two most important types of Buddhist paintings in China: "Cao family style is like a character wearing a silk dress rising out of the water, and Wu family style is like a silk ribbon flying in a breeze." Most of Cao Zhongda's works have not survived but a rare sculpture of Buddha Shyakmuni in Luye Garden has his signature wet-dress style. The Wus' looser-fitting attire, with flowing sleeves and ribbons moving gently like a celestial being of Chinese legend, can often be seen in the murals in Dunhuang.

Shaping Buddhist art to fit in China was not complete until the Sui and Tang Dynasties, but most of its important art works were finished during this transformation process, and by the end of the Tang Dynasty, the format became truly Chinese.

Buddhism flourished in China during the Wei and Jin Dynasties, a period of political instability and wars with the provinces divided. Dynasties came and went without effective control or authority. The people, living in turmoil and chaos, lost their faith in the decadent ruling class and in the traditional Chinese philosophical teachings, Confucianism. Metaphysics became fashionable. Ideologically, it was one of the most active periods in Chinese history. Into this maelstrom, Buddhism arrived and soon gained tremendous popularity; from the emperor and court officials to the ordinary people, there was remarkable enthusiasm for this new religion. The whole country constructed

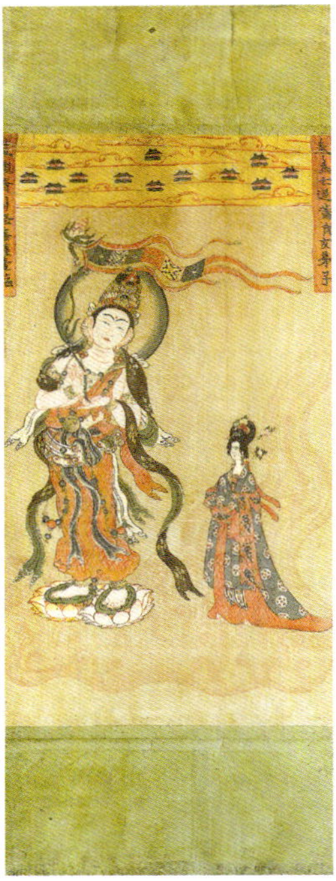

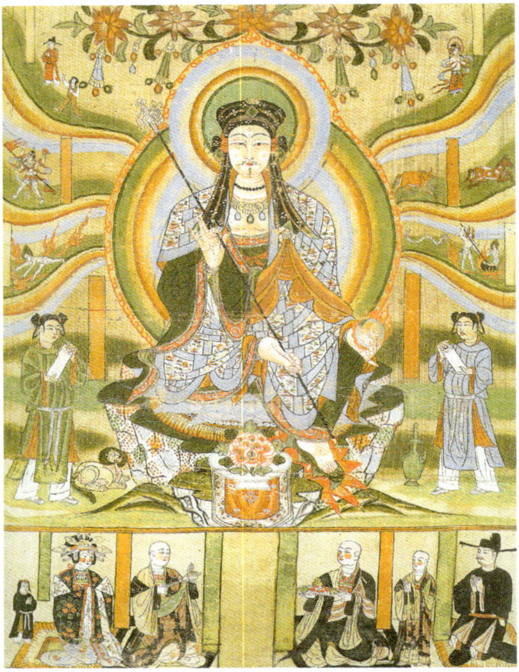

(left) Mother Buddha silk scroll, from Buddhist manuscripts at Dunhuang Mogao Caves, Guimet Museum, Paris.
(right) Bodhisattva silk scroll, from Buddhist manuscripts at Dunhuang Mogao Caves, Guimet Museum, Paris.

religious buildings, creating tens of thousands of temples, pagodas, towers, and caves. During the Northern Wei period (386–534), the ruling class installed Buddhism as the state religion. Most of the important caves were made at this time, including Bingling Temple Caves, Yungang Caves, and Maijishan Caves, together with majority of the sculptures and murals in them, and major parts of Mogao Caves, including the colored chambers. The paintings and sculptures mainly depicted legends and the life stories of Buddha and Bodhisattvas, emphasizing penance and enduring hardship to seek enlightenment. The murals and sculptures were often constructed to complement each other. Profiles are simple and elegant, with many of the original Indian features, and succinct geometry.

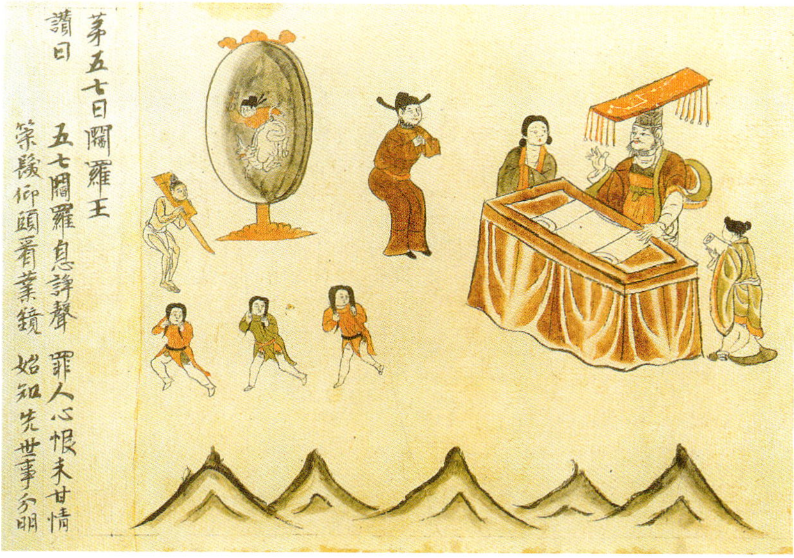

Scroll, Buddhist manuscript from Dunhuang Caves, National Library of France.

The simplicity and sincerity of the North Wei Dynasty were gradually replaced by lavishness and elegance during the Tang Dynasty. Many elements of the original Indian Buddhist art disappeared and the incorporation of local Chinese features in Buddhist images took place quietly but steadily, as the national confidence returned and there was a rediscovery of traditional Confucianism. Prosperity, economic power, and national confidence combined with inspired artistic imagination and provided a perfect setting for many magnificent artistic projects. The scale, the enthusiasm, and the order of these projects is impressive. The murals of this period are mainly of the *Western Paradise of Amitabha*, depicting its celestial abundances, a Buddhist utopian ideal, and the *Dhammapada Scripts*. Illustration was used to teach Buddhist scripts, with the addition of elements of ordinary daily life in China. These murals are often solemn, yet lavish, and majestic, but also with secular delights and poeticized details of daily life. The portraits of Yan Liben, the *Qiluo* Characters of Zhang

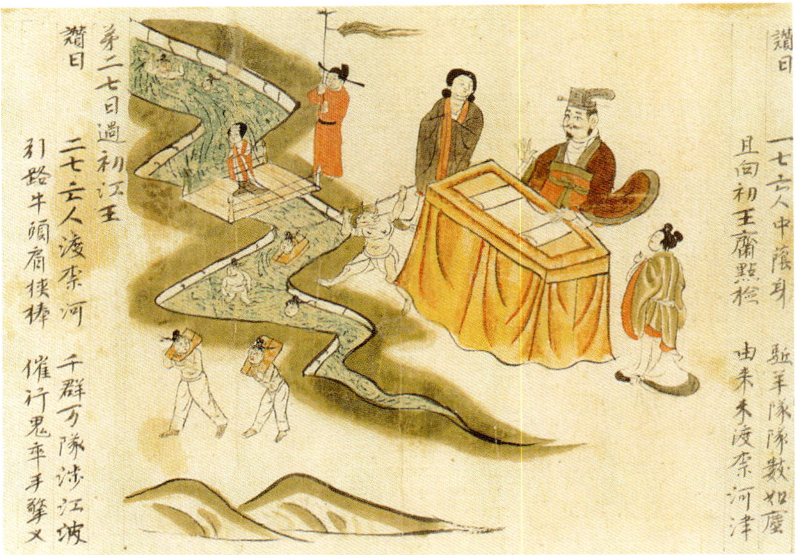

Scroll, Buddhist manuscript from Dunhuang Caves, National Library of France.

Xuan and others, and the paintings by Wu Daozi defined major characteristics of paintings during the Tang Dynasty, and many of these can also be found in the religious murals. Spiritual Buddha and Bodhisattvas were created out of the same molds as secular emperors and court ladies.

In comparison to the simplistic and bold but unsophisticated expressions of the North and South periods, the techniques used in the murals in the Tang period are more refined and artistically imaginative. Many were learned from the court officials and imperial painters; some of the latter had directly contributed to the religious projects, and brought with them their cultural perspectives and techniques. The Maijishan and Mogao Cave murals have pure colors and are full of variety, while the compositions are heavy and complicated. The characters are modeled from court officials and ladies of that period, dignified, gracious, and used to luxury. The musicians and musical instruments displayed in front of Bodhisattvas are more

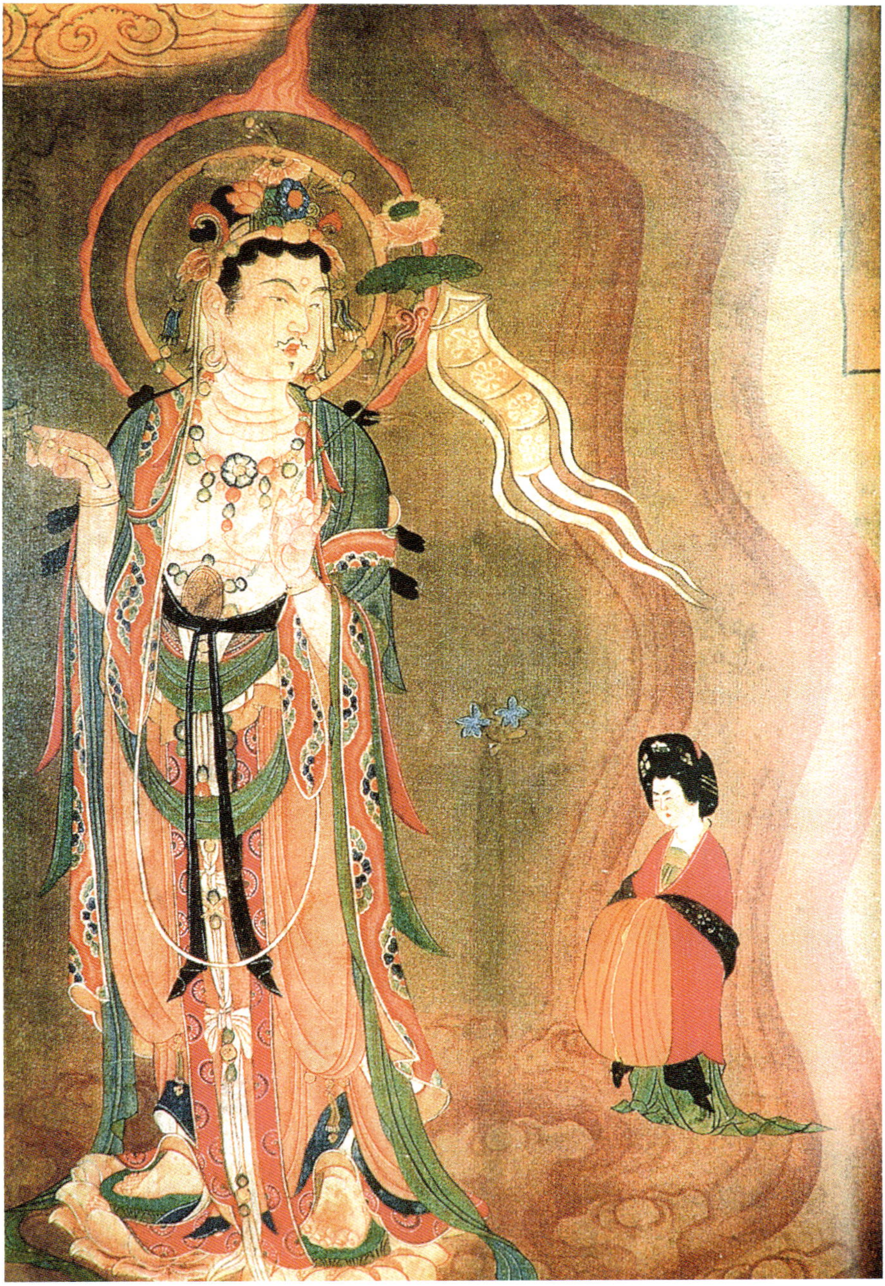

Bodhisattva guiding a dead woman to heaven, silk scroll of the Tang period, from Dunhuang Caves.

extravagant than the murals in Ajanta. The Seven Pagodas, flowers, musicians, lotus ponds, trees, and birds in the western paradise of Amitabha are a fantasy of luxurious and lavish living of celestial abundance, in sharp contrast to the need for strict penance to seek enlightenment. The Buddhas, Bodhisattvas, and other celestial beings have full sturdy figures, with red cheeks, and display grace and elegance, a reflection of the fashionable aesthetic standards of the Tang Dynasty. The mural creators were able to plan and portray complicated scenes and to provide balance in the colossal size. They used the positions of palatial pavilions and mansions to indicate depth, exploited shading colors, controlled the width and variety of lines of individualize characters, and also included delightful details of secular daily life to enrich and humanize paradise.

The enthusiasm for depicting the Pure Land of the western paradise led to the creation of many magnificent religious pictures of the celestial world and pushed their creators to an unprecedented level of sophistication. But then excessive aestheticism and overindulgence finally broke down the spirit of the religion in the paintings. Some artists went back to the traditions of simplicity and sincerity, and others made religious paintings without any deep essence. So it is not surprising that Buddhist art went into decline during the Song Dynasty.

Dunhuang Mogao Caves

The Mogao Caves are built on the cliffs between the Mingshao and Sanwei Mountains to the southeast of Dunhuang, and measure 1,618 meters in length from south to north. The building and carving started in AD 366 and continued for about a thousand years, during which time all the dynasties participated but the most active was the Tang Dynasty. There are 45,000 square meters of murals, and 2,000 colored sculptures have survived and constitute the largest and best-preserved collection of Buddhist cave art and treasures in the world. Dunhuang was a strategic point on the Silk Road from the west frontier of China, so it was important for the exchange of people and culture between China and the western regions (*xiyu*).

The Dunhuang Mogao Cave treasures include architecture, color sculptures, murals, as well as books and records, with the art in three integrated groups. The colored sculptures and murals from the Northern Wei and Western Wei Dynasties (535–556) are the highest achievement of the early period of Dunhuang arts, with thirty-six caves belonging to this period. The murals are painted on the walls, ceilings, and supporting pillars. Apart from a few decorative paintings, most murals in the Mogao Caves illustrate Buddhist stories, the birth of Buddha, and Buddhist doctrine. There are many images of Bodhisattvas, celestial beings, and musicians and dancers. For example, *Prince Sattva Feeds Himself to the Hungry Tigress* in cave 254, *Conversion of the 500 Robbers* in cave 285, *Buddha's Preaching* in cave 249, *The Nine-colored Deer Saves the Drowning Man* in cave 257, and *The Buddha's Life Stories* in cave 290 are all delicately painted with rigorous composition, and all are masterpieces of high artistic value and achievement.

The murals have kept many original elements of Buddhist art in subject and painting methods. The Buddha's life and Jataka stories all come directly from the Buddhist classics, and similar murals and subjects are found in caves in India. The images and features from a foreign land were kept unchanged, as they were viewed as representative of the gods and accepted as the spiritual essence of Buddhism – for example, the half-naked images and postures of Buddha and various gods. The "Indian coloring method" of using

Dunhuang Frescos

The internationally acclaimed Dunhuang No. 1 Cave was first built in 366. The frescos and color figures in the early caves were heavily influenced by India and Central Asia. "The unique Dunhuang style" was developed during the Northern Wei Dynasty, while the influence of the Central Plains culture was most significant in the Western Wei Dynasty. Works from this era mostly depict local versions of tales of Jataka and Buddhist monks and nuns, while subjects from India and Central Asia integrated with Chinese themes and styles in the same cave, as seen in cave 249, built in the final years of the Northern Wei Dynasty, where the main Buddha sculpture is flanked by Bodhisattva and Apsaras, and surrounded by many smaller Buddha sculptures, known as "The Thousand Buddhas." The colored niche for the Buddha above the main Buddha depicts Apsaras playing musical instruments. Representative Dunhuang caves include cave 275 (from the Sixteen Kingdoms Period), caves 257 and 254 (Northern Wei Dynasty), cave 428 (Northern Zhou Dynasty), and cave 285 (from the Western Wei Dynasty).

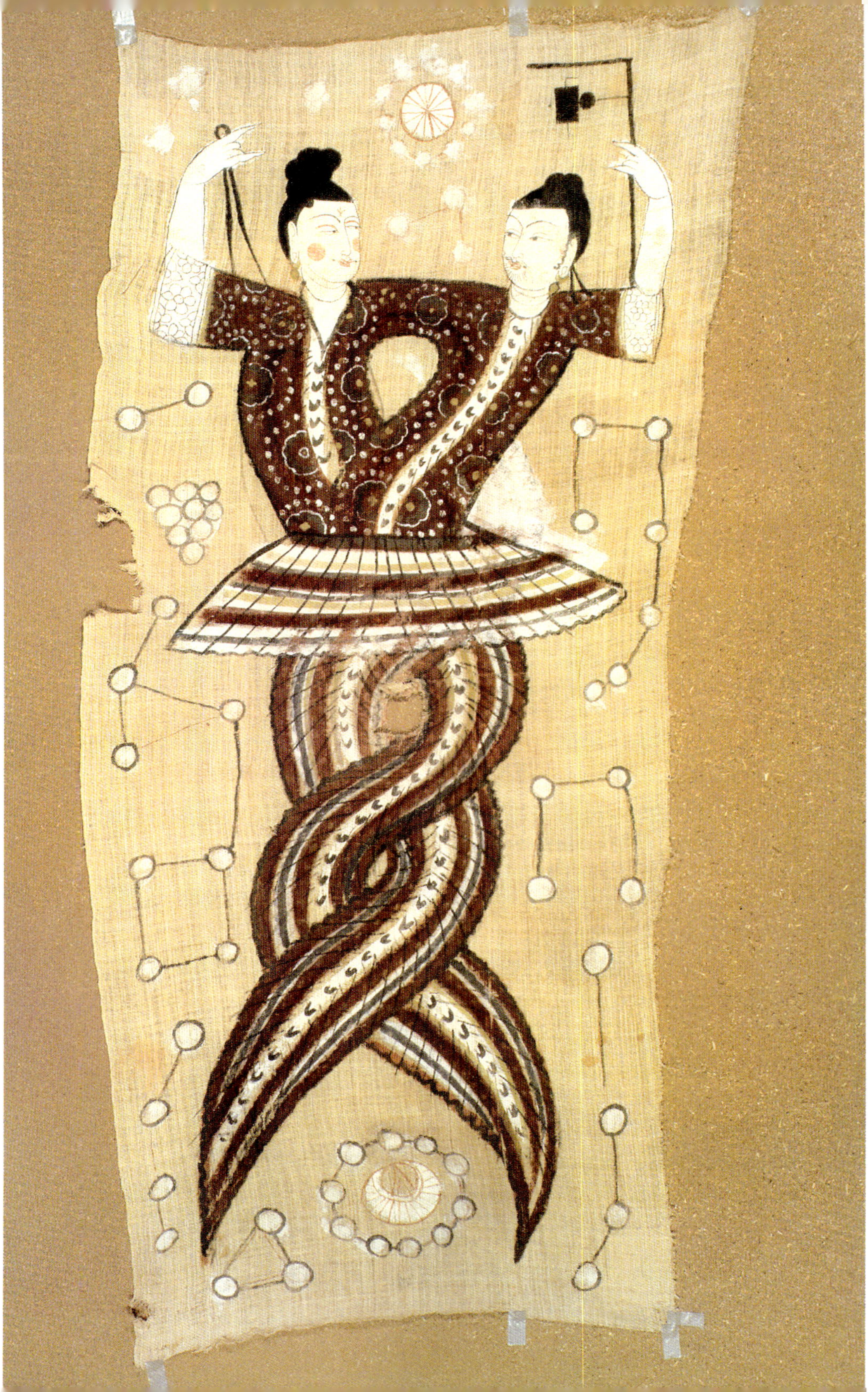

dark and light shades to depict a sense of three dimensions is another example. However, small details were left more or less to the imagination of the painters who used their own experience – for example, the hunting scenes and clothing and body features. Musicians, celestial beings, and minor Bodhisattvas have become half Indian and half Chinese, but more realism was inhibited during the Northern Wei Dynasty because of the deep respect and admiration for the religion from a foreign land. Consequently, the mural figures are very bold and unconstrained, and the conception and colors are generally very pure with an overall decorative effect.

The murals in the Ajanta caves in India have scenes of entertainment and performance, banqueting and drinking, and games and matches. All the Bodhisattvas are dressed lavishly in bright colors and are placed in a variety of postures. Even the devils look like part of a stage setting and do not show horror or fear. In contrast, murals in the Northern Wei period are more frightening and ghastly in depicting such subjects, such as penance, feeding tigers, and robbers taking eyes, and although the composition and colors are bold and unconstrained, there is no sense of gentleness or loveliness.

Blazing fires depicted on the murals in Mogao caves 249 and 257 radiate heat and flame, which reminds us of the Gothic style of Christian paintings. They were an extension of ancient Chinese

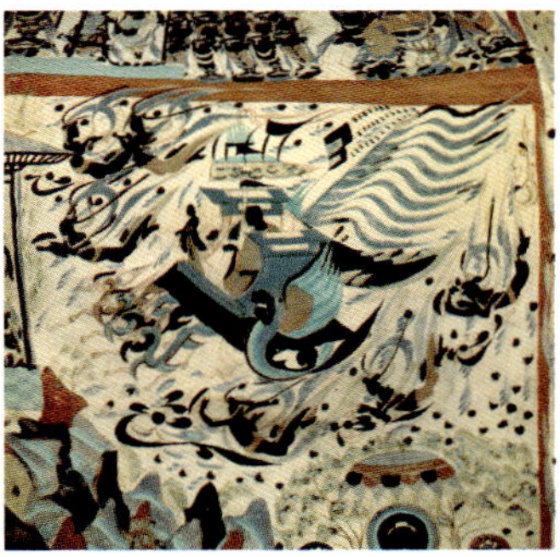

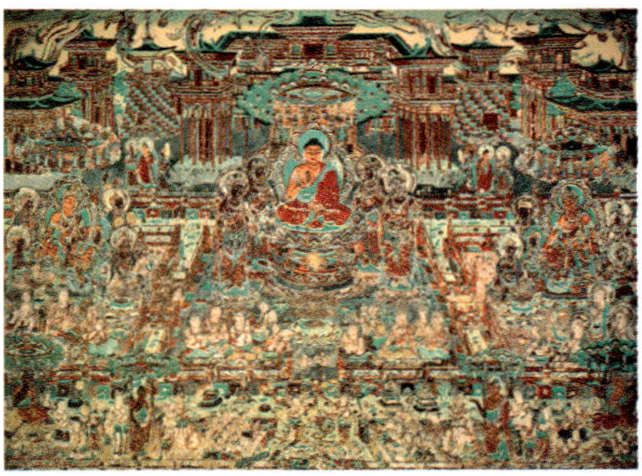

(left) Cave 423 of Dunhuang Mogao Caves, carved during the Sui period, with the inscription: "*on Mogao Caves*."
(right) Sutra of the Buddha of Infinite Life, cave 217, carved during the height of the Tang Dynasty, mural from Dunhuang Mogao caves.

< Fuxi and Nuwu, silk scroll from Buddhist manuscripts, Dunhuang Mogao Caves, Guimet Museum, Paris.

silk and brick-plate paintings in the Han period, seen in the paintings of Gu Kaizhi. Similarly the Bodhisattvas, Buddhas, and celestial beings look like saints and angels in Christian teachings, except they combine Indian figures with Chinese elements such as silk dresses and ribbons, and spreading flower petals, which adds vividness and mysticism to a rather sincere and plain subject. Several hunting murals and *The Nine-colored Deer Saves the Drowning Man* again combine the Buddhist story with the scenes of brick-plate paintings: an imaginative and symbolic expression of people and animals, with the mountains and trees in the background painted with the local red clay and other heavy colors, a technique often used in gold and silver art wares and on murals in tomb chambers during the Han period.

In *Illustration of Defeating the Evil King* in cave 254, a whole story is told. Shakyamuni is sitting solemnly in the middle and by his side stand the evil king, his three evil beauties and other demons,

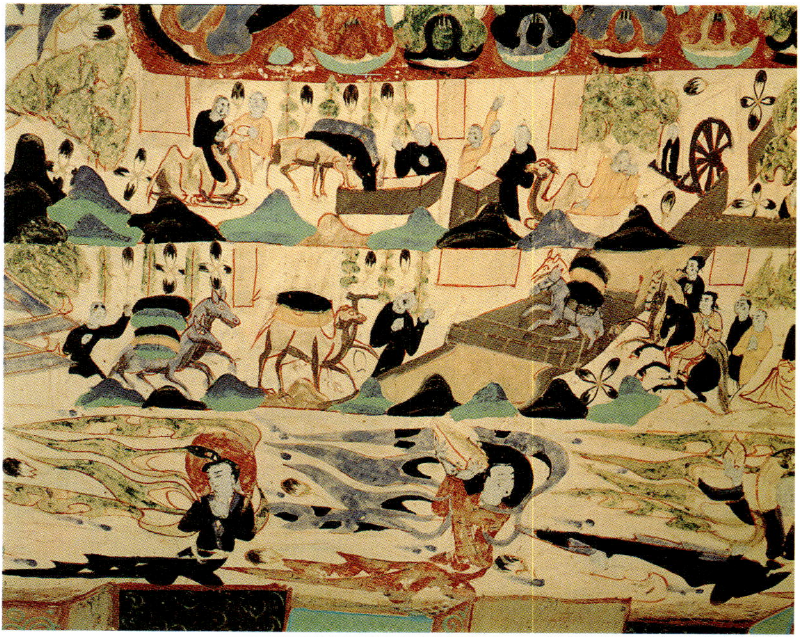

Cave 296 painted 557-581 in Dunhuang Mogao Caves. Top and bottom sections depict the trade route of the Silk Road.

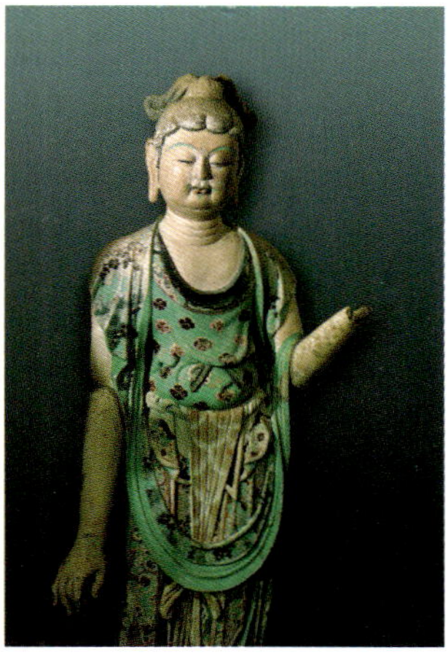

Colored statue in cave 194 of Dunhuang Mogao Caves of the Tang period. Most Buddhas have chubby cheeks, plump bodies, and light clothing, a reflection of the aesthetic standard of the period.

and it depicts Buddha avoiding the temptation of beauty and defeating the force of evil. When the evil king's plots failed, he fell to the earth, and the three "beauties" reveal themselves as old women. The earth is trembling and the mountains quake. The heads of other demons fall from their shoulders, and their bodies run away as quickly as they can. The style is relatively simple and plain, mainly relying on the contrast between the shaking of the earth and mountains and the violent demons with the serenity of Shakyamuni. The scenes of terror are almost as if the painter had temporarily lost his sanity, disregarding conventional and secular aesthetic standards.

The Mogao murals of the Sui and Tang periods concentrate more on the Purification of the Buddha Field, illustrations of the Buddhist scripts, and portraits of Buddha and Bodhisattvas, rather than sacrifice, penance, liberation, and the Jataka Stories. They are much richer in content, have clearer colors, and are more expressive. Since the western paradise was a fashionable concept, there are about 228 murals depicting the Purification of the Buddha Field. Even other topics, for example *Musicians on the Pure Land* and *Paying a Debt of Gratitude*, adopt the western paradise as a background. There are 207 Mogao caves carved during the Tang Dynasty, which is usually divided into four periods, the early, the great, the middle and the late Tang: examples are cave 220 built in the sixteenth year of Zhenguang period (642); cave 335 built in the second year of Chuihong period (686), and caves 130 and 172 built during the Kaiyaung and Tianbao periods; cave 112; and cave 156, respectively.

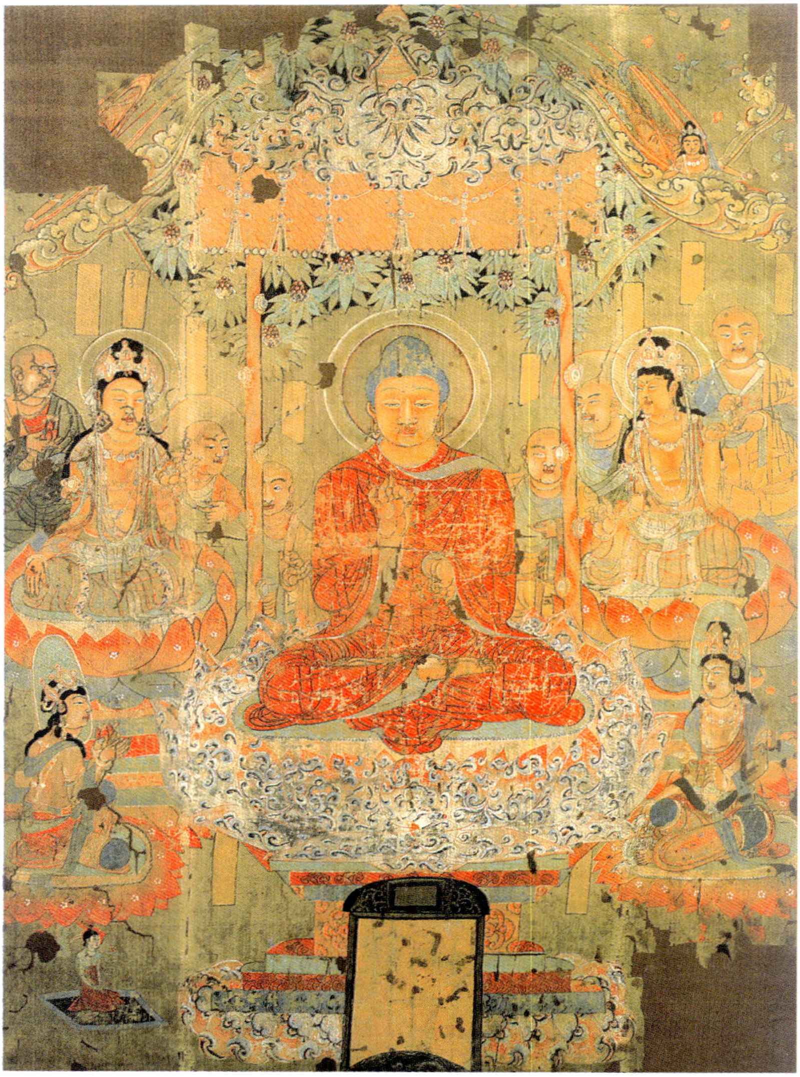

The Amitabha silk painting, from Dunhuang Mogao Caves, British Museum.

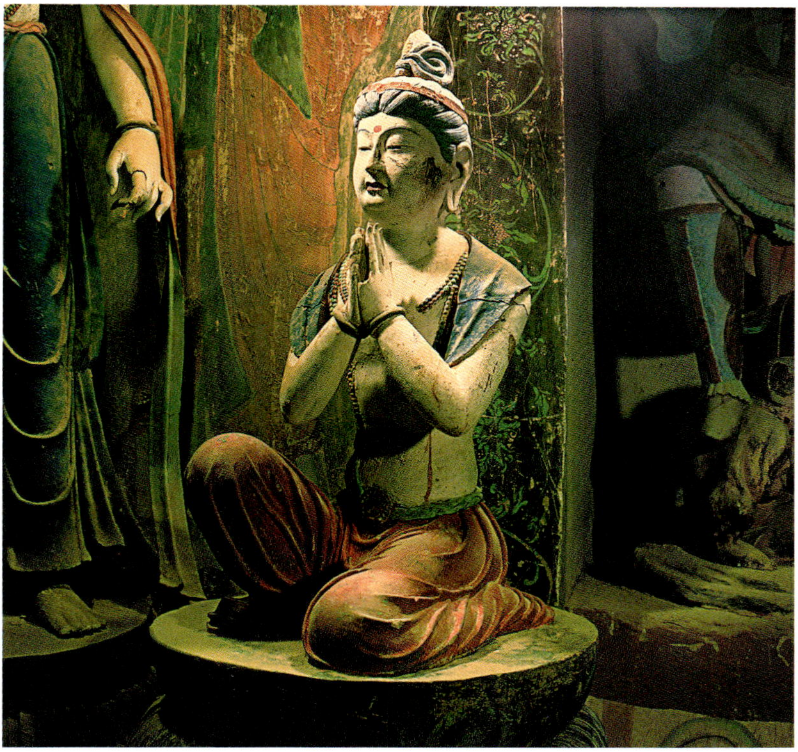

Bodhisattva color statue, in cave 384 of Dunhuang Mogao Caves, carved at the height of the Tang Dynasty.

All these caves have many magnificent works and they are the most representative of Buddhist art in the Tang period.

The main characters in murals of the Sui and Tang periods moved from bold, symbolic representation, a tradition of the Northern Wei period, to showing full facial features. For example, *The Bodhisattva Portrait* in cave 103 has the usual grace and elegance, and the face and clothing associated with traditional benevolent characters in Chinese paintings, and little trace of foreign elements. Court ladies in the murals in cave 285 look very similar to those in Gu Kaizhi's paintings. The portraits of emperors in cave 220 are almost exact copies of *Thirteen Emperors*. While the lavishness and exuberance seen in western paradises of the Promised Land in Buddhist teaching are present, the subjects have more earthly elements and origin; for example, hunting, banqueting, carriage, boating, theater, performance, cultivation, farm animals, commerce, and medical treatment are all modeled on real life. Many murals also have landscape as background, so art historians have decided that the Tang Dynasty is when Chinese landscape painting finally became an independent genre. However, very few works solely of landscape have survived, and therefore the mural landscapes are important source material to study its development during the Tang Dynasty. Many of their mural *shanshui*s still have elements of wilderness, fanciful mountains and sharp cliffs decorated with pine forests and waterfalls, with wild animals running.

Caves 158, 159, 217, and 220 portray *The Western Paradise of Amitabha*. The Buddha who is presiding over the western paradise sits on a lotus throne at the center, with the Bodhisattva Avalokiteshvara and the historical Buddha along with other bodhisattvas by his side. In front of the throne are dancers and other artists, either in pairs or on their own, with musicians playing instruments on either side of them. There is a pond at the center and a series of palatial mansions in the background, with gold and silver floors and colored glazes which mirror the reflections of the bright lights. Children play in the pond, celestial court ladies spread flower petals, and the lotus is in full blossom. In an extravagance of abundance, Amitabha sits tranquily, graceful and elegant.

During the Tang Dynasty, people enjoyed extravagance and lavishness in sharp contrast to the Buddhist teachings of sacrifice and penance. The Buddhist murals tried to teach the traditional concepts of Buddhism, for example, those illustrating *The Saddharmapundarika Sutra*. This sutra promotes the goal of total enlightenment and in order to achieve this, one has to endure a life of suffering and hardship. Ordinary people would give up, so *The Saddharmapundarika Sutra* used the story of a mirage city to teach people to continue until they reached the final enlightenment. A

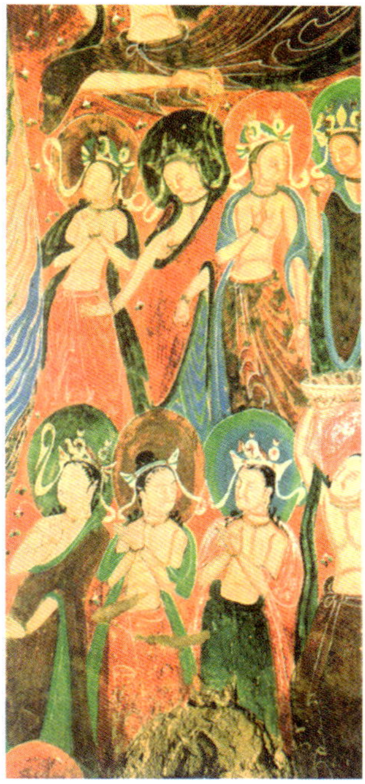

Group portrait of Bodhisattva, in cave 285 of Dunhuang Mogao Caves, painted AD 535–556.

group of people travelled to a faraway place to seek its treasure and had to overcome many obstacles and endure unimaginable sufferings. After a while, the people became exhausted and lost interest, and decided to return home. At this moment, a wise guardian produced the mirage city in front of them, with palatial mansions and pavilions, gardens and rivers. The people were delighted and went into the city, thinking they had found the treasure and there was no need to go further. The wise guardian made the mirage disappear and told the people that it was only a place to take a rest, and they needed to continue their journey to get to the treasure. The murals in cave 217 vividly rebuild the mirage city, with many details and a broad landscape.

The sponsors of mural projects were another important subject for the paintings. The most famous example is *Traveling* in cave 156. It depicts a hunting trip Zhang Yichao, the highest ranking political official in the northwest region where Dunhuang is located, took with his family and their triumphal return. Zhang is riding a red saddle horse and is accompanied by columns of knights on horseback on each side, with trumpets and drums playing, and hunting dogs and Mongolian gazelles running around: all in all, a splendid hunting day. In another mural *Song State Queen (the wife of Zhang Yichao) Going Out*, Zhang's wife rides on a brilliant white horse, accompanied by maids and servants, dancers and musicians; these are the traditional Saddle Horse Characters of the Tang Dynasty, just like those in *Shepherd Horse's* and *Night-Shining White*. Also in this mural a group of magicians are trying to climb to a column, with a whole orchestra in the background. That such an extravagant mural was painted to commemorate the sponsor illustrates both an important social relationship during the Tang Dynasty and the relationship of Buddhism to its followers.

The murals in Mogao Caves mark the complete assimilation of Buddhist art in China. They show the unification of traditional Chinese painting techniques and Buddhist teachings, which have been modified to fit the national and social characteristics. The bold and unconstrained conceptual style of the Northern Wei period has been enriched both in technique and composition. The elegant use of lines and colors balances the imposing magnificent scale with clear and quiet details. The murals in cave 220 are the best preserved in Dunhuang and illustrate the achievement of the early Tang period.

Pure Mountains and Remote Streams

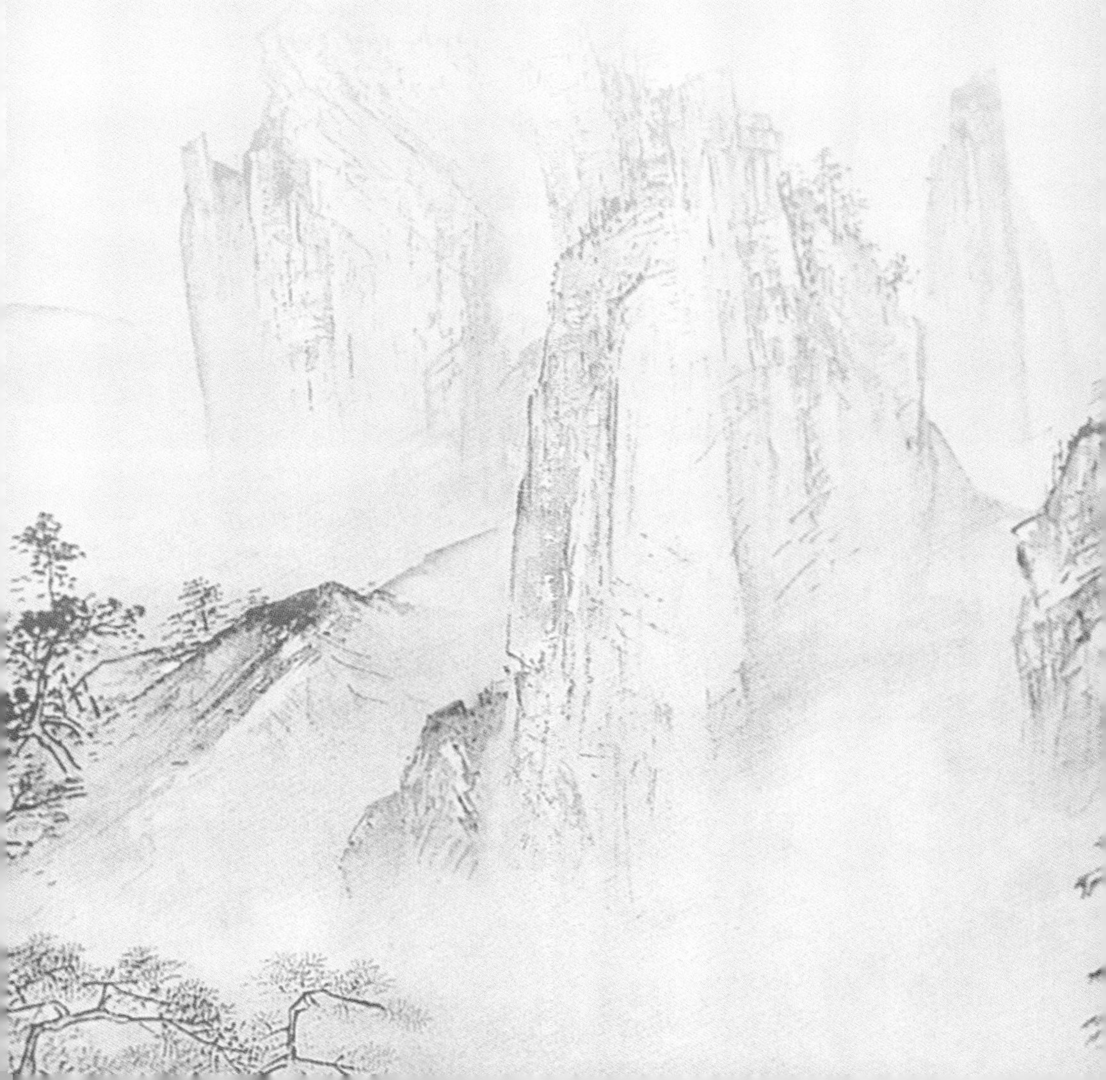

Northern Painters and Southern Painters

In *Famous Paintings Record of Past Dynasties*, Zhang Yanyuan writes that *shanshui* (Chinese landscape painting) was initiated by Wu Daozi and matured with Li Sixun (651–718) and his son Li Zhaodao (dates unknown). None of Wu's original paintings have survived, but several major original works of the two Lis have. Li Sixun's *Sailing Boats and Pavilions* (*Jiangfan Louge Tu*) has tourists strolling by the river, azure skies, boats on the misty river, and exquisite buildings at the foot of hills, features that symbolize vastness and tranquility. The tree trunks, twigs and veins of the leaves are painted using the "double outline technique," used by Zhan Ziqian, a Sui Dynasty painter. The trees and rocks are drawn in great detail as if they were copies of nature. The main colors are blue and green, but where the ink lines turn, they are decorated with gold, a sharp contrast to the overall tone. The style embodies the clarity and colorfulness in Zhan's *Spring Outing* (*You-Chun Tu*). Li Zhaodao reached a new level of sophistication with his father's style. His *Journey in the Spring Mountain* (*Chunshan Xinglv Tu*) and *Emperor Xuanzong's Journey to Sichuan* (*Minghuang Xing Shu Tu*) are both painted on vertical silk scrolls in light colors, and feature changing mists, remote valleys, rushing waterfalls, lush forests, and leisurely tourists on horseback. Despite their small size, the compositions are vividly depicted.

For the "double outline technique," ink lines, usually two strokes, either side by side or one above another, merge in the center, and are used to draw the

Painting Academies in the Song Dynasty

The Song Dynasty witnessed the apex of China's painting academies. They had the most complete organizational form and comprehensive systems in art education in various areas, such as the development of discipline and examinations. With an improving economy, the Northern and Southern Song Dynasties saw the rapid expansion of painting academies, which would become the exemplary models for such schools in subsequent dynasties. Emperor Huizong of Song, Zhao Ji, is credited with bringing painting academies to their pinnacle: he started painting studies in the third year of the Chongning Reign (1104) and officially incorporated them in the imperial examinations in order to identify skilled painters. The painting focused on six major subject matters: Buddha, human figures, landscapes, birds and beasts, flowers and bamboos, and houses. Questions in the examinations were based on ancient poems and verses. Painters employed by the painting academy were divided into six ranks and treated well. The *Xuanhe Collection of Paintings*, which contains Song Dynasty imperial painting and calligraphic works, remains important for studying China's history of ancient painting.

outlines. Then transparent colors are used to create a pastel shade and opaque mineral colors are applied. Before the Song Dynasty, painters from Gu Kaizhi on often employed this method in their landscapes, figure paintings, and flowers and birds. "Double outline" is also evident in Chinese calligraphy in imitation of painting. After the Song Dynasty, many painters devoted themselves to landscape. They used the main section or the side of the brush to make strokes that imitate the grain of rocks and tree bark, an approach that is known as the "stroke technique." To depict the surface of different kinds of rocks, painters developed a number of highly individualistic stroke techniques, such as "hemp fiber" strokes by Juran, "straight rubbing" strokes by Guang Tong and Li Cheng, and "raindrop" strokes by Fan Kuan. These terms, first used by art critics, became the accepted terms.

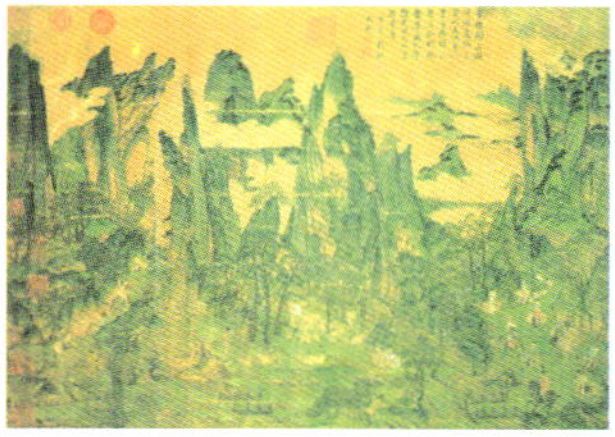

Emperor Xuanzong's Journey to Sichuan by Li Zhaodao (55.9 cm x 81 cm), Taipei Palace Museum.

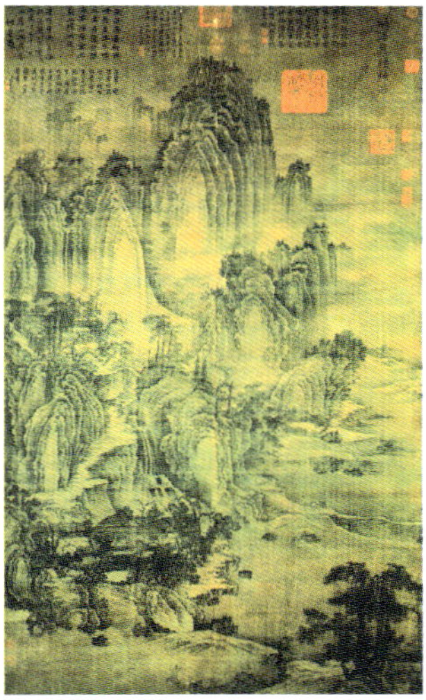

Lushan Mountain by Jing Hao (185.8 cm x 106.8 cm), Taipei Palace Museum.

The transition period between the Tang Dynasty and the Northern Song Dynasty is called the Five Dynasties (907–956), and it was then that the status of landscape was settled. We live with nature, but for Chinese painters it also embodies the *Dao* (The Truth). The Northern School, represented by Jing Hao and Guan Tong, was famous for the grand compositions of large mountains and broad rivers. However, the signature style of the Southern School, represented by Dong Yuan and Juran, is their simple depiction of southern China, a world of constant mists, drizzly rain and light breezes. Traditional "blue and green *shanshui*" declined in popularity. Scholar painters began to emphasize the use of the brush and the application of ink. Ink-and-wash landscapes, without any color or with only some light coloring, reached its maturity. Painters also began to explore the philosophical dimension of their work.

Jing Hao (dates unknown), art name Haoran, was a native of Qinshui in today's Shanxi Province. He retreated to the Honggu Valley of Taihang Mountain at the end of the Tang Dynasty and thereafter called himself Honggu Zi. His paintings used the traditional brush-and-ink skills developed in the Tang Dynasty. *Lushan Mountain* (*Kuang Lu Tu*) is a majestic but careful balanced composition, with a sense of depth and horizon perspective. It is a typical "panorama *shanshui*," as defined by the painters of the Song Dynasty. From the land at the foot of mountains to the remote peaks, Jing emphasized the magnificence of the peaks while focusing on the details of the foreground. The mountains are shown as separate and yet harmoniously related in the scroll, which is regarded as a model for Chinese landscape painting. Viewing the scroll from bottom to top, there are several distinct sections. At the foot of the mountain are trees, cottages, rivers, stone paths, men on a boat, and muleteers. Further up are the peaks, waterfalls, pavilions, bridges, and forests in mist and clouds. Contrasted with the surrounding mountains, the central peak appears higher and precipitous, soaring into the sky. Jing integrated organically the three methods of outlining, broad strokes, and shading, thus highlighting texture, composition, and the three-dimensional feel, while illustrating the artistic charm of ink-and-wash painting.

Jing realized the careful use of ink could create the impression of colors. Clouds, mists, and waterfalls drawn with thin lines had a romantic and symbolic feel, as used by Gu Kaizhi and Zhan Ziqian, but Jing began to use different shades of ink to depict mountain mists. He wrote, "Wu Daozi uses the brush but not ink, whereas Xiang Rong uses ink but not the brush. I will try to use both and find a balance and create a style of my own." He aimed to identify and maximize the various features of brush-and-ink skills. As more scholars participated in painting, "precise brush and romantic ink" became a core criterion for judging art. Jing's approach to perfect balance was very practical: for example, while in a waterfall, the rigidness of lines and strokes could be softened using ink shades.

Guan Tong (dates unknown) was born in Chang'an. When he was young, he learned from Jing Hao, and in his later years he was respectfully entitled "chulan," meaning "better than his teacher." They were called "Jing-Guan" collectively. Guan often visited Qinling and Huanshan Mountains, and he preferred painting mountains in autumn, forests in winter, and rural village life. His style was very simple strokes, but giving a strong sense of purpose and meaning. His paintings include *Journey in the Mountains* (*Guanshan Xinglv Tu*) and *Waiting for the Boat at a Mountain Stream* (*Shanxi Daidu Tu*); both are in the Taipei Palace Museum. *Journey in the Mountains* shows high mountains and deep valleys covered by clouds. In the mountains is a small temple, and in the foreground a small bridge and a guesthouse, with many tourists and traders; it is full of life and rural freshness.

Dong Yuan (d. 962) of the Southern Painting style, artist name Shuda, was born in Zhongling (today northwest of Jinxian, in Jiangxi province). He mostly painted scenes south of the Yangtze River with vibrant grasses and trees, usually using thin, long wet strokes, which was called the "hemp fiber" stroke, and sometimes using dots. *People of the Suburb of Longsu* (*Longsu Jiaomin Tu*) has round mountains, thick grasses and trees, and at the foot of the mountains, a family hangs lanterns on trees for a festival. The characters were painted meticulously with strong color, while the mountains and water used "hemp fiber." *A Summer Mountain* (*Xiashan Tu*) in Shanghai Museum, *Waiting for the Boat at the Xiajingshan Pass* (*Xiajingshankou Daidu Tu*), and *Xiaoxiang River* (*Xiaoxiang Tu*), all illustrate his typical style of simple inks and harmony of shape and shade, mostly painting the mountains of south China, a land of exuberant growth and contrasts of mist and bright light.

Mi Fu, calligrapher and art critic of the Northern Song Dynasty was an admirer of the simple style of Dong Yuan's paintings,

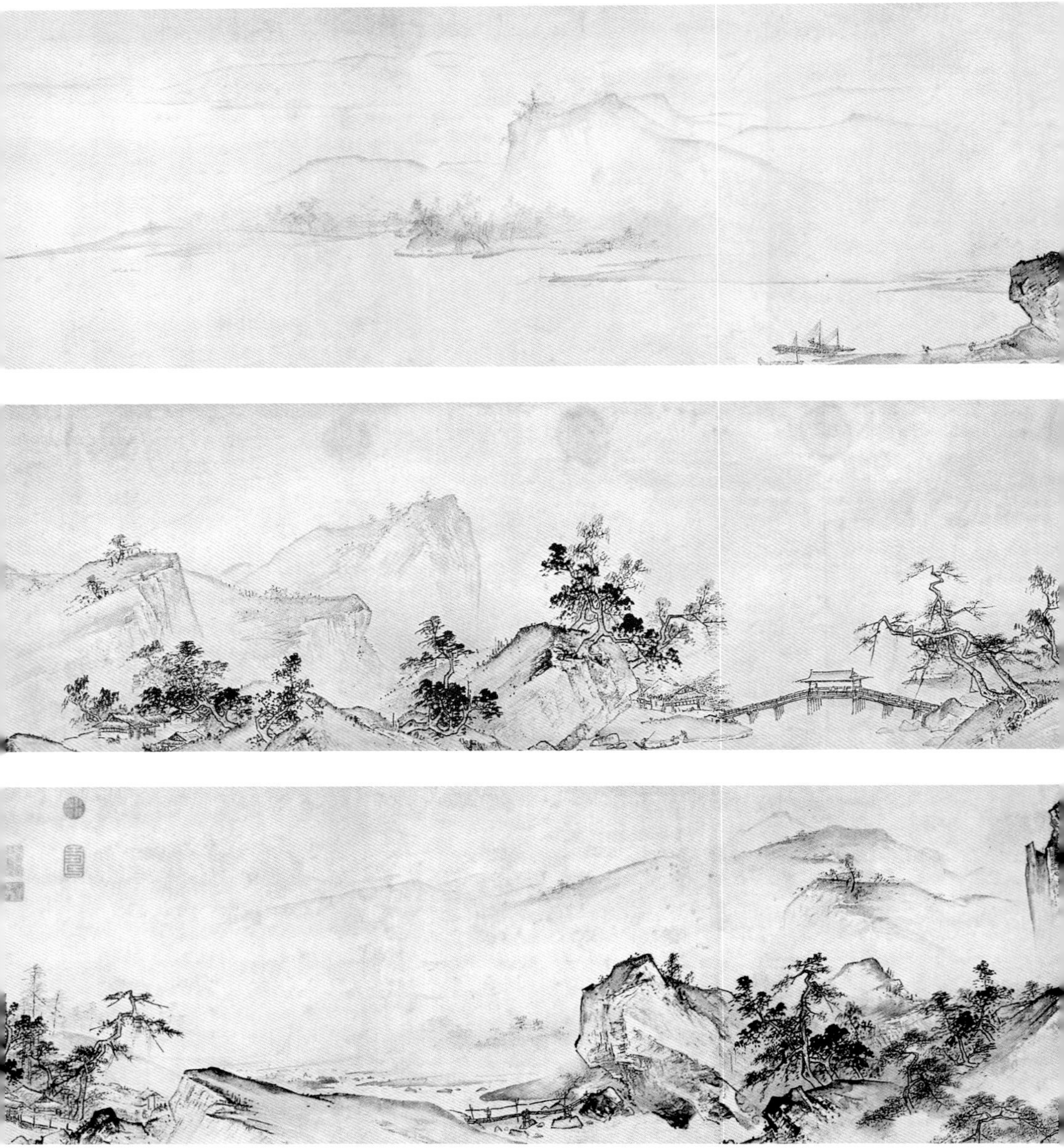

Pale Mountains and Remote Streams, scroll, by Xia Gui (185.8 cm x 106.8 cm), Taipei Palace Museum.

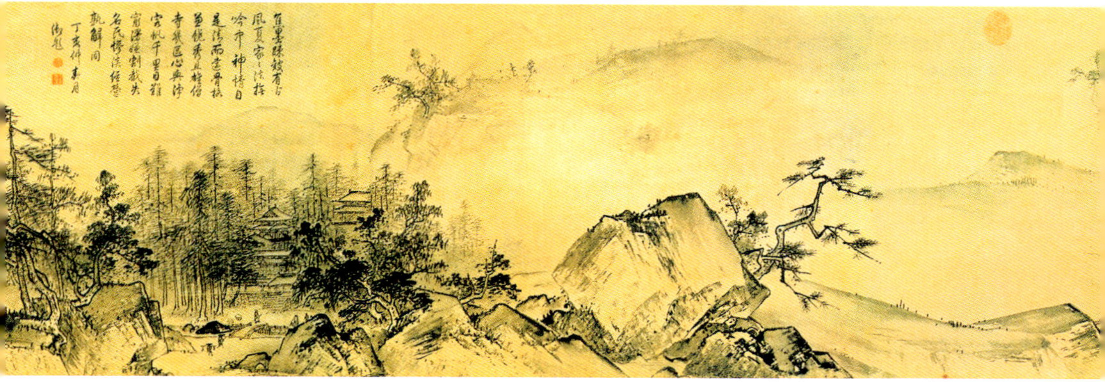

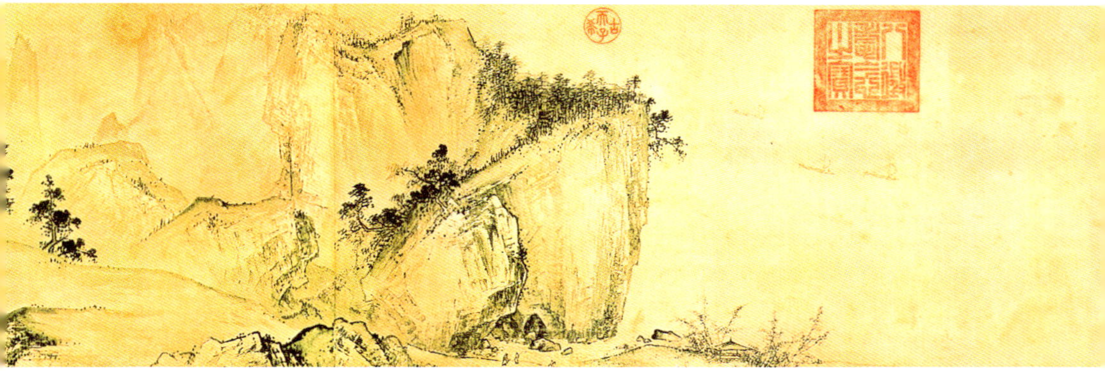

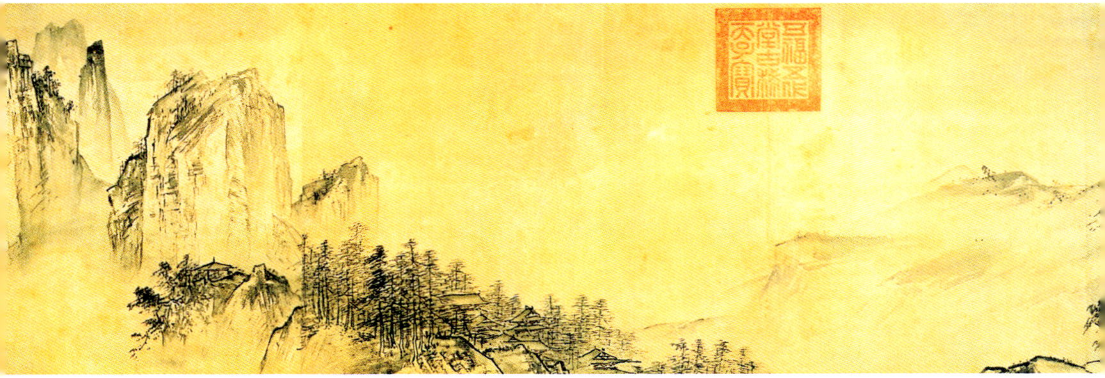

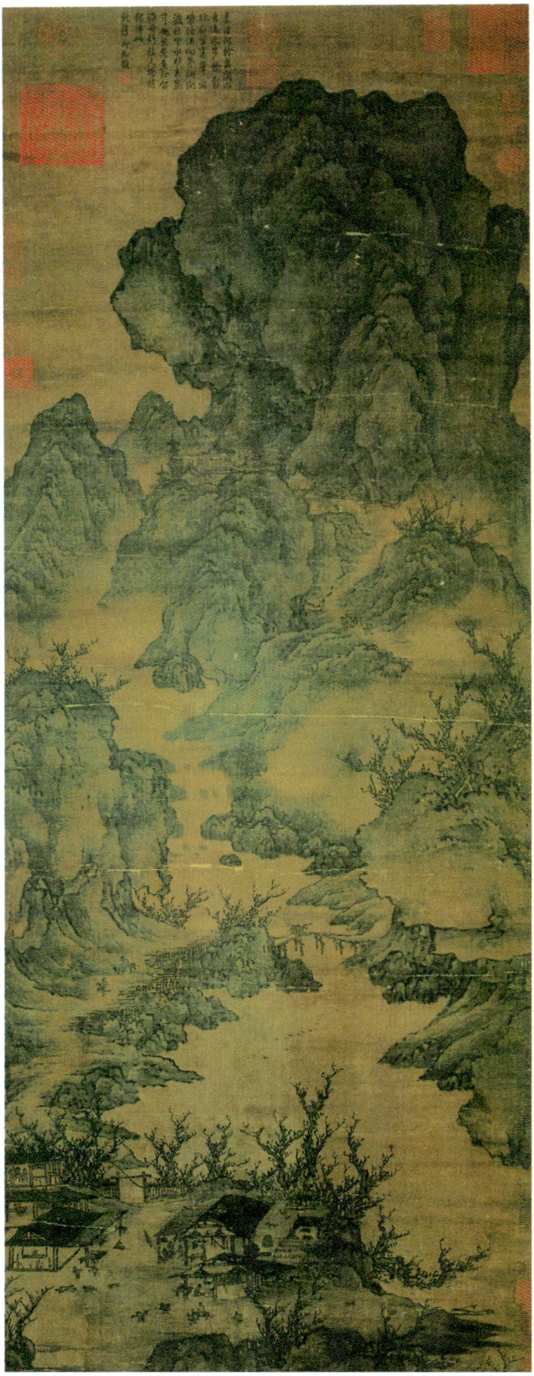

Journey in the Mountains by Guan Tong (144.4 cm × 56.8 cm), Taipei Palace Museum.

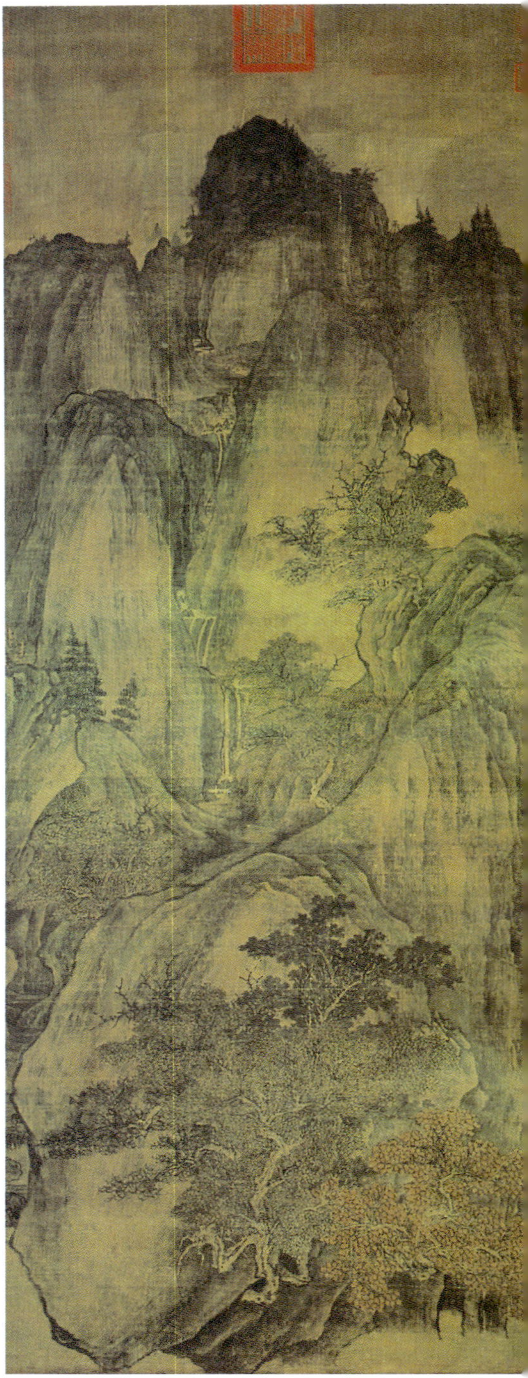

Waiting for the Boat at the Xiajingshan Pass, scroll, by Dong Yuan (50 cm × 320 cm), ink and color on silk (detail), Liaoning Museum.

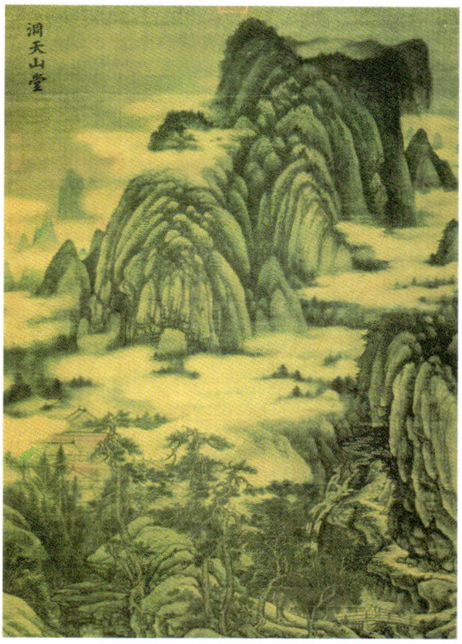

Asking for Directions in an Autumn Mountain by Juran (165.2 cm × 77.2 cm), Taipei Palace Museum.

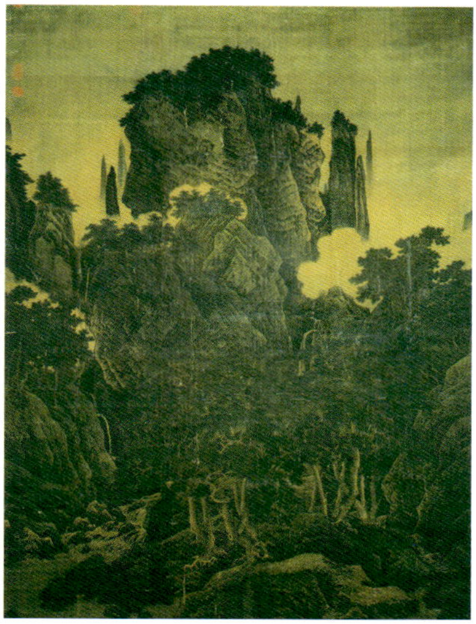

Whispering Pines in the Mountains by Li Tang (165.2 cm × 77.2 cm), Taipei Palace Museum.

which reproduced what he saw. In *Xiaoxiang River*, he abandoned the use of color and there are no mountains. Instead, we see the vast river, the misty sky, a lofty view, and on the river, small boats carry people, fishermen throw out fishnets, and on the riverbank, people engage in a religious ceremony. Shen Kuo of the Song Dynasty commented on Dong Yuan's paintings, "The strokes are few in his paintings. A close look shows they are not what they seem to be. But viewed from a distance, they are a magnificent representation of what was intended." His innocent style and the fact that the views need to be appreciated from a distance indicate his realistic intentions. Since the Han and Tang Dynasties, the grand painting style of north China had been the mainstream of painting, philosophy, and practice, Dong's realistic attempts to depict mountains and waters gave fresh light on painting.

Juran (dates unknown) was born in Jiangning (Nanjing) and was a Buddhist monk at Kaiyuan Temple there, and his active career continued into the Northern Song Dynasty. He was a student of

Dong Yuan, good at painting with simple ink and wet brushwork, and "hemp fiber" strokes were his specialty. Many of his original works have survived, including *Asking for Directions in the Autumn Mountains* (*Qiushan Wendao Tu*) in Taipei Palace Museum, *Valleys and Pines Trees in Wind* (*Wanhe Songfeng Tu*) in Shanghai Museum, *Rocks and Bushes* (*Cengyan Congshu Tu*), in Taipei Palace Museum, *Xiaoji Zhuanlanting Pavilion* (*Xiaoji Zhuanlanting Tu*) in Taipei Palace Museum, and *Buddhist Retreat by Stream and Mountain* (*Xishan Lanruo Tu*) in Cleveland Museum of Art. Juran developed Dong Yuan's style of light ink and depiction of mist. He often used watery ink to achieve his intended results.

During the Tang and Song Dynasties, Zen was popular in China and painters of Southern China advocated its spirit of quietness and innocence. Dong Yuan's and Juran's paintings did not have a sense of magnificence. Mi Fu praised their paintings, "Their paintings have a clear and moist scent, with innocent outlines," and "Juran's paintings with joyful lands are full of life and freshness." Mountain ranges extended into the distance and the valleys were dotted with farmhouses with open doors, and a small path in the foreground wound its way into the valleys. There were lines of trees in all directions, rocks in the rivers were beaten by the waves, and grasses danced in the wind. As a Buddhist monk, Juran had a more eccentric attitude to life than Dong Yuan, and thus Juran's paintings had fewer, lonelier people and deserted scenes. His paintings make people feel more isolated from society. The artist concentrated more on the universe in his heart and mind and much less on the material world at large. The scholars in later generations admired Juran's work, mainly because they loved his Zen philosophy.

Painting history always associates Jing, Guan, Dong, and Ju with the Five Dynasties and the early Northern Song Dynasty, but they actually inherited the highest level of sophistication of landscapes from both Northern and Southern China, so they had a unique place in art history. Northern China style had many followers in the North Song Dynasty and produced many masters, but because Southern China style was promoted by scholars, it gained popularity in the Yuan Dynasty. In the Ming and Qing Dynasties, when discussing landscape, Dong and Ju were mentioned and the Northern China style of "panorama *shanshui*" was gradually forgotten.

Song Emperor Huizong and His Period

Following the achievements of the Sui, Tang, and the Five Dynasties, imperial court painting, scholar-officials' painting, and folk painting, each with distinct features but also each influencing the others, jointly defined painting in the Song Dynasty.

The Northern Song Dynasty unified the country, ending the turmoil caused by fighting between the feudal states and ushering in a period of social stability. As commerce and the handicraft industry underwent rapid development, urban civilization flourished. Zhao Ji, also called Huizong, the eighth emperor of the Northern Song Dynasty, is known in history for his political incompetence and his obsession with art. When the Northern Song was overthrown by the northern nomads of the Jin Dynasty in 1127, Emperor Huizong and his son Zhao Heng, known as Emperor Qinzong, were captured and died miserably years later. The imperial court retreated to the south where they established the Southern Song Dynasty (1127–1279) with Lin'an (today Hangzhou in Zhejiang province) as the capital. Immigrants from the north exploited the rich natural resources of the south and with the locals created a period of sustained economic and cultural developments.

Bianliang (today Kaifeng in Henan province) and the capital of the Northern Song Dynasty, Lin'an, were both prosperous commercial cities. As well as aristocrats, both places were home to large numbers of merchants, craftsmen, and ordinary urban dwellers, and boasted a colorful cultural life. Painting became commercial and handicrafts an industry, with artists selling their works in marketplaces. In the busy fairs held in Bianjing's

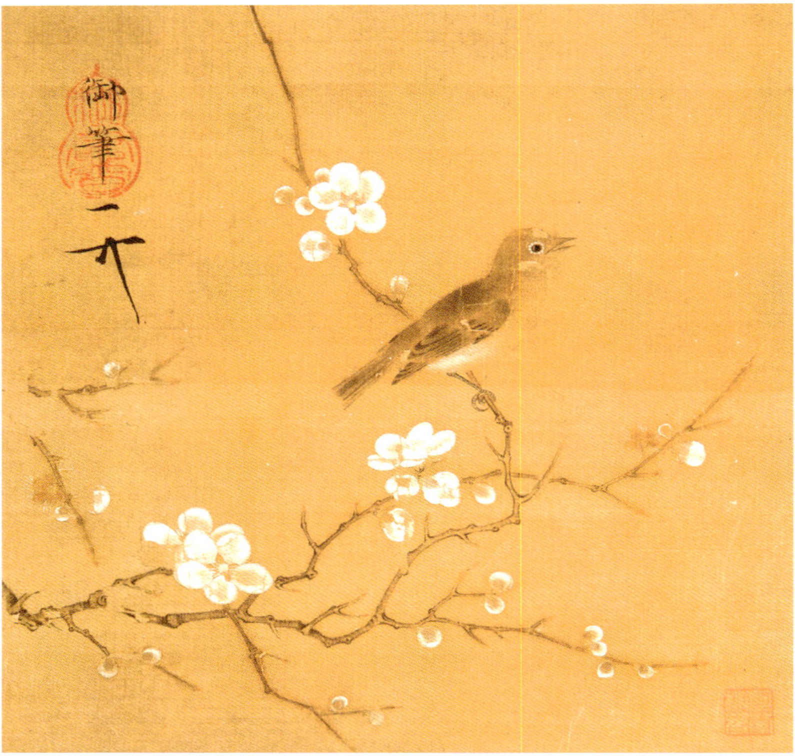

Plum Blossoms and a White-Eye by Zhao Jie (24.5 cm × 24.8 cm), Beijing Palace Museum.

Daxiangguo Temple five times a month, there were stalls offering books and paintings. In the night market of Lin'an, painted fans were sold. Many restaurants in the two capitals and other cities were decorated with paintings to attract customers. When arranging a banquet, urban residents could rent screens, hanging scrolls, and calligraphy works for decoration. *Pictures of the Door God and Zhong Kui* were tremendously popular for celebrating the Spring Festival. Block printing developed and Bianjing, Lin'an, Pingyang, Chengdu, and Jianyang became centers of the printing industry. Illustrated books and Buddhist scriptures were published, and many survive from the Song and Jin periods, such as Buddha portraits, Mantras of the Dharani Sutra, *Pictures and Eulogies of*

Sudhana's Journey to the South (*Foguo Chanshi Wenzhu Zhinan Tuzan*) and *Zhaocheng Tripitaka* (*Zhaocheng Zang*).

Ancient Chinese painting peaked in the Song Dynasty, especially in the depiction of real life. The Song artists established techniques, styles, forms, and theories that were found in the later Yuan, Ming, and Qing Dynasties, a testament to the maturity and flourishing of the Song painters. They emphasized the emotions of the human figures, intriguing plots, and the creation of distinctive images. While painters specializing in flowers, birds, mountains, and rivers strived for a pleasing artistic composition, they also wanted the details to be true-to-life. Scholar-official painters contributed to subjective expression and the exploration of calligraphic effects. Court paintings also enriched the nationwide painting boom.

The Imperial Painting Academy was established during the reigns of the Emperors Huizong and Gaozong, originally named Zhao Gou (1127–1162). While most of the emperors of the Song Dynasty showed some interest in painting, Emperor Huizong recruited painters through nationwide examinations and became rather too preoccupied with painting. At a time when his country was gravely endangered by domestic troubles and foreign aggression, the emperor, well-established as a calligrapher and painter in his own right, scoured the nation not for able men to help save the country but for experts for the Imperial Painting Academy and searched for important paintings to add to his imperial collection. Many excellent folk painters established themselves and were recruited to the academy, which made it a magnet for master painters. While maintaining some connections with ordinary society, court painters ultimately needed to please the emperor, and so they followed the traditional style of the court art developed during the Tang Dynasty, but at the same time their works inevitably exhibited typical Song Dynasty characteristics, such as decadence, fragile beauty, and simplicity. As well as Huizong's collection of calligraphy and paintings, his ministers and scholar-officials acquired rich art collections, as recorded in

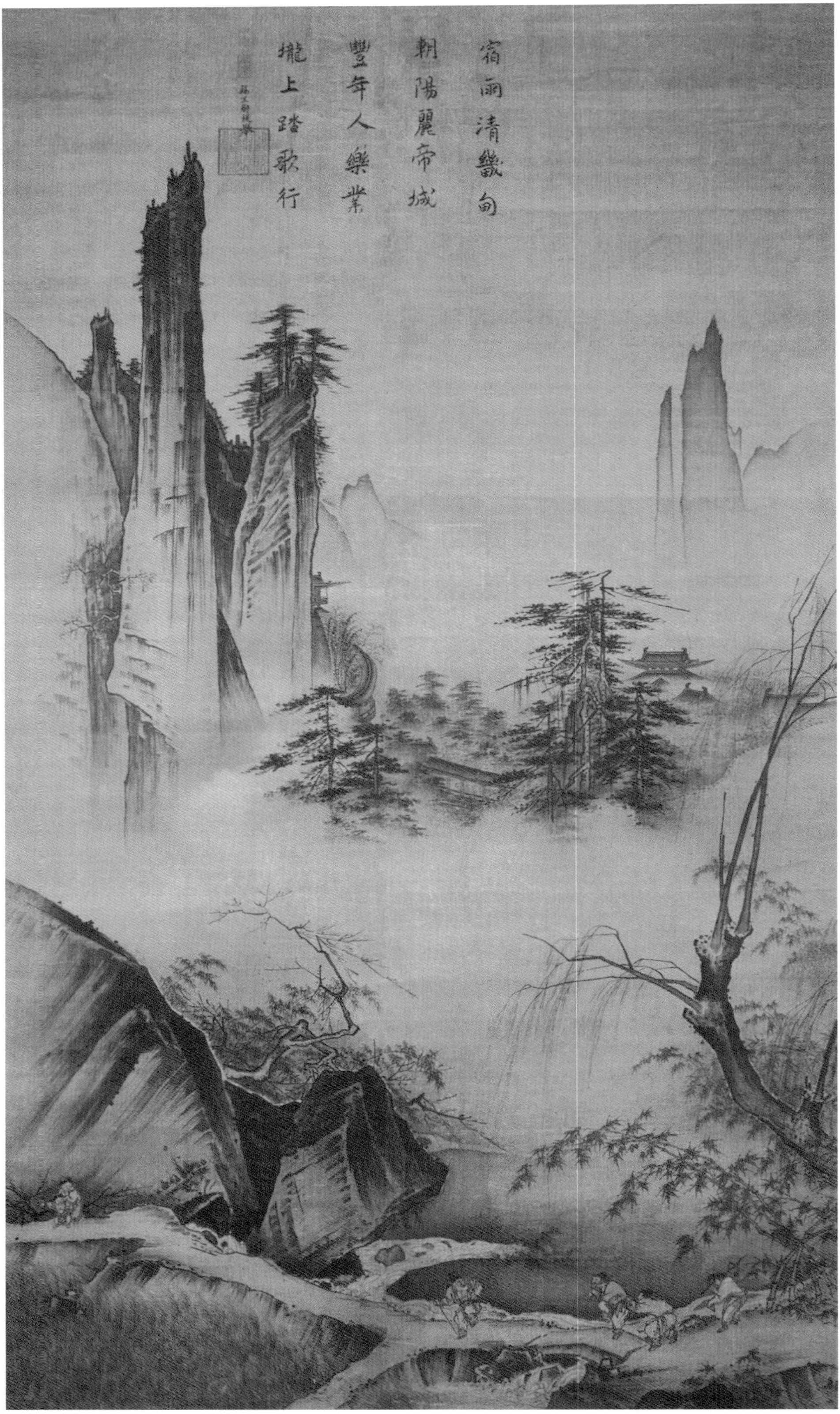
宿雨清畿甸
朝陽麗帝城
豐年人樂業
壠上踏歌行

the *Xuanhe Collections of Paintings*. When the Northern Song Dynasty fell, the Jin troops looted Bianjing, and took some court painters and the court collection back with them to the north, so these men and works had a major influence on the painting in Jin-controlled regions. Other painters went south as refugees and were employed there in the Emperor Gaozong's Imperial Painting Academy, and enhanced the cultural development south of the Yangtze River. Famous court paintings of the Song Dynasty include Guo Xi's *Early Spring* (*Zaochun Tu*) and *Spring Snow in the Mountains* (*Guanshan Chunxue Tu*), Zhang Zeduan's *Along the River During the Qingming Festival* (*Qingming Shanghe Tu*), Wang Ximeng's *Thousand Li of Rivers and Mountains* (*Qianli Jiangshan Tu*), Li Tang's *Plucking Roses* (*Caiwei Tu*) and *Whispering Pines in the Mountains* (*Wanhe Songfeng Tu*), and Ma Yuan's *Singing and Dancing* (*Tage Tu*) and *Waters* (*Shui Tu*).

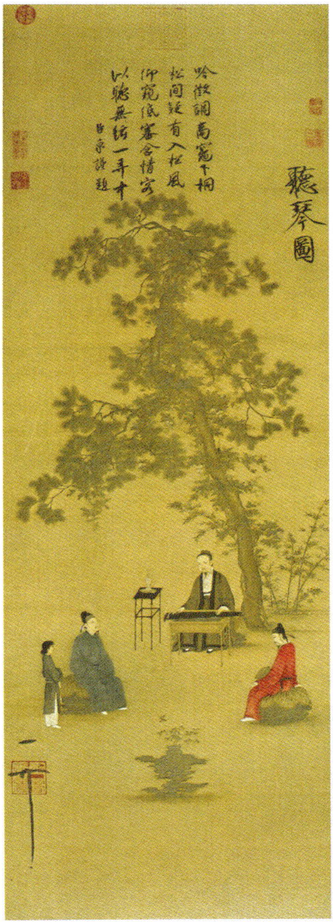

Listening to Guqin by Zhao Jie (147.2 cm × 52.3 cm), Beijing Palace Museum.

Scholar painting first appeared in the Tang Dynasty and then became a major influence in the middle and late Northern Song Dynasty, when there was a widespread interest in collecting and critiquing paintings by scholars and scholar-officials. Quite a few of them took up painting as well, because like composing poems, art was seen as a way of expressing their unique being. Scholar painters had new ideas on the choice of subject and form, for example, inscribing phrases and poems as decoration on their paintings. In the Northern and Southern Song Dynasties, Chinese plum blossoms by Zhongren and Yang Wujiu, bamboos by Wen Tong, bizarre trees and stones by Su Shi, cloudy mountains by Mi Fu and his son Mi Youren, and daffodils by Zhao Mengjian were particularly well known. An important contribution

< *Singing and Dancing* by Ma Yuan (192.5 cm × 111 cm), Beijing Palace Museum.

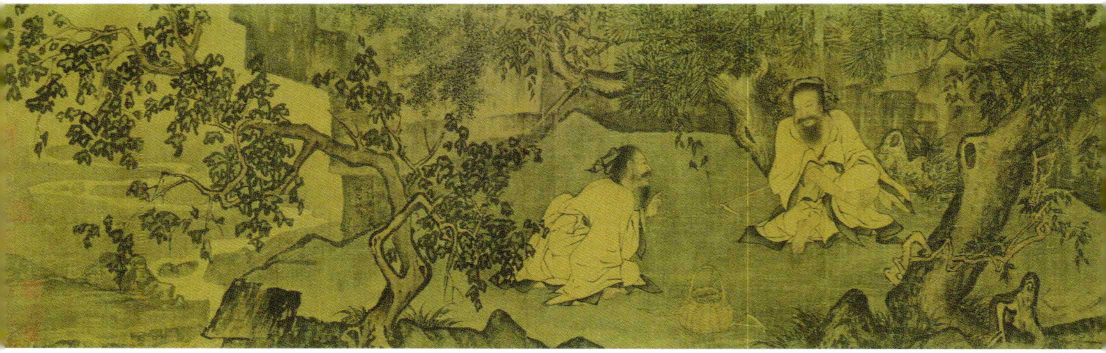

Plucking Roses by Li Tang (27.2 cm × 90.5 cm), Beijing Palace Museum.

made by scholar-officials of the Northern Song Dynasty to scholar painting was their theoretical research. Ouyang Xiu proposed to pursue an aesthetic atmosphere of "desolateness and asceticism." Su Shi denied that painting mainly aimed at imitating nature. Scholar-officials had long formed a network, through which their paintings and the ideas of Su Shi and others spread rapidly, even to Liao and Jin territories ruled by ethnic minorities, and were a precursor of the scholar painting of the Yuan and Ming Dynasties.

Along the River During the Qingming Festival (Qingming Shanghe Tu)

Figure paintings of the Five Dynasties and the Northern and Southern Song Dynasties encompassed more subjects than earlier periods, including religious mythology, historical stories, and scholar life. The later painters emphasized their figures' facial expressions to convey inner feelings and mental state. Painting skills evolved in two directions: a meticulous style with fine brushwork and rich colors, represented by Li Gonglin and Zhang Zeduan; and the ink-and-wash school, with a freehand style represented by Liang Kai.

In the Tang and Song Dynasties, Chinese painters tended to use subtle coloring and simple, unsophisticated strokes. Following Gu

Kaizhi and Wu Daozi, Li Gonglin (1049–1106), in the North Song Dynasty, was famous for outline drawing characterized by "supple brushwork, diluted ink, and absence of color and wash." Outline drawing is similar to sketching in Western painting, and can be very effective without the use of colors. *Taoist Gods Visiting the Primeval Lords of Heaven* (*Chaoyuan Xianzhang Tu*) by Wu Zongyuan, is the most famous painting in this style in the Northern Song Dynasty, which has been preserved thanks to the efforts of the modern Chinese painting master Xu Beihong. Li Gonglin was also a master of outline drawing, including *Five Horses* (*Wuma Tu*), *Illustrations of Jiuge* (*Jiuge Tu*), *Portrait of Vimalakirti* (*Weimojie Tu*), and *Imitating Wei Yan's Herding the Ranch* (*Lin Weiyan Fangmu Tu*), images depicted by simple brush strokes are not only vivid but as rhythmic as calligraphy.

Gong Kai (ca. 1222–1304), of the outline drawing school in the Southern Song Dynasty, also learned from Wu Daozi, but adopted a freer style. He liked painting ghosts, and his *Zhong Kui Traveling with his little Sister* (*Zhongshan Chuyou Tu*) depicts an excursion of two sedans carried by ghosts. Despite the evident gloominess, the painting is full of glamor. Gong's paintings were usually rife with punchy satire, and critics in the Yuan Dynasty believed they were not to be taken lightly. Liang Kai (dates unknown), in the Southern Song Dynasty, was once in the Imperial Painting Academy, and was also skilled at human figures in the outline drawing style, but according to historical records, he changed in middle age to ink-and-wash freehand painting, an unconstrained style of painting comparable to free cursive calligraphy and characterized by varying shades of ink. His paintings in the latter style include *The Six Patriarchs* (*Liuzu Tu*), *Immortal in Splashed Ink* (*Pomo Xianren Tu*), and *Li Bai Chanting Poems to the Moon* (*Taibai Xingying Tu*).

Zhang Zeduan's *Along the River During the Qingming Festival* is painted on silk with pastel colors, with most of its images outlined in black ink, producing the characteristic neatness and delicacy of the style. As a court painting, it is unlike ordinary "folkloric paintings,"

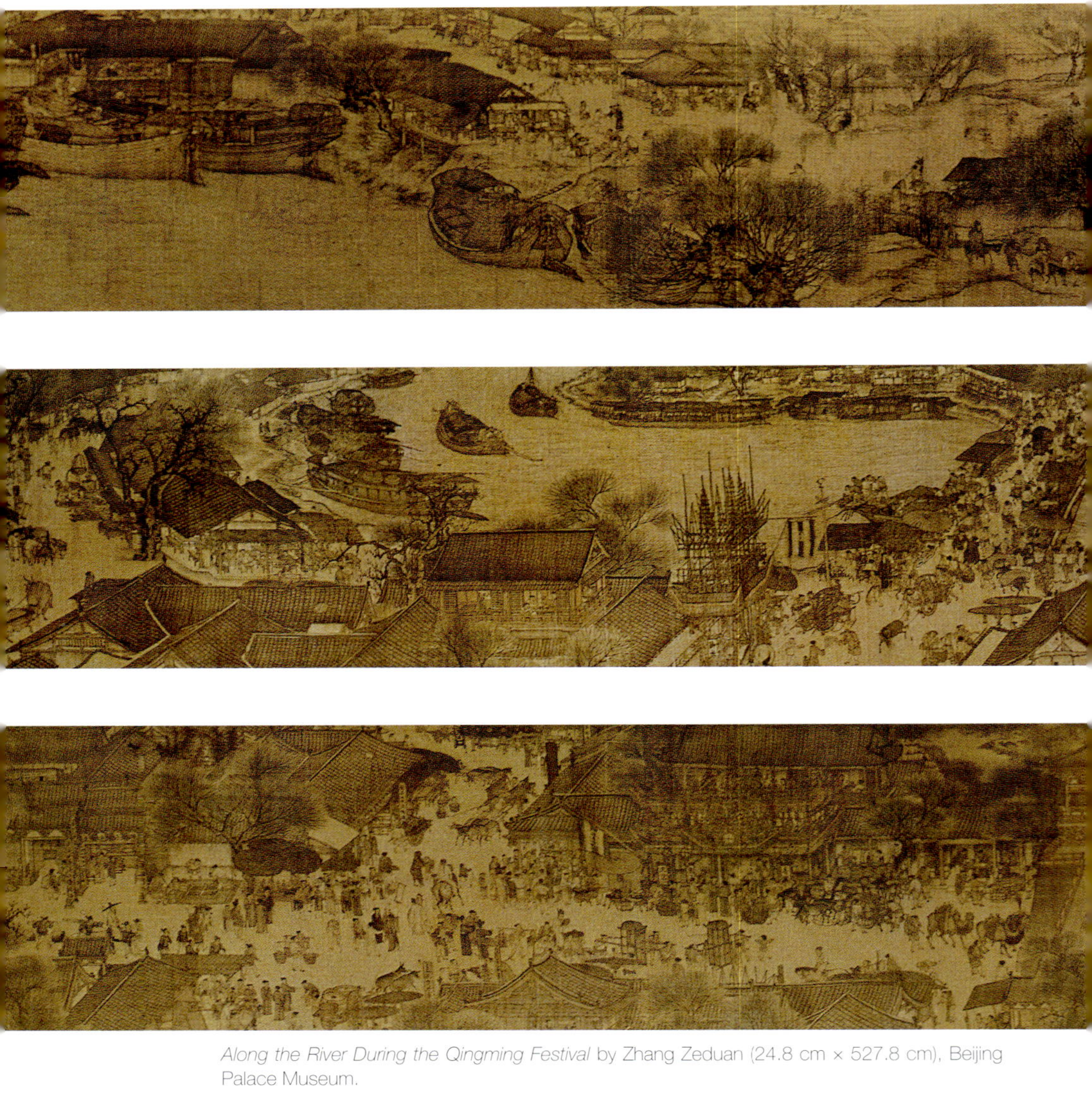

Along the River During the Qingming Festival by Zhang Zeduan (24.8 cm × 527.8 cm), Beijing Palace Museum.

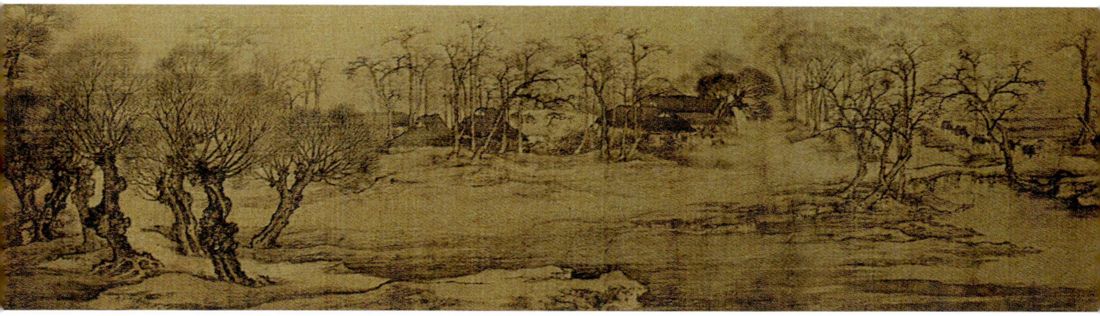

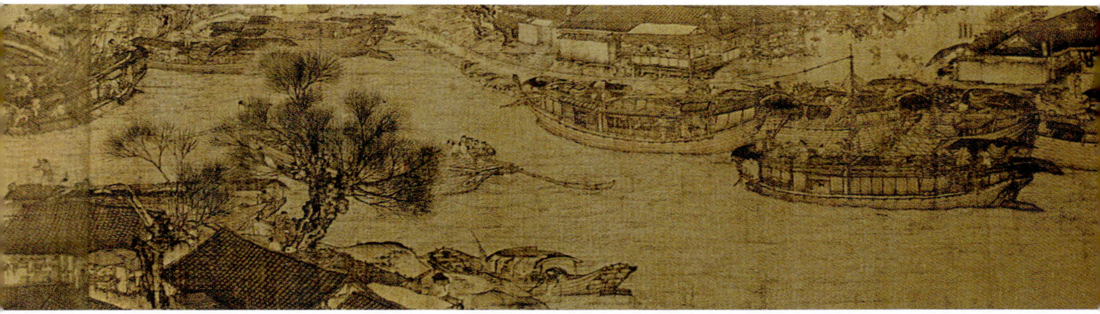

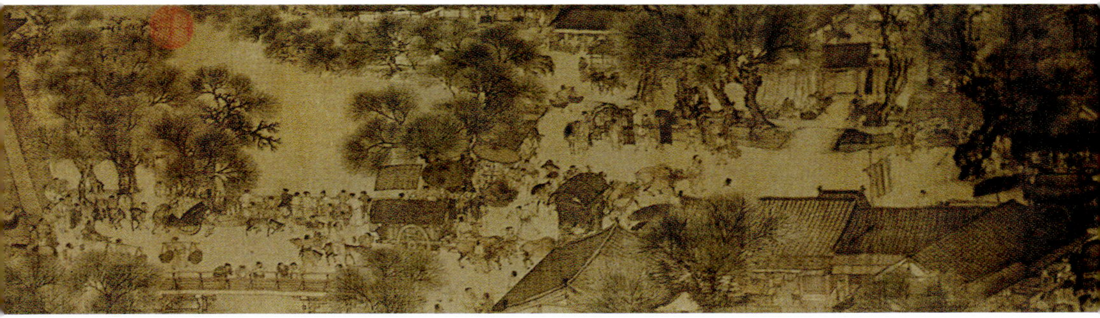

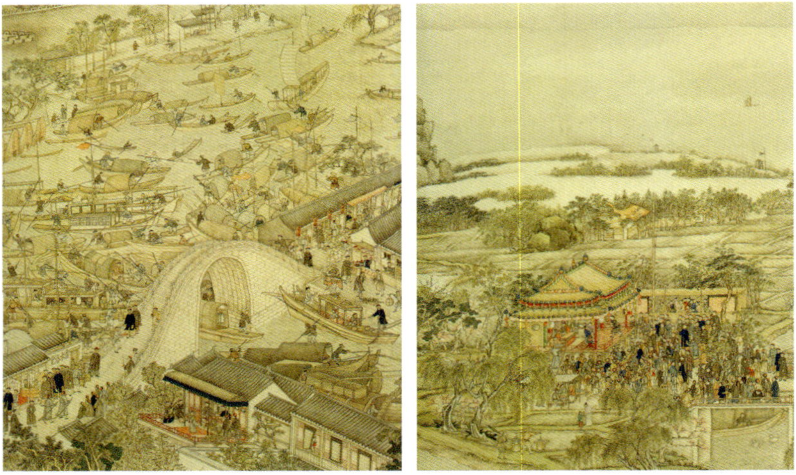

Along the River During the Qingming Festival (details).

in which lively, humorous folk scenes of ordinary people can be found in *Itinerant Vendors* (*Huolang Tu*), *Children at Play* (*Xiying Tu*), and other paintings by lesser painters such as Su Hanchen and Li Song. However, in the *Qingming* scroll, Zhang Zeduan gives a panoramic and objective depiction of all the activities during the Qingming Festival in prosperous Bianjing from a bird's-eye view, making this spectacular painting a historical epic. The scroll includes scholars, farmers, business people, doctors, fortune tellers, Buddhists, Taoists, petty officials, women, boat trackers, cattle, horses, camels, shops, rivers, ports, lakes, swamps, boats, official compounds, large mansions, and thatched houses. Boasting a keen observation of life, an acute mind, and an excellent mastery of painting composition, Zhang was well rounded in his work, skilled at portraying human figures, mountains and rivers, and various architectural styles, as evidenced by lifelike expressions, deftly painted natural features, and the seamless transition from one scene to another. The scroll seems complex yet is orderly and thoughtful, and using exaggeration and a comic atmosphere typical of folkloric paintings, he reproduced the social customs and lifestyles of the time, from transportation on the Bianhe River to the hard life of the working people.

The *Qingming* scroll does not carry the painter's signature. In his postscript on the scroll, Zhang Zhu of the Jin Dynasty ascribed it to Zhang Zeduan (dates unknown), a native of Dongwu (in today's Shandong province), who pursued studies in Bianliang and was admitted to the Imperial Painting Academy. According to Zhang Zhu, he was good at "boundary painting," a type of landscape or figure painting with architecture as the background and used to depict cities, streets, and boats. Many reproductions of the scroll were available in the Southern Song Dynasty; they were sold in Lin'an galleries at one gold coin each, testifying its special popularity.

Panorama *Shanshui*

By the Song Dynasty, landscape dominated Chinese painting. Painters traveled extensively to forests and mountains, where they observed nature so as to be able to accurately reproduce it in different places, seasons, and weather. Guo Xi, a landscape painter in the Northern Song Dynasty, wrote in *Spirituality by the Forest Stream*: "To capture the essence of nature requires a keen interest in painting, hard work, and extensive traveling." From sublime mountains and rivers dotted with splendid buildings, aristocrats' excursions in luxurious gardens, and scholar-officials' secluded life, to rural scenery, ordinary people driving a cart, operating a watermill, ferrying, farming, fishing, logging, and riding on a mule, as well as to places such as Buddhist and Taoist temples and wine shops in deserted cities. Painters classified *shanshuis* into various categories, with distinctive characteristics; for example, the scenery "in the north" and that "south of the Yangtze River" differed greatly. Other subjects included "morning mist," "evening green," "summer mountains," "cold forests," "remote valleys," "gentle breeze and light rain," "waters and skies blending into one color," "rivers rushing through a valley," "evening sun in sparse forests," "light snow in a fishing village," "desolate temples in autumn mountains," "buffalo boy returning home by a willow-lined river," and "fishing

Appreciation of Masterpieces
Chinese painting masterpieces are to be evaluated in three ways: the paintings themselves, including style, composition, brushwork, and color; the calligraphic standard of the painters' calligraphy, including position, font, size, and the consistency between handwriting and painting style; and the style, size, and school of the painters' seals, the matching of characters cut in intaglio and relief, and the position of the seals, as well as the correctness of the texts and the correlation between the texts and the painting.

alone in winter." They also illustrated ancient poems through realistic depiction of actual landscapes while still using their imagination.

In the Song Dynasty, northern panorama *shanshui*, started by Jing Hao, during the Five Dynasties, continued to enjoy wide popularity. His vertical scrolls were symbolic to those longing for a secluded life in that the towering mountains illustrate their long-coveted sense of freedom from the real world beset with disturbances and disasters. Three painters of the Northern Song Dynasty, Li Cheng, Guo Xi, and Fan Kuan, brought this genre to its peak. Since the Six Dynasties, Chinese landscape painting had been influenced by Confucianism, Taoism, and Buddhism, with the combination of Confucian rationalism and Taoist non-action as its fundamental feature. Either becoming an official after taking the imperial civil service exam or living a secluded life was the goal for scholars. For example, according to historical records, Li Cheng was a "knowledgeable and talented" man who had "big ambitions since childhood." Of course, "big ambition," does not mean that he wanted to become a successful artist, but refers to his political hopes. However, as he "failed one exam after another, getting nowhere in the end," Li decided to "devote himself to painting," "spending most of his days in mountain caves painting cold forests." Guo Xi also pointed out in *Spirituality by the Forest Stream* that gentlemen enjoyed mountains and rivers because these natural landscapes make them "feel closer to the hermits living as fishermen and loggers in isolation from the troublesome world."

Li Cheng (919–967) was almost a contemporary of Jing Hao and Guan Tong and their student.

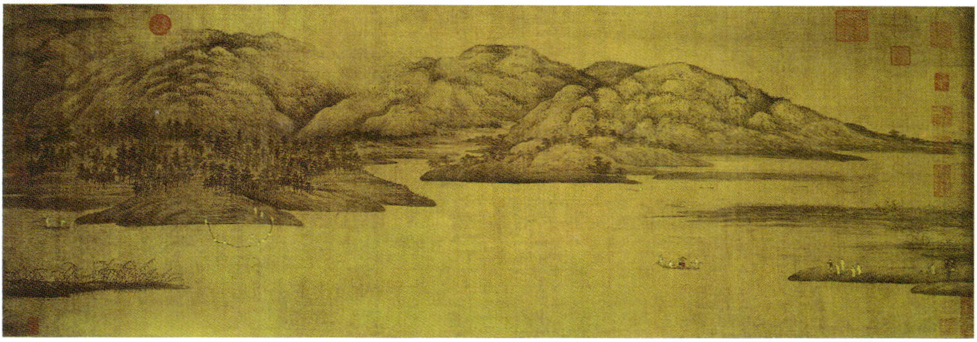

Xiaoxiang River by Dong Yuan (50 cm × 141 cm), Beijing Palace Museum.

A descendant of the royal clan of the Tang Dynasty, he lived in Chang'an but later moved to Yingqiu, in Qingzhou (today's Shandong Province), gaining the nickname of Li Yingqiu. Li Cheng was good at writing poems, playing the zither and chess, but never held an official position, and he developed his own style as he concentrated on depicting actual landscapes, mostly of cold forests from a "level-distance perspective," or from near mountains across to distant ones. They were distinguished by their sharpness and the use of diluted ink. His early works were not too much influenced by stereotypes; for example, *Level-Distance View of Pines* (*Qiaosong Pingyuan Tu*) features true-to-life scenery, and is a rarity as it conforms to the laws of perspective, with the nearby pine trees appearing much higher than the far-off mountains. Li Cheng was so faithful to his observations of nature that he adopted the level-distance perspective in most of his works, thereby giving the scenes a sense of breadth. Following Jing Hao in terms of brushwork, he focused on the "backbone" of the mountains and trees to create a feeling of desolateness, serenity, and remoteness. What is remarkable about his work is that he stressed realism in forests and rocks, as in *Reading the Tablet by a Jagged Rock* (*Dubei Keshi Tu*). It shows a slope on which is an ancient tree, whose sparse branches are covered by vines. There is nothing in the background as if this limitless place has been lying barren for a long time. A towering tablet sits on a tortoise-shaped pedestal and has dragon carvings on top. A man wearing a hat and sitting on a mule is reading the inscriptions, while a boy, presumably his valet, stands beside him holding a long pole. The trees and the stones were outlined before they were painted with ink.

Li Cheng, Guan Tong, and Fan Kuan represented three major schools of landscapes in north China during the Five Dynasties and the Northern Song Dynasty. But by the Northern Song Dynasty, Li Cheng's paintings had become rare (Mi Fu went as far as suggesting there were no genuine Li paintings). *A Solitary Temple Amid Clearing Peaks* (*Qingluan Xiaosi Tu*) in Nelson-Atkins Kansas City Museum of Art, Kansas, is attributed to Li Cheng. His style can be studied in the paintings of his many followers, of which the best-known disciples are Wang Shen, Xu Daoning, and Guo Xi.

Guo Xi, artist name Chunfu, a native of Wenxian in Henan Province, was admitted to the Imperial Painting Academy in middle age and served as a court painter until his death. He was said to be a favorite courtier of Emperor Shenzong of the Northern Song Dynasty. A disciple of Li Cheng and an outstanding landscape painter in his own right, his painting is characterized by vigorous brushwork and a clear ink-and-wash style. He depicted mountains and rocks using light ink strokes so they look like rolling clouds, while the dangling twigs resemble crab legs. He employed an exquisite style in his early years, but later he shifted to a more imposing one. He was particularly good at towering precipices, pines, winding rivers, cliffs, and sheer peaks shrouded in mist. He is often linked with Li Cheng as "Li-Guo." Guo's representative works include *Early Spring* (*Zaochun Tu*), *Spring Snow in Mountains* (*Guanshan Chunxue*), *Level-Distance View of Rocks* (*Keshi Pingyuan*), and *Silent Valley* (*Yougu*). In *Spirituality by the Forest Stream*, a collection of his essays on painting complied by his son Guo Si, Guo Xi suggested that a landscape should give viewers the feeling they were actually present in the scene, where they could

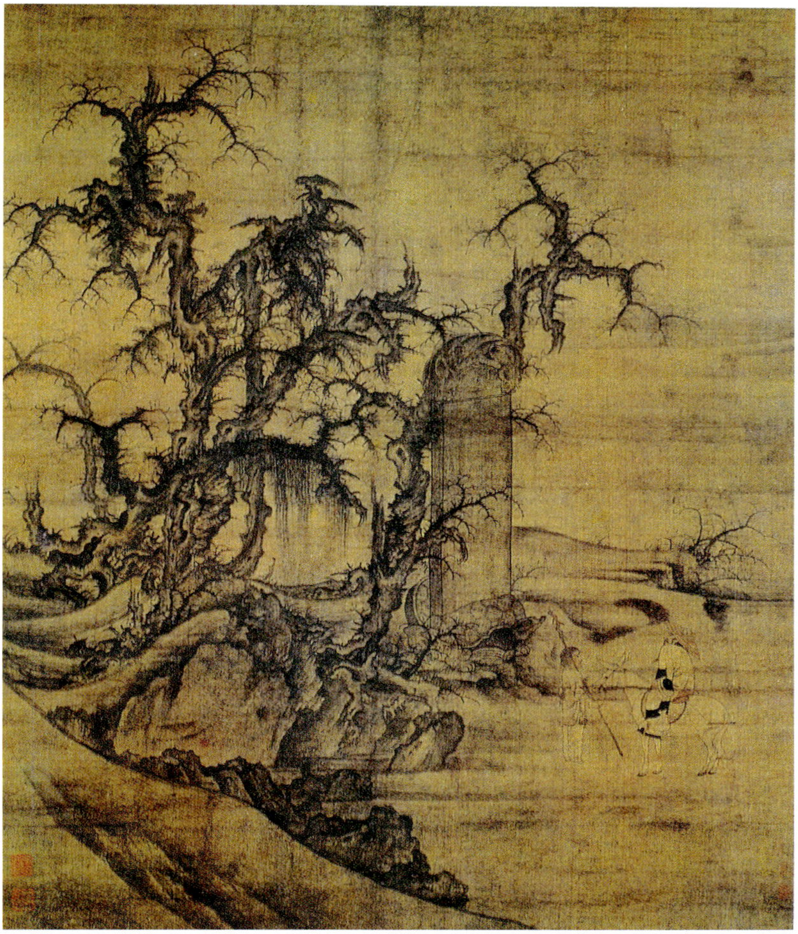

Reading the Tablet by a Jagged Rock by Li Cheng (126.3 cm × 104.9 cm), Municipal Museum of Art.

take a stroll, feast their eyes, have fun, and enjoy a brief retreat. He encouraged painters to travel extensively and observe closely so as to learn from nature. He also classified painters' observation skills in three perspectives: remoteness in height, depth, and horizon.

Early Spring depicts mountains teeming with new life, and features thin mists, new leaves, and limpid rivers, with the figures, boats, and buildings arranged according to the major theme. It has a distinctive layout and is quiet and spacious in conception with

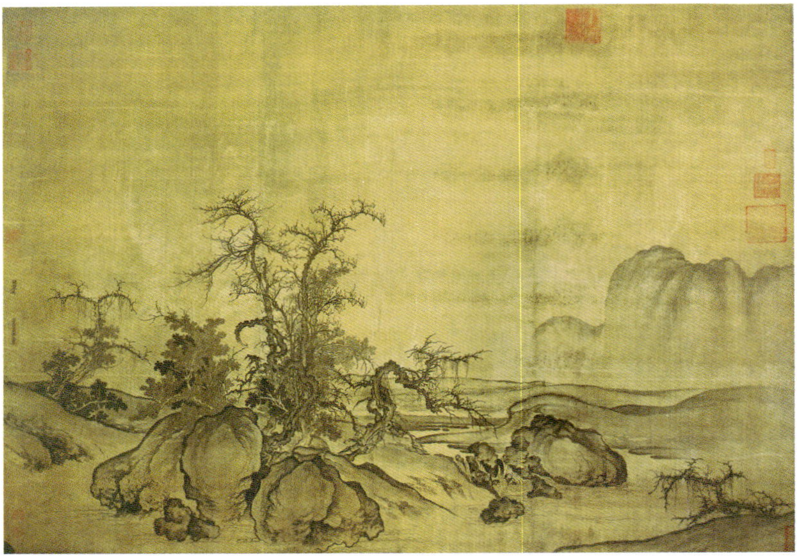

Level-Distance View of Rocks by Guo Xi (120.8 cm × 167.7 cm), Beijing Palace Museum.

strangely shaped rocks and striking mountains. Guo Xi tried to keep his painting as close as possible to the actual deep wilderness while exploiting the magnificent style of landscape in north China and the regular style typical of court painters. He used the three perspectives alternately, with mountains far and near setting off one another amidst the lingering, graceful mist. "The painting easily generates a sense of 'remoteness' – a space nourishing to the heart of the viewers. However, judging from this painting, which highlights paths in mountains, boats on the rivers and pedestrians on the roads, the painter's proposal of giving viewers a feeling as if they were present on the scene, where they can view, walk, travel and live, is nothing but an assumption, or an ideal that may not necessarily be put into practice." As a matter of fact, vertical scrolls constrained early attempts to convey the relative remoteness, but as the style reached maturity, along with their observation of and experience with nature, the painters improved in showing depth.

More realistic and less grand paintings by Guo Xi have a different aesthetic conception. *Level-Distance View of Rocks* (1078) uses only the horizontal perspective, and the relative relationship between the nearby pines and rocks to the far-off mountains is reminiscent of Li Cheng's work. With the simpler perspective, the dimness of the view is manipulated and adapted by the painter, and leaves more room for expressing his personal feelings. Guo maximizes the use of varying ink tones. The foreground objects are outlined in firm strokes and filled in with "curled cloud lines," while the distant mountains are painted in light ink using the "boneless method," meaning to draw an object directly without drawing its outline. Guo's paintings from a "corner view" laid the groundwork for the painting style of the Southern Song Dynasty.

Fan Kuan (dates unknown), a native of Huayuan (today's Yaoxian in Shaanxi Province), had a mild temper, which earned him the name by which he is known (Kuan means "mild tempered"). He lived during the early Northern Song Dynasty and was one of its three most famous landscape painters. Fan learned from Li Cheng and Jing Hao before he retreated to mountains in the belief that "Nature is a better teacher than people." He established his own style based on his observation of nature, becoming a representative of the "North School" along with Li Cheng. Fan would sit in remote mountains all day long, examining the landscape all around and pondering over "real nature." He was very good at scenes of the four seasons, travelers, and imaginative views of winds, the moon, clouds, and skies after rain or snow. All his paintings are landscapes of Shaanxi and Gansu provinces, painted on broad scrolls with striking mountain views. He liked to draw lush forests on the top of the mountains and protruding rocks in the middle of rivers using "raindrop strokes," which underscore the tangible structure and texture of the mountains. His best-known works include *Travelers in Streams and Mountains* (*Xishan Xinglv Tu*) and *Snow in a Cold Forest* (*Hanlin Xuejing*).

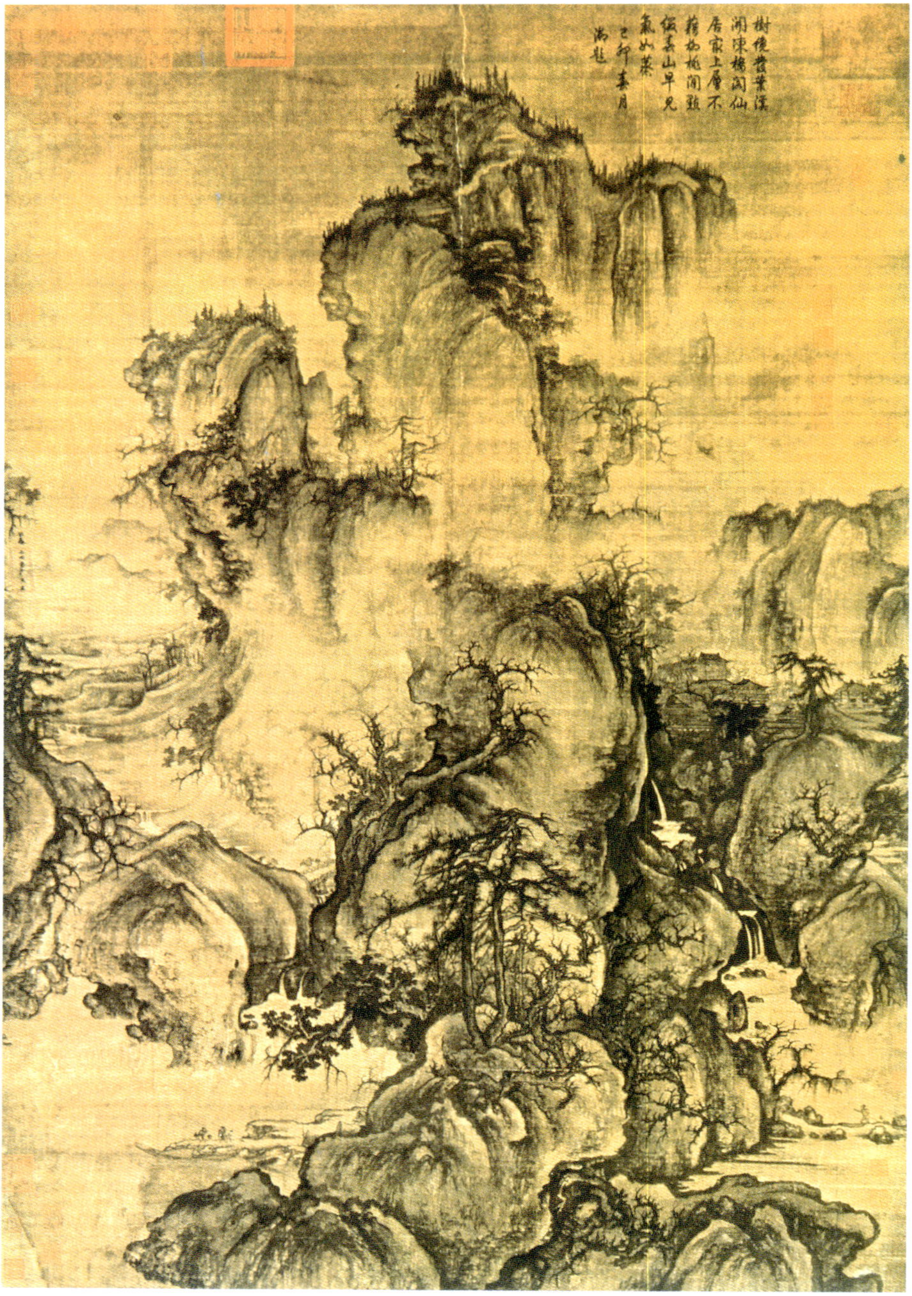

Early Spring by Guo Xi (158.3 cm × 108.1 cm), Taipei Palace Museum.

Travelers in Streams and Mountains was painted on silk in ink. On the side is a note by Dong Qichang of the Ming Dynasty: "*Xishan Xinglv Tu* by Fan Zhongli of the Northern Song Dynasty." The painting depicts a spectacular view of Qinglong Moutains, vibrant forests and grasses, imposing rocks, and undulating ridges. It seems that Fan paid no heed to traditional layout that would have emphasized depth; instead, he put the steep precipice in the center, indicating its "existence" was of great importance to the hermit in the painting. For him, the mountain is what a philosopher would call an "entity" and symbolizes the "spiritual enlightenment" that he pursues. The hermit completely integrates himself into nature. Despite the use of "raindrop strokes," which can be interpreted as an appropriate way to express his feelings, Fan devoted great attention to impressive details. He portrayed rivers in the valley, broad riverbeds, and roads at the foot of the mountain, donkeys carrying firewood, and wayfarers hurrying on their journey in a regular manner, like dry-point works of European rural life in the seventeenth century.

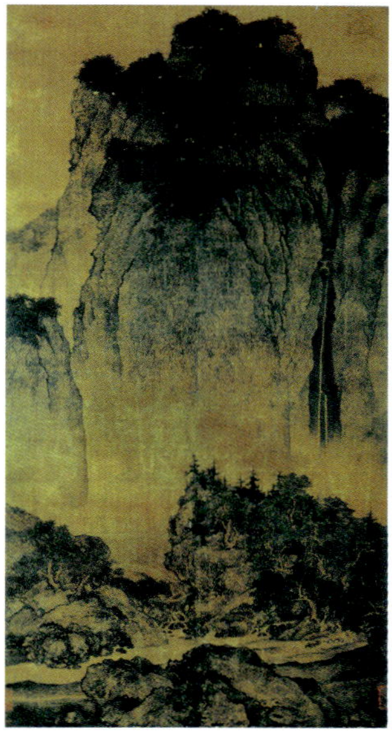

Travelers in Streams and Mountains by Fan Kuan (206.3 cm × 103.4 cm), Taipei Palace Museum.

In the Five Dynasties and the Northern Song Dynasty, landscape painters, from north China's Jing Hao, Li Cheng, Fan Kuan, and Guo Xi to Dong Yuan in the south, established a full set of patterns for landscapes, but realism remained their main concern. They were trying to find a perfect expression for the landscapes and they constantly attempted to improve the work with direct observation and personal experience of nature. The grand scale and composition of the works and the implicit philosophic meanings are unrivaled by later paintings. However, *shanshuis* are fundamentally different from Western landscapes, which aim to reproduce natural scenes in a physical sense through illusion and imitation, while the nature reflected on silk or paper scrolls in ink is suggestive – and are often perceived by Western viewers as expressionist.

Su Shi and Mi Fu

As a great author, frustrated politician, and amateur painter, Su Shi occupies a significant position in the history of Chinese painting, despite the fact only a few of his works have survived. This is because Su, active during the Northern Song Dynasty, proposed the concept of "scholar painting," and practiced it, and the style gradually became the mainstream of Chinese painting.

Su Shi (1037–1101), artist name Zizhan and also known as Dongpo Jushi, was a native of Meishan, in Sichuan Province. He entered the civil service as a youth and was promoted to a prominent position in the imperial court; however, in middle age he was jailed for his involvement in a political incident and then exiled several times and did not receive amnesty until he was on the verge of death. Having experienced so many ups and downs in his life, Su had a complex philosophical view, encompassing "the golden mean" and "the heavenly fate and destiny" of Confucianism, the serenity and the contentment without disgrace of philosophical Taoism, the detachment and enlightenment of Buddhism, and the metaphysical pursuit of longevity of religious Taoism. Not a professional, Su's occasional paintings, were mostly of withered trees, bamboos, and bizarre stones. His surviving works are all embellished by the writings and poems of Mi Fu and Liu Zuoliang, which have ensured their identification.

Poetry and painting were purely hobbies for Su. However, according to the Confucian standards of a "gentleman," he strongly believed: "Artistic skill is the nearest equivalent to the truth." This means that in addition to physical and mental relaxation, scholars can gain a deeper understanding of the truth by studying fine arts.

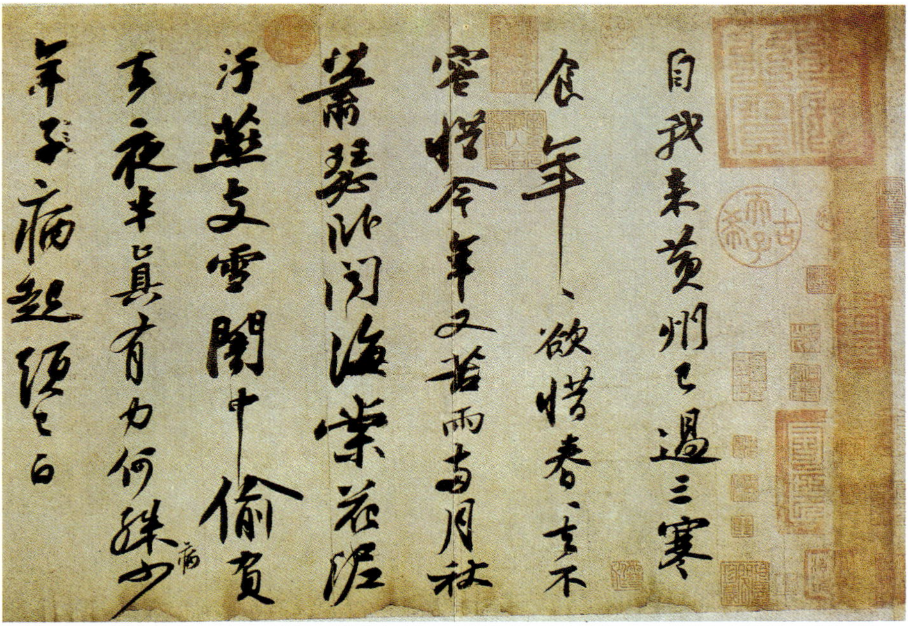

Handwriting on *Poem of the Hanshi Festival in Huangzhou* by Su Shi (detail), (34.2 cm × 18.9 cm), Taipei Palace Museum.

Su said nature images are changeable and therefore imperfections serve as evidence of their multifaceted nature, adding that violation of the common principles of truth will lead to a complete failure.

Su commented on a painting by his friend Wen Tong (1018–1079): "When Wen Tong paints bamboo, all he sees is bamboo. As he integrates himself into the bamboo, his paintings look endlessly fresh." Unlike laypeople and craft painters who tend to focus on every detail, Wen Tong concentrated solely on bamboo so that he could integrate himself into its nature and achieve a harmony that would show his feelings towards nature, a style that Su Shi highly appreciated. When scholars enjoy natural landscapes, they will immediately go beyond the physical existence to reach a spiritual dimension. Su sneered at painters who mechanically pursued the likeness of nature. "Despite his superb expertise, Wu Daozi is merely a craft painter," he commented bluntly. The painters Su admired were well-educated scholar painters who were

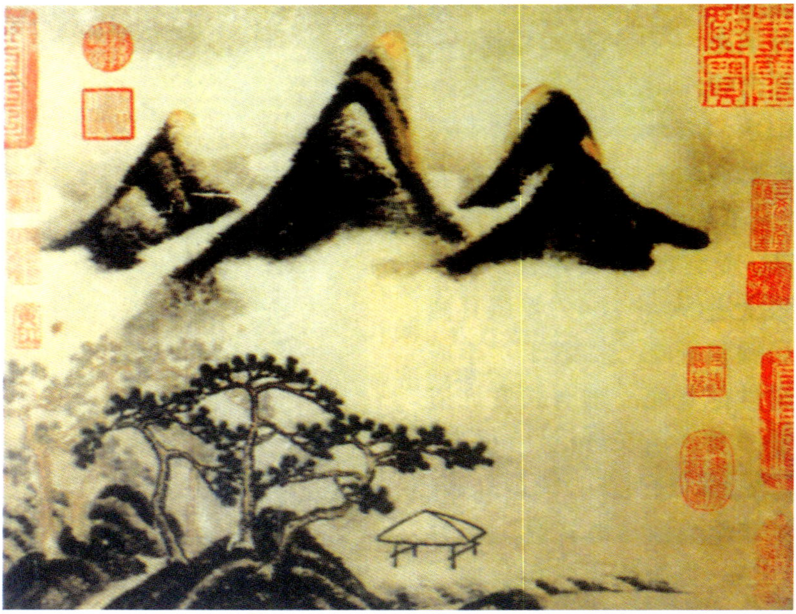

A Lucky Pine in Spring Mountains by Mi Fu (62.5 cm × 44 cm), Taipei Palace Museum.

capable of "going beyond the images," such as Wang Wei and Wen Tong. These painters could transcend formal likeness to arrive at "common principles," using natural images as a means to express their inner feelings and their unique self. A gentleman can think about an object, but should not be obsessed with it, for if he does, he will be burdened by an insignificant object, while taking no pleasure from a valuable one.

What matters to scholar painters is how to express what is in their mind through images, but they should transcend these images, and not be confined to them. If they give too much attention to images, they will become subordinated to them, and find themselves frustrated in their pursuit of happiness. However, if they can go beyond the images, they can take pleasure from them, no matter how insignificant they are. Su's values were a negation of the criteria of the Northern Song Dynasty for the refined paintings. He distinguished scholar painters from craft or career painters. It was his belief that the scholar painters who

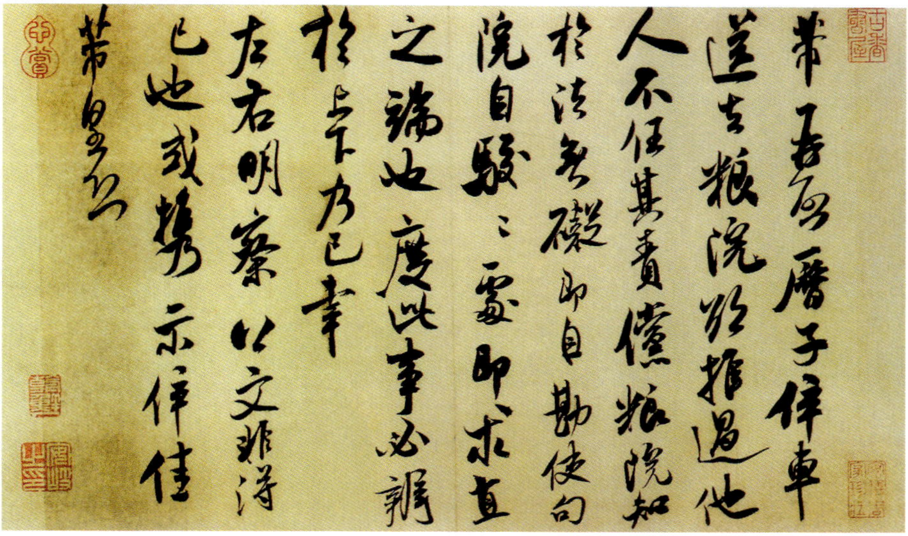

Handwriting on *Tiaoxi Brook Poems*, scroll by Mi Fu (detail), (189.5 cm × 30.3 cm), Beijing Palace Museum.

concentrated on the "spirit" only touched on the "surface." Seeking likeness to nature is the goal of craft painters, and scholars should not bother about this, but instead concentrate on improving morality and nurturing spirituality. In Su's opinion, the reason why likeness is not to be valued is that pursuing it will result in further moving from the "truth." What scholar painters seek to express is the "common principles" embodied in their characters and aspirations that only other outstanding talents can understand. As a person with remarkable accomplishments in literature and a distinctive personal charisma, Su was qualified to put forward this view, but whether his paintings illustrate it is a slightly different matter. For Confucian scholars, poetry, calligraphy, and painting are all forms of art which they enjoy as a means of relaxation. Su said, "What cannot be fully expressed by poetry can be expressed by calligraphy or painting, both of which are ink creations." His casually painted *Bamboos and Stones* (*Zhushi Tu*) may be deemed as an example of scholar painters' improvised calligraphic painting. It is reminiscent of Liang Kai's freehand-style paintings of poets and celestials in the Southern Song Dynasty. Despite the prevailing painting style of the court and the Imperial Painting Academy at the time, the theories and works of eminent intellectuals such as Su Shi and Mi Fu clearly indicated a shift of painters' focus.

Mi Fu (1051–1107), artist name Dong Yuan, a friend of Su's, was good at poems, essays, calligraphy, and painting. He was also expert at verifying the authenticity of paintings and a collector of famous works. Mi and Su were both masters of calligraphy, and were part of the "Four Great Calligraphers" of the Song Dynasty, together with Cang Xiang and Huang Tingjian. Mi exhibited an innocently irregular style in his landscapes, most of which were in ink. Mi Youren (1086–1165), Mi Fu's son, or "junior Mi" as he is usually called, carried on the family tradition and was particularly adept at painting mountains in clouds. He made a slight change to his father's style, giving birth to a new school of landscape. Terms such as "Mi's mountains," "Mi's cloudy mountains," and "the Mi school" are often used in the study of Chinese painting history. Mi's mountains usually consist of short strokes and are enveloped in changing clouds. Mi Fu said, "I paint in a casual manner. Most of my paintings feature trees and rocks hidden behind clouds and mists and are not a literal representation of nature." In a similar fashion, junior Mi often humorously called his paintings "games with ink" in his notes.

In terms of artistic conception, Su Shi stood for "remoteness, freshness, brevity, and detachedness," while Mi Fu advocated "naturalness," "innocence," and "classical taste." Their viewpoints coincided, but Mi, being aggressive in nature, was more outspoken. Widely recognized masters of the landscape of the Tang and Song Dynasties were mostly from northern China, including Wu Daozi, Li Cheng, and Guan Tong. Mi Fu, however, said that his paintings "are not as vulgar as those of Li Cheng and Guan Tong" and "have definitely no similarity to Wu Daozi's style." He also showed disapproval of court painters such as

Guo Xi. However, he was ready to sing the praise of Su Shi, for his few paintings of trees, bamboos and rocks. He was particularly fond of another painter also called Dong Yuan, a neglected artist in southern China, repeatedly lauding him, seemingly because Mi Fu found a similarity between Dong's paintings and those of a hundred years earlier: His comments also served as an artistic manifesto of the scholar landscape painters. Dong Yuan, with his natural and innocent style, was unrivaled in the Tang Dynasty and is even better than Bi Hong. His works have no match in recent years for their profound spiritual dimension, featuring rolling mountains and changing clouds and mists, his unembellished paintings convey a sense of innocence. Dark green mists and sturdy twigs are also vividly depicted. With streams, rivers, bridges, isles, and fishermen, the paintings represent typical scenery of southern China.

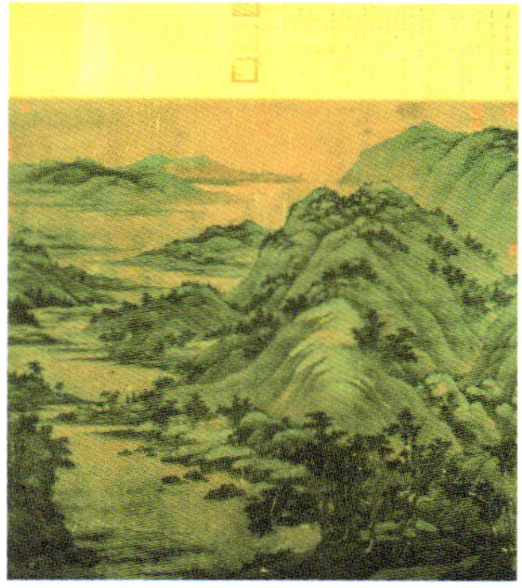

People of the Suburb of Longsu by Dong Yuan (156 cm × 160 cm), Taipei Palace Museum.

The notion of "painting cloudy mountains as a game with ink" proposed by Mi Fu and his son Mi Youren is an indication of the scholar-painters' style. Mi Fu's comments on Dong Yuan can be used to characterize his own paintings. Some critics point out that while Dong tried to capture the structural changes of actual mountains and trees, Mi only played with ink casually, making almost no effort in that regard. That is because they were strongly influenced by Su Shi's uninhibited style of painting. In Mi Youren's *Clearing Clouds Over Distant Peaks* (*Yuanxiu Qingyun Tu*), the remote mountains are not even outlined but are shaped with different shades of ink. Based on a transient scene in the mind, this ink-and-wash painting embodies an unaccountably mysterious taste, or an alleged "real interest" of nature. One should note that Mi Youren used lines typical of Gu Kaizhi and Zhan Ziqian to depict the clouds and mists in this painting, a fact that shows scholar painters like him not only tried to convey the "real interest" directly but also attempted to re-enact some classical painting styles.

Scholar Paintings

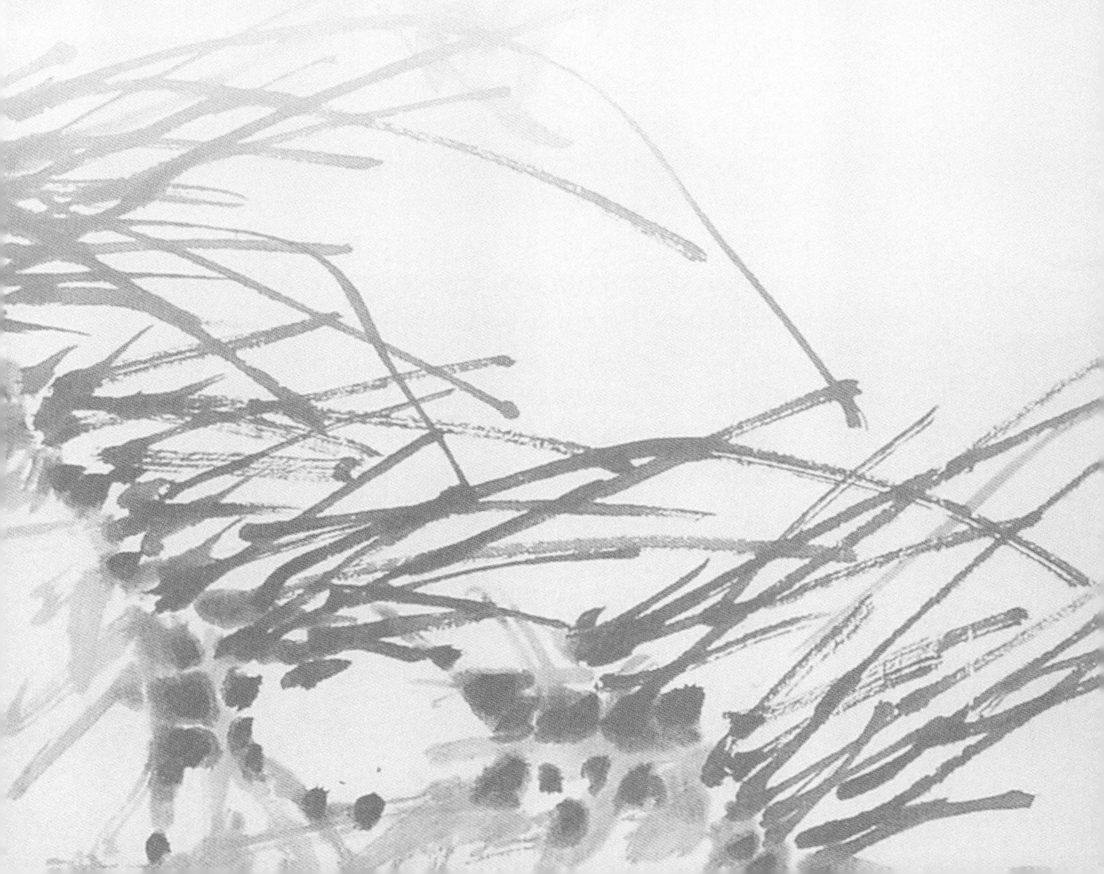

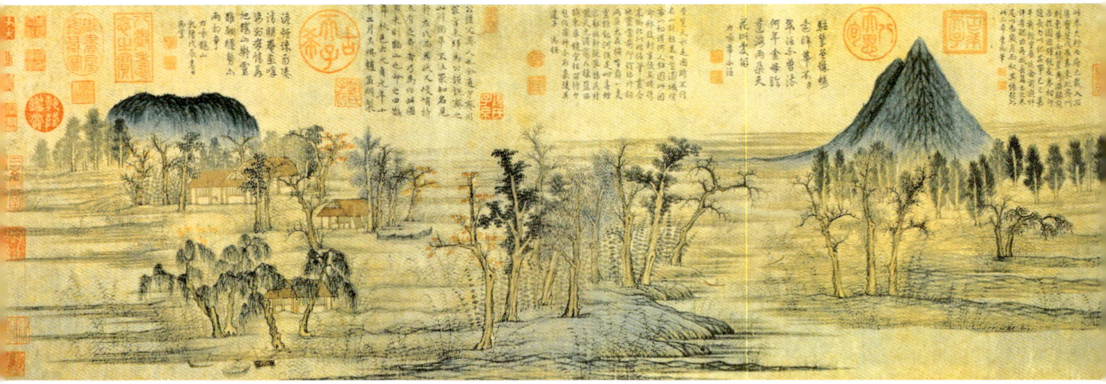

The Autumn Colors on the Que and Hue Mountains, scroll, by Zhao Mengfu (28.4 cm × 93.2 cm), Taipei Palace Museum.

Zhao Mengfu and the "Four Masters of the Yuan Dynasty"

The theory of scholar painting of the Northern Song Dynasty did not have much influence in the Southern Song Dynasty. Under great pressure from the Kingdom of Jin in the north, the south was on the verge of being conquered. The intellectuals of the Han ethnic group who believed in Confucianism canvassed for support in resisting the aggression of the foreign ethnic groups, putting their patriotic passion and anger into their poetry and statements, and found the gentle painting style unsuitable for their emotions. The Imperial Art Academy of the Southern Song Dynasty had only some second-class painters, who tried to express their anger through unrestrained and incisive brushwork.

Genghis Khan united Mongolia in the thirteenth century and continued these conquests. In 1271, Kublai Khan established the Yuan Empire in Dadu (today's Beijing) and conquered the Southern Song Dynasty in less than twelve years, thus assuming authority over the whole of China. During the early stage of the Yuan Dynasty, in order to consolidate his rule, Kublai Khan studied the art of government from Confucius' works and was courteous to Confucian officials. His successors continued to respect Confucius and Taoism and established Kui Zhang Ge. The painting collector Ke Jiusi (1290–1343) was appointed as Court Academician of Book Appreciation to check and classify all the books in the imperial collections. When the Yuan Dynasty was in place, society re-established some normality, and scholar painters reacted violently against the narrowness of the painting style of the Southern Song Dynasty. Their representative was Zhao Mengfu (1254–1322), artist name Zi'ang, also known by his literary name Songxue Daoren. He was a descendant of the royal family of the Song Dynasty, and after its fall, he was recommended to the imperial court and was appointed a court official, since the new empire was particularly interested in utilizing the descendants of the previous dynasty; he only resigned after Kublai Khan died. Zhao Mengfu followed Dong Yuan and Li Cheng in painting mountains and water and Li Gonglin and Tang Ren in painting portraits and horses. His ink-bamboo and flower-and-bird paintings were famous, showing his style of using rounded and vigorous brushwork. He painted stones with hollow strokes and bamboo in calligraphic style. Dong Qichang of the Ming Dynasty commented: "His paintings had the style of painters of the Tang Dynasty, but not that thin, and were as vigorous as paintings of the Northern Song Dynasty, but not that

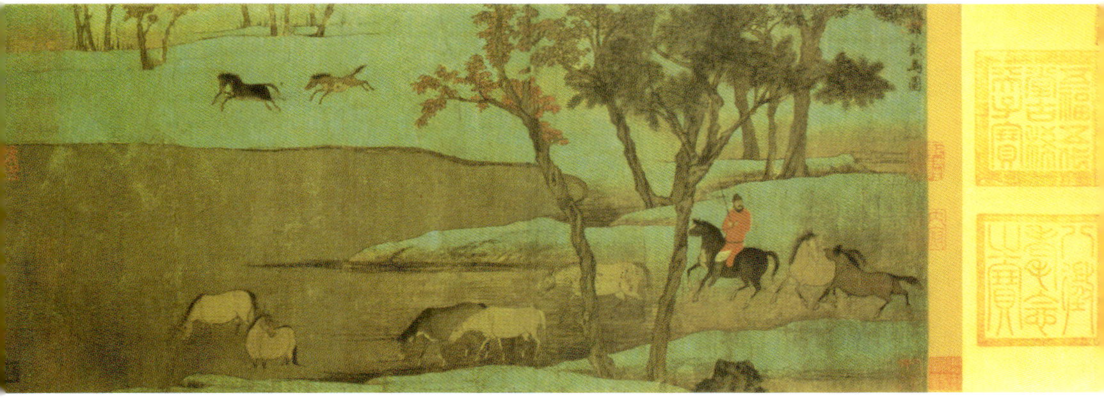

Horse Drinking Water in a Suburb in Autumn, scroll, by Zhao Mengfu (23.6 cm × 59 cm), Beijing Palace Museum.

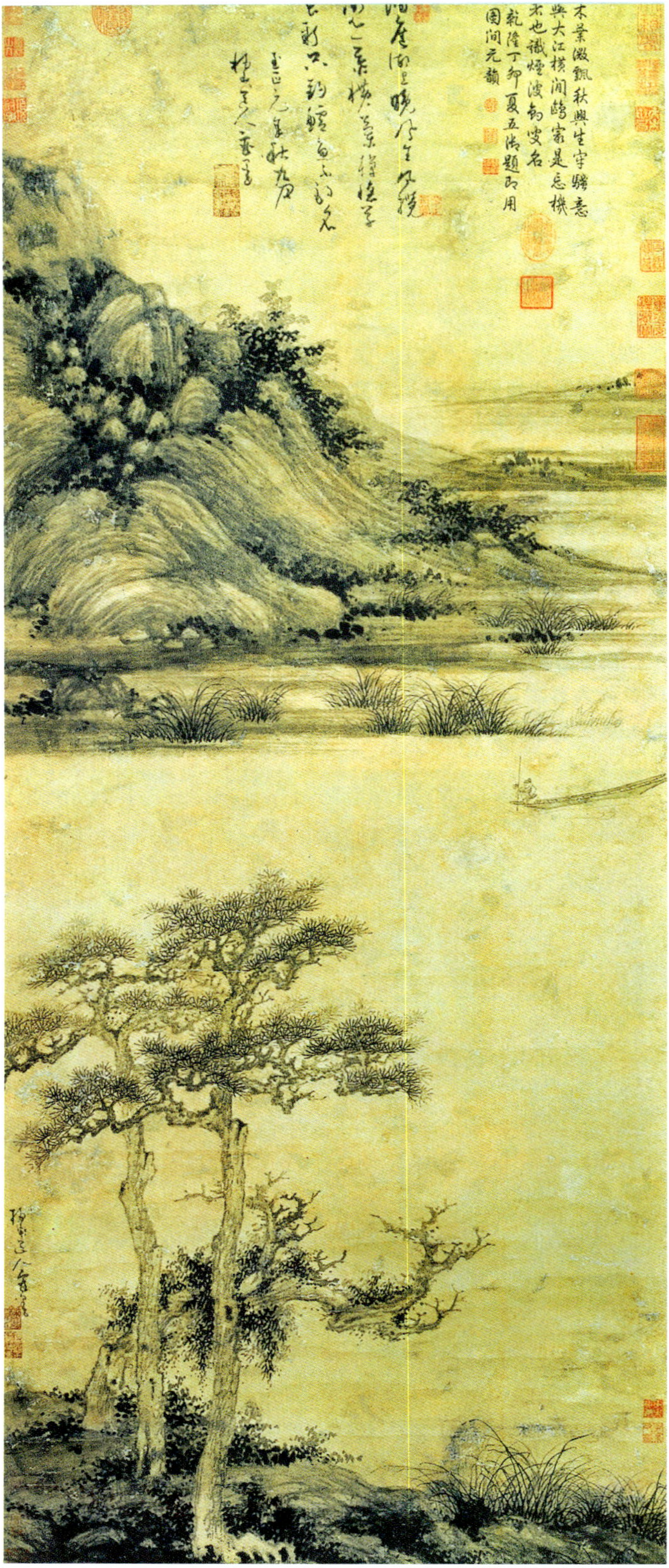

Fishermen on Dongting Lake, scroll, by Wu Zheng (146.6 cm × 58.6 cm), Taipei Palace Museum.

boorish." He wrote quiet poems and made seals. His paintings included *The Autumn Colors on the Que and Hue Mountains* (*Quehua Qiuse Tu*), *Painting of Red-Clothed Arhats* (*Hongyi Luohan Tu*), *Horse Drinking Water in a Suburb in Autumn* (*Qiujiao Yinma Tu*), and *Happiness of Fishermen at the Riverside* (*Jiangcun Yule Tu*). His writings fill ten volumes of *Songxue Zhai Wenji* (*Collected Works of Songxue Daoren*).

Zhao Mengfu insisted on reforming the painting style of the Imperial Art Academy of the Southern Song Dynasty and believed that paintings should have a sense of tradition; otherwise, they lacked any value even they were carefully painted. The Yuan Dynasty abandoned the academy, and with his special status, Zhao Mengfu's proposal, to abandon the tradition established in the Southern Song Dynasty and go back to the cultural roots of previous dynasties, pleased the rulers of the Yuan Dynasty. His impressive paintings led to the development of a trend of "going back to the ancients."

Zhao Mengfu had two distinctive painting styles: fine brushwork with strong colors and bold and unconstrained brushwork in ink-and-wash. The first style illustrated his respect for the paintings of the Jin, Tang, and Northern Song Dynasties, and in his early work, he frequently used green. *Youyu Qiuhe Tu* is a good example: he sketched the lines first and added color afterwards (without dots), which was a traditional style. *Horse Drinking Water in a Suburb in Autumn* and *Washing Horses* (*Yuma Tu*) followed the style of the Tang Dynasty with carefully designed patterns and the utilization of colors to make a warm tone. *Birds' Luster and the Color of Autumn* has a simple, remote landscape, which, according to Dong Qichang, followed the painting style of Dong Yuan. Modern art historian Wang Bomin (b. 1924) went to look at the Huabuzhu and Queshan Mountains that were painted in *Birds' Luster* and confirmed that Zhao was a master at painting real scenery. The ink painting *Water Village* (*Shuicun Tu*) is a beautiful scene of range upon range of mountains covered with clouds and

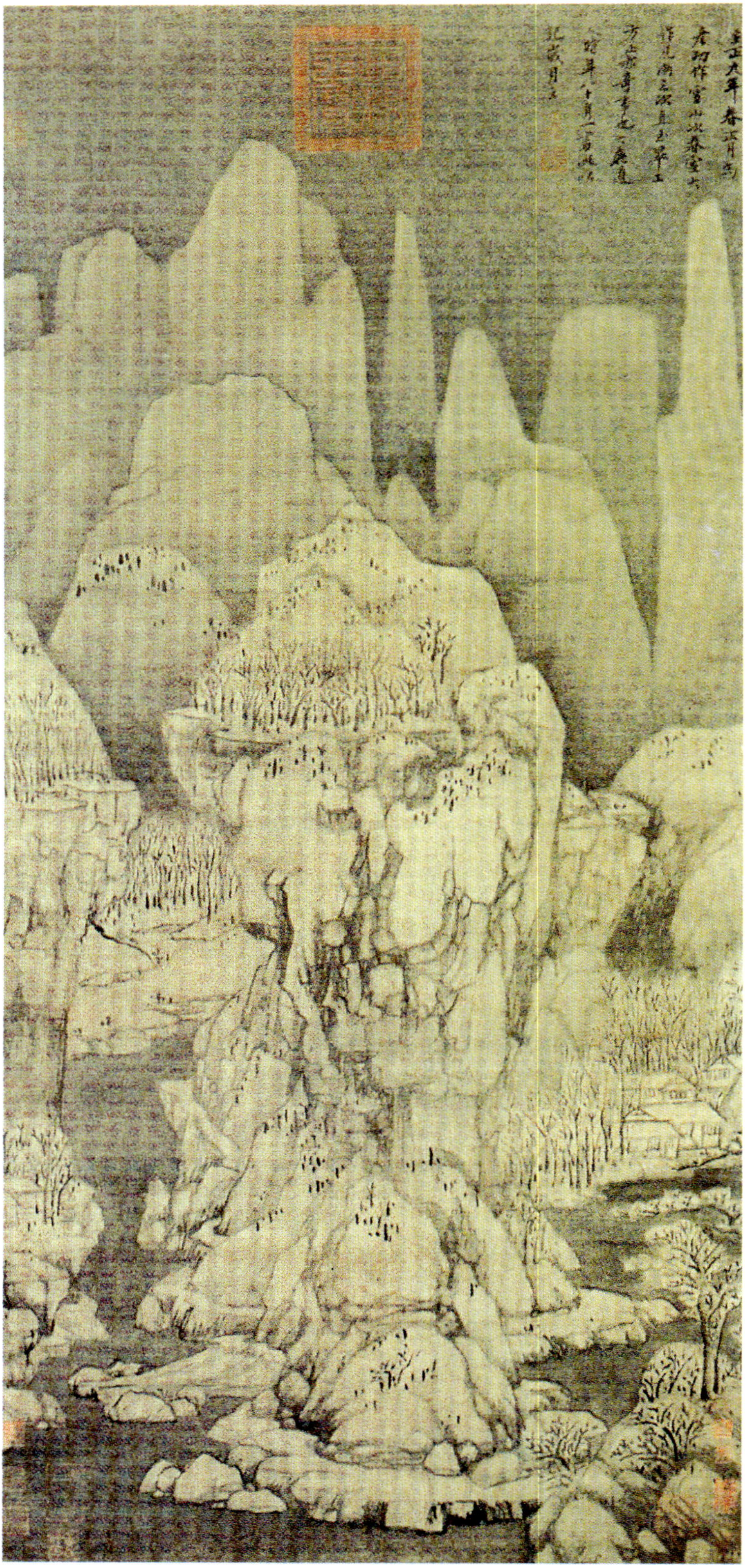

villages encircled by rivers. Zhao recovered the skill of using the center of the brush and abandoned the Southern Song painters' practice of using its sides. His ink landscapes followed Li Cheng and Guo Xi, enabling him to rectify the shortcomings of hollowness in Mi Fu's method. To express his respect for Su Shi and Wen Tong, he also imitated their styles and painted several bamboo and stone paintings, using cool brushwork to remedy the abruptness of Su Shi's painting. He consciously exhibited calligraphic skill and included long poems. Experts say that scholar painting "started with Su Shi, and the gate was opened widely by Zhao Mengfu."

Most of the non-official scholar painters of the Yuan Dynasty retired from the secular world and exercised painting freely in their spiritual world, illustrating their way of living, and their interests and ambitions. Thus, mountains and waters, withered trees, bamboo and stones, plum blossoms and orchids were their favorite subjects, while figures that directly reflected social life lost out. These scholar officials would stress the spirit of the scholar, the sense of history, and the grace of non-convention and would object to any sense of manipulation or artisanship. The ink paintings of freehand brushworks of Su Shi and Mi Fu were regarded as the best examples to demonstrate this philosophy. They would pay great attention to calligraphic skills while painting, integrating poem and calligraphy into their work. Calligraphy was used as the criterion to judge their success, because scholar painters believed that painting was just the extension of calligraphy skills. Scholar painters in the Yuan Dynasty pursued the painting theories of Wen Tong, Su Shi, and Mi Fu, advocating the abandonment of realism and seeking spiritual resemblance in simplicity. Scholars still asserted that painting was only a hobby; landscape painter Wu Zhen reiterated that "painting was simply an activity of interest while scholars were composing poems." Zhao Mengfu with Huang Gongwang, Wang Meng, and Wu Zhen of the middle and late Yuan Dynasty were regarded as the "Four Masters of the Yuan Dynasty." In the late Ming Dynasty, Dong Qichang listed Zhao Mengfu

< *Nine Peaks after Snow* by Huang Gongwang (117.2 cm × 57.5 cm), Beijing Palace Museum.

separately as the grandmaster and substituted Ni Zan as the fourth. While the four inherited the landscape tradition of the Five Dynasties and the Northern Song Dynasty and were influenced directly and indirectly by Zhao Mengfu, they developed their own distinct characteristics.

Huang Gongwang (1269–1354) was the first of the masters. He was a child prodigy who read many classical and historical works and showed talent in calligraphy, music, and non-dramatic songs. He served as a local official in the Yuan Dynasty and was prosecuted by mistake in middle age. After he was released, he sought to live in seclusion, and began to paint at the age of fifty. Huang Gongwang exceeded the achievements of Dong Yuan and Juran, and he learned to use a texture stroke, but later he changed his painting style. His paintings are more charming than those of Zhao Mengfu. His surviving works include *Living in Fuchun Mountain* (*Fuchunshan Jutu*), *Cliff of Tianchi* (*Tianchi Shibi Tu*), and *Nine Peaks after Snow* (*Jiufeng Xueji Tu*).

Wang Meng (1301–1385), artist name Shuming and also known by his literary name Xiangguang Jushi or Huangheshan Qiao, was Zhao Mengfu's nephew. He was born into a family with calligraphic and painting traditions. He served as an official but later resigned and chose to live in Huangheshan Mountain in Linping (today's Yuhang in Zhejiang Province). After the fall of the Yuan Dynasty, he worked again as an official in Tai'an in Shandong Province, but he was arrested in 1385 and died in prison. He had a remarkable memory and read extensively, and had a solid training in poetry, writing, calligraphy, and painting. He often received advice from Huang Gongwang, and he too modeled Dong Yuan's and Juran's style. He mainly painted in ink and developed cow-hair strokes. He was regarded as a creative landscape master, and learned from his work. His surviving paintings include *Living in Summer Mountains* (*Xiari Shanju Tu*), *Living in Seclusion in Summer* (*Xiari Gaoyin Tu*), and *Gezhichuan Yiju Tu* (*Moving to Live in Gezhi Valley*).

Living in Summer Mountains is ink on paper (118.1 cm x 36.2 cm), now in the Beijing Palace Museum. In the distance are ranges of mountains; the center has a magnificent mountain peak, thrusting into the clouds; the foreground has ancient pine trees beside the hill with a pool of calm water beside the trees. On the rocks, is a hill with its foot extending into the water. The hills are divided into three groups with little pieces of sand dotting the spaces in between. It mixes vague images and clear focus, and the whole is carefully arranged so it is completely different from the paintings of the Yuan Dynasty. Judged from the postscript, the painting was completed in his later years.

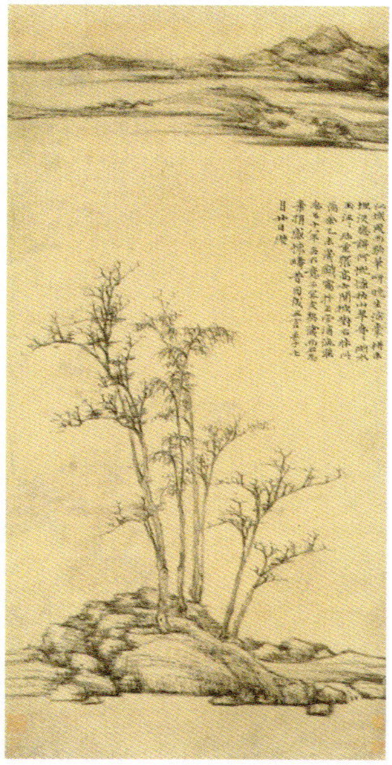

Fishing Village after Rain by Ni Zan (96 cm × 47 cm), Shang Hai Museum.

Wu Zhen (1280–1354), artist name Zhonggui, and also known as Meihua Daoren, Meihua Shami, and Meihua Heshang, was born in Jiaxing in Zhejiang Province. In middle age he lived in seclusion and poverty, making a living by divination. Consequently, he was both a "master of Taoism" and a "monk of Buddhism," which was not unusual given his social background and the times. Wu Zhen modeled his work on Dong Yuan, Juran, and occasionally on Jing Hao and Guan Tong. Yun Nantian, a landscape painter in the Ming Dynasty, commented on Wu's paintings: "Meihua Anzhu (Wu Zhen) and Yifeng Laoren (Huang Gongwang) learned from Dong Yuan's and Juran's painting style together. Wu promoted obscurity while Huang adhered to simplicity. They had different aesthetics but similar artistic achievements." Wu's paintings were mostly about fishermen, reflecting his life and social attitude.

Ni Zan (ca. 1306–1374), also known as Yunlinzi, Huanxiazi, Jingmanmin, and Jingchu Yinzhe, was born in Wuxi to a wealthy family. He built Qingbi Pagoda in his garden and stored all his collections there. In his old age, he longed for a secluded life and sold his land during a chaotic period, and lived on boats for twelve years. Then he devoted himself to painting and formed his own landscape style. But he was arrested and died soon after his release. He was influenced greatly by Dong Yuan, and also by Jing Hao and Guan Tong, and learned from Li Cheng to paint mountains, stones, and trees. He painted the scenery around Tai Lake. Most of his paintings followed a pattern where the low, near section is flat hillside with bamboo, trees, and huts or pavilions; the middle is calm water; and the top, far section is mountain ranges. He often used dry brushes with simple ink. His painting style showing complexity and richness through simplicity exerted great influence on scholar painters of the Ming and Qing dynasties. His surviving paintings include *Poem of Du Lin* (*Dulin Shiyi Tu*), *Shizilin Garden* (*Shizilin Tu*), *Fishing Village after Rain* (*Yuzhuang Qiuji Tu*), and *Six Men of Honor* (*Liu Junzi Tu*).

The ink-and-wash landscapes of the "Four Masters of the Yuan Dynasty" completed the change of interest in landscape from the Northern Song Dynasty. As Dong Qichang summarized: "The four masters, Huang, Ni, Wu, and Wang all started learning from Dong Yuan and Juran," that is, their own painting style was enlightened by Dong Yuan. They established a direction for later landscape painters, who greatly respected the painter Shi Tao, of the Qing Dynasty, who was famous for his egotism, commented: "The achievements of Dachi (Huang Gongwang), Yunlin (Ni Zan) and Huanghe Shanqiao (Wang Meng) exceeded those of the painters before them." Their followers respected them for their virtues and personalities. The four had very different personal circumstances, but reached the same goal in the end. They appreciated each other and shared a similar philosophical way of thinking. The four masters sought a life aloof from secular society and avoided the restraints of political ambitions and material temptations. They were devout Taoists and Buddhists, and they dreamed of living with nature. Their greatest joy was lying in forests and by rivers and rocks, watching the white clouds going by: landscape was their religion.

Plum Blossom, Orchid, Bamboo, and Chrysanthemum

During the Yuan Dynasty, scholars and artists were no longer appreciated at the imperial court, except for a favoured few. Most poets, artists, and scholars chose to leave Hangzhou for other cities, including Suzhou and Yangzhou, as did the "Four Masters of the Yuan Dynasty." But Wang Meng and Ni Zan could not escape and were implicated in court scandals, and died unnaturally. The political and literary persecution and the corruption of the mandarin class further alienated the intellectual elites and they sought self-gratification in pursuing art that did not have political implications. The plum blossom, orchid, bamboo, and chrysanthemum were favorite subjects, and they implicitly explored the commonly accepted characteristics associated with these plants. Orchid and bamboo represented moral loftiness, and plum blossom and chrysanthemum principles and justice. Traditionally, they have been humanized, and bamboo called "gentleman" and orchid "beauty." Su Shi often painted bamboo, withered trees, and strange stones in a very casual style, about which the philosopher Zhu Xi of the Song period commented, "Su's paintings appear to be unplanned and very leisurely but a close examination will reveal their proud and aloof characteristics, which are a reflection of Su's own personality."

Plum blossom, orchid, bamboo, and chrysanthemum attracted a new generation of painters and marked a historical change in painting. During the Tang and Song Dynasties, flower-and-bird and landscape became independent genres, with a varied range of subjects. Some art historians consider flower-and-bird paintings to begin with the paintings of plants and animals on the pottery of the Neolithic Age, which later attracted the interest of the imperial

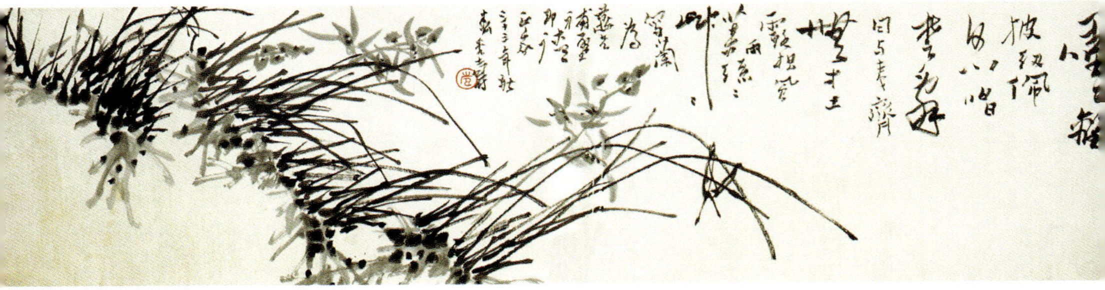

Green Orchid for Hai Yan by Pan Tianshou (33 cm × 126 cm), Pan Tianshou Museum

court. There are more than eighty artists listed in the official records in the Tang Dynasty as specialists in painting flowers, trees, birds, and animals, and many of them painted only flowers or birds. During the Five Dynasties (907–960), the imperial painter Huang Quan's (903–965) works featuring delicate brushwork and strong color was representative. He lived at the imperial court for most of his life and was famous for his paintings of rare birds, animals, flowers, and stones, which were in the royal collections. But Xu Xi, another important painter of the same period, considered Huang's imperial topics and style extravagant and wasteful and instead explored ordinary rivers and forests and painted the outside world. He was famous for light color and ink paintings of flowers, birds, fish, insects, and fruits and vegetables. However, both the rich imperial style of Huang Quan and the loose and wild style of Xu Xi attached great importance to sketching real objects. While few of their paintings have survived, during the heyday of the Imperial Art Academy in the Song and the Ming Dynasties, Huang Quan's style was followed and promoted by the imperial artists, while Xu Xi's style was copied and developed among the folk painters. A close examination of these flower-and-bird paintings leads one to feel a similar sense as when studying the landscapes of the Five Dynasties and Northern Song Dynasty: a sense of "natural theology." In this regard, the *Xuanhe Collection of Paintings Flowers and Birds* commented:

"The peony flower and the phoenix and the peacock represent wealth and honor, while the pine tree, the bamboo, the plum blossom, the chrysanthemum, the gull, the egret, the wild goose, and the wild duck all represent freedom and leisure. The honorable dignity of cranes, the brave struggle of hawks, the exquisite grace of aspen, willow, and phoenix trees, and the eternal morality of pine and cypress all can be vividly expressed in paintings. A person who appreciates the intention of painters would marvel at the implicit fineness of their shapes and lines and the spiritual fancy of the images in their minds. He could often gain much by studying the paintings as by experiencing the real world."

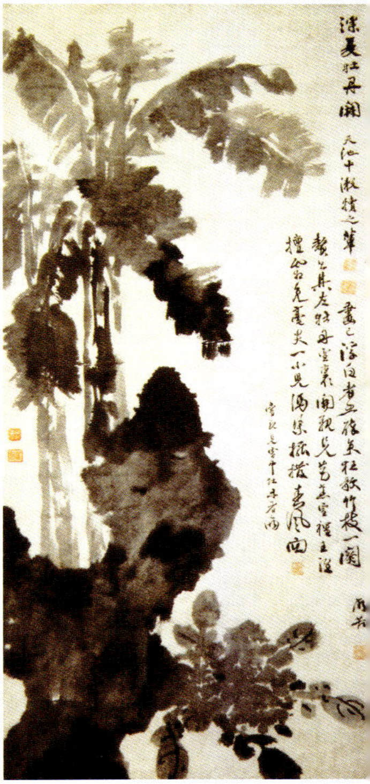

Peony and Rocks by Xu Wei (12.0.6 cm × 58.4 cm).

Meticulous flower-and-bird painting style continued to develop, especially in the imperial court. Painters still devoted themselves to portraying vividly flowers, grass, birds, and animals. Plum blossom, bamboo, stone, orchid, and grape became an independent painting genre and fashionable in scholar paintings. According to the *Xuanhe Collection of Paintings*, "Some paintings of light ink do not seek to give the actual likeness, but rather the spiritual resemblance. They are usually not painted by craft or career painters, but by scholars." These last included Su Shi and Wen Tong, who did not want to copy meticulously the natural objects as did their craft and career counterparts, and they disregarded the imperial style of the court. They chose objects such as unusual stones and withered trees to reflect their spiritual thinking. Compared with landscapes, flower-and-bird paintings could enable them to work better with ink, and provided a painting format for them to combine the calligraphy of poetry, painting, and seal-engraving art in one piece, fully exhibiting all of their abilities. There was also another sort of painter whose status was between the imperial craft painters and the scholars. They appreciated the

Ink Grapes by Xu Wei (116.4 cm × 64.3 cm), Beijing Palace Museum.

scholar painters' elegance and meticulous paintings, and they too delicately painted only with ink. The flower-and-bird paintings of Wang Yuan (dates unknown) and Bian Wenjin (dates unknown) of the Ming Dynasty, Lin Liang (1426–1495) of the Yuan Dynasty, and Shen Zhou, Wen Zhengming, and Tang Yin of the "Wu School" in the Ming period all belonged to this category.

The freehand brushwork of ink paintings with the themes of plum blossom, bamboo, and flower and bird in the Yuan Dynasty are outstanding achievements. To those scholar officials who kept far from the reality of political affairs, Xu Xi's style could bring comfort to their hearts. Zhao Mengfu of the early Yuan Dynasty and three of the "Four Masters of Yuan," Wang Meng, Ni Zan, and Wu Zhen, were all famous for painting bamboo and stone. The imperial scholar painter Ke Jiusi used ink paintings of bamboo to judge whether such a painting was scholar painting." Wang Mian (1287–1359), born into a simple farmer's family, chose to live a secluded life in his hometown after failing the imperial examinations, and called himself Meihua Wuzhu (Master of Plum Blossom House). His ink paintings of plum blossom in a refreshingly pure style were of great natural charm. Xu Wei (1521–1593), a poet, painter, and dramatist in the mid-Ming Dynasty, was regarded as the artist who completed the transformation of flower-and-bird paintings from the classical style to the scholar-painter style and inspired "greater freehand ink paintings" in the following generations.

Xu Wei, artist name Wenchang, also called Tianchi and Qingteng, was born in Shanyin (now

Shaoxing), Zhejiang Province. His poetic drama *Si Sheng Yuan*, written early in his life, was appreciated by the great dramatist of the Ming Dynasty, Tang Xianzu. Xu lived in poverty all his life and failed the imperial examinations several times, which finally disordered his brain. He killed his wife, and was arrested, and only in his declining years, was released from the jail; he died at the age of 73. His actual painting life spanned ten years. His poem describes himself:

"Wandering aimlessly for half a life, I am getting old;
Standing alone at my study in night wind, I whistle bold;
Looking at the bright pearls under my pen, nowhere to be sold;
Throwing up and down among wild canes idly, I walk in cold."

Xu's flower-and-bird painting and calligraphy, known as the "green cane style," incorporated the elements of the Song and Yuan Dynasties and of Shen Zhou and Lin Liang. In contrast to the idleness and grace of the "Wu School," it directly expressed his surge of feelings. He boldly broke the limit of the shapes and injected the subjects with his powerful personal feelings. Taking full advantage of Chinese painting paper (*xuan* paper), he wrote and painted freely depicting the spiritual likeness of subjects in wet and flowing ink. His surviving masterpieces include *Peony and Rocks* (*Mudan Jiaoshi Tu*), *Putao Tu* (*Grapes*), *Ink Flowers* (*Mo Hua Tu*), and many others. The painter Zheng Xie of the Qing Dynasty, who was one of the "Yangzhou Eight Eccentrics," highly appreciated Xu Wei's paintings and said, "I would offer fifty pieces of gold for a branch of megranate of Tianchi (Xu Wei)." He engraved a seal, reading "Running Dog at the Door of the Green Cane," to express his admiration of Xu. Qi Baishi of modern times expressed his respect for Xu by saying he wished he had been born three hundred years earlier to "tidy the papers and grind the ink blocks for the Green Cane." Xu's style had great influence on many painters of the Qing Dynasty, including Zhu Da, Shi Tao, and the "Yangzhou Eight Eccentrics," and the painters of modern times including Wu Changshuo and Qi Baishi.

"The Southern and Northern Schools"

Zhao Mengfu of the early Yuan Dynasty supported the idea of "ancient value," aiming at resuming the interest in the ancients that had been lost at the end of the South Song Dynasty and initiating a new style through studying the classical paintings. Zhao and the "Four Masters of the Yuan Dynasty" completed the change of painting styles, but, during the Ming and Qing Dynasties, the negative influences of the doctrine of "back to the ancients" became evident. In copying their work, even trivial painters could label themselves the admirers of Huang Gongwang. In the Ming Dynasty painters abandoned completely the study of nature, but treasured it as shown in ancient paintings. They were keen to illustrate how their painting styles, their brushwork, their mountains, stones, and trees could be traced back to painters in earlier dynasties. They believed copying paintings was the best way of achieving pleasure in painting. Meanwhile, commercial prosperity in the South reduced the attraction of returning to nature, which was now considered to be unnecessary.

The Ming Dynasty restored the Imperial Art Academy and so the center of scholar paintings moved back to the Yangzhi River. The "Four Masters of the Wu School" at nearby Su Zhou, namely Shen Zhou (1427–1509), Wen Zhengming (1470–1559), Tang Yin (1470–1523), and Qiu Ying (1493–1560), represented the highest level of scholar paintings, but were replaced in the late Ming Dynasty by the Huating School in Shanghai, with Mo Shilong (1539–1587) and Dong Qichang (1555–1636) as its representatives. The Wulin School, or the Zhejiang School, in Hangzhou, of Daujin (1388–1462), and Lan Ying (1585–1664), was, to some extent, the continuation of the painting style of the South Song Dynasty represented by Ma Yuan and was also unavoidably influenced by the scholar painting of the Yuan Dynasty. In the Ming Dynasty, there was a trend to formalize the style of the scholar painters of the Song and Yuan Dynasties, who had themselves been against the formal painting style of the

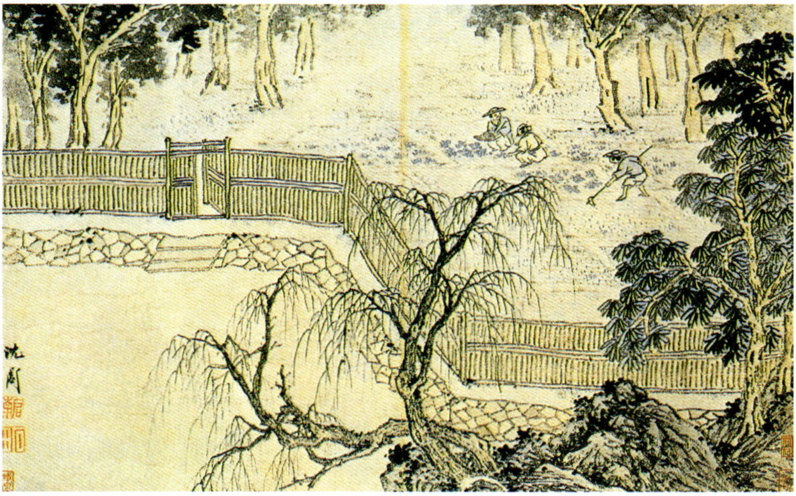

Picture Album of Mountains-and-Waters Painting (detail), by Shen Zhou.

imperial art academy and considered it merely the skill of carving and following the pattern of conventions; for them, painting was the leisurely pursuit of brushwork. Painters, such as Su Shi, painted only for fun, as well as to express his viewpoint or an experience, or as a means to seek The Truth (*Dao*). The scholar painters of the Song Dynasty just tried to copy and to imitate the success of the ancient classical works. Calligraphers, painters, and critics alike in the Ming Dynasty indicated that after Mi Fu and his son in the Song Dynasty and the Four Masters of Yuan Dynasty, the development of painting and stopped. They thought they should just interpret and follow the works, the traditions, and the skills of the scholar paintings.

The diverse, meticulous painting styles of Shen Zhou and Wen Zhengming of the Wu School were representative of this period. Shen was a professional scholar painter and devoted his whole life to painting, poetry, literature, and calligraphy. One of his two paintings currently in the Taipei Palace Museum, *Lushan Mountain* (*Lushan Gao Tu*) is majestic, and uses textural methods, a skill initiated by Wang Meng of the Yuan Dynasty. Obviously, the goal of Shen's painting was to illustrate Wang Meng's painting skill, and he did not use it in any other painting. The other painting, *Sitting at*

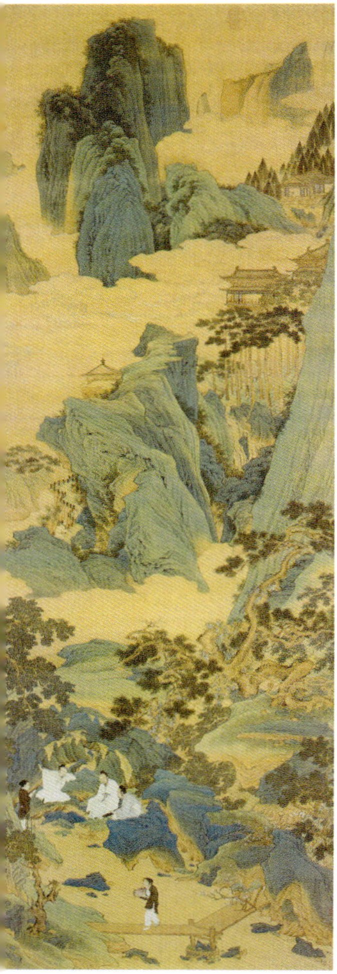

Fairy Land of Taoyuan by Qiu Ying (175 cm × 66.7 cm), Tianjin Art Museum.

Night (*Yezuo Tu*), is a mountain at night, with cottages at its foot and a man sitting by candlelight. This time, Shen used a steadier wet brushwork, a skill of Wu Zhen, another member of the "Four Masters of Yuan Dynasty." Shen kept the aloof, proud style of the Wu. At the top of the painting, he wrote a prose piece with the same title, of more than 400 Chinese characters, making it an integrated part of the painting, a perfect example of the practice of combining literature and calligraphy with painting. The prose, of a refreshingly pure style and full of implicit philosophical meaning, narrated the reflections of the painter in his cottage at night, listening to the sounds of nature, and demonstrated a harmony of "outside silence and inner tranquility," which contrasts with the sounds and noises of the world at large. Shen copied his contemporary Daijin's works and we can only speculate that Shen was accidentally exposed to Dai's work and was inspired by it to find a better way to follow and copy the paintings of previous generations.

Wen Zhengming came from the same town as Shen and was his student. Both of them had no desire to become mandarins but were local celebrities who had mastered poetry, calligraphy, and paintings. Wen mainly painted landscapes with thin, precise brushwork, and he often used dark blue and green with a meticulous graceful and elegant style. His paintings of plum blossom and bamboo seem to radiate fresh, exquisite scents. Shen and Wen both came from wealthy families and shared a similar attitude to a life of simplicity and relatively uncomplicated experiences, which ensured they enjoyed their life as scholar painters.

Dong Qichang of a slight later period had a more aggressive style of art criticism. He had learned the essence of Dong Yuan, Juran, and Mi Fu of the Five Dynasties and the Northern Song Dynasty, and Ni Zan and Huang Gongwang of the Yuan Dynasty, and painted vivid pictures of mountains, water, trees, and stones. However Dong's influence in fine art history was mainly from his proposal to divide Chinese paintings into the "north and south schools." Dong Qichang, artist name Xuanzai, also known Sibai or Xiangguang Jushi, was born in Huating (now Songjiang County of Shanghai City). He was a successful candidate in the highest imperial examinations, served as a minister, and was once appointed as a teacher to the crown prince. He was not only a famous artist, but also an important art connoisseur and collector. He collected many masterpieces of the "Four Masters of the Yuan Dynasty," including Huang Gongwang's *Living in Fuchun Mountain* (*Fuchun Shan Ju Tu*), as well as Dong Yuan's work, which was even in his day very rare. He also wrote many books discussing the theories of paintings and was a keen promoter of scholar paintings. He explained in detail the origins of different painting styles and gave the criteria to judge scholar painters. But Mo Shilong, also from Huating, had been the first to discuss the extension of north and south sects of Chinese Buddhism into an analysis of painting history. He wrote:

"Buddhism was divided into north and south schools from the Tang Dynasty. Paintings were divided into south and north schools, also from the Tang Dynasty. However, painters should not be divided."

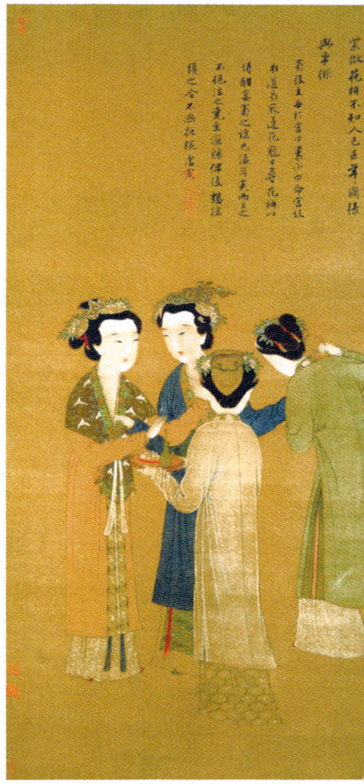

Court Ladies of Houshu Kingdom by Tang Yin (124.7 cm × 63.6 cm), Beijing Palace Museum.

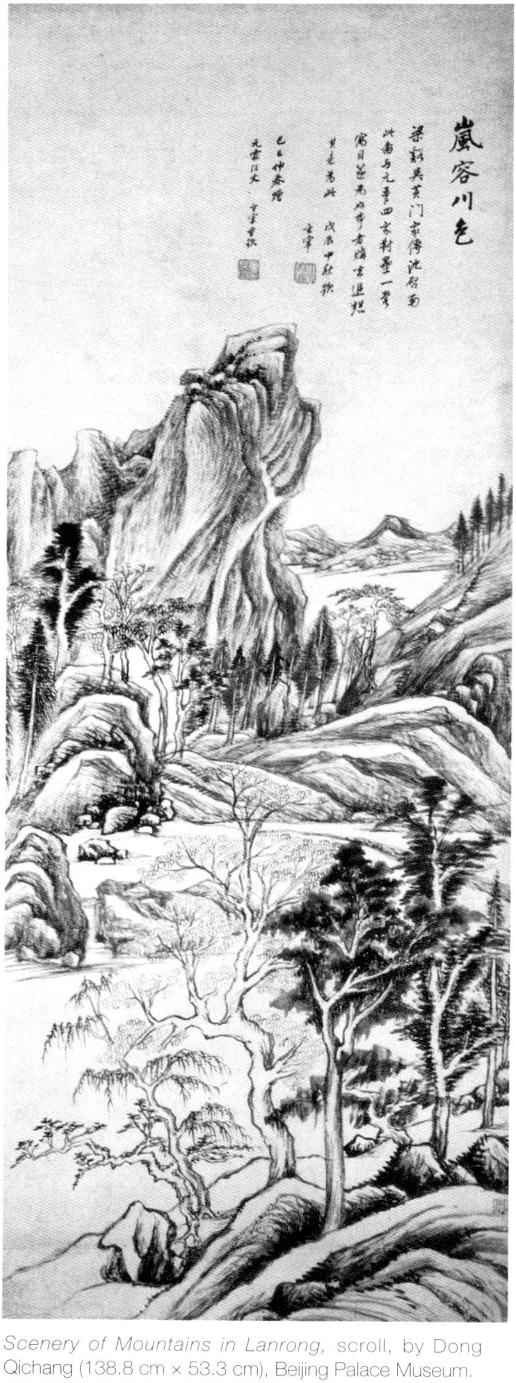

Scenery of Mountains in Lanrong, scroll, by Dong Qichang (138.8 cm × 53.3 cm), Beijing Palace Museum.

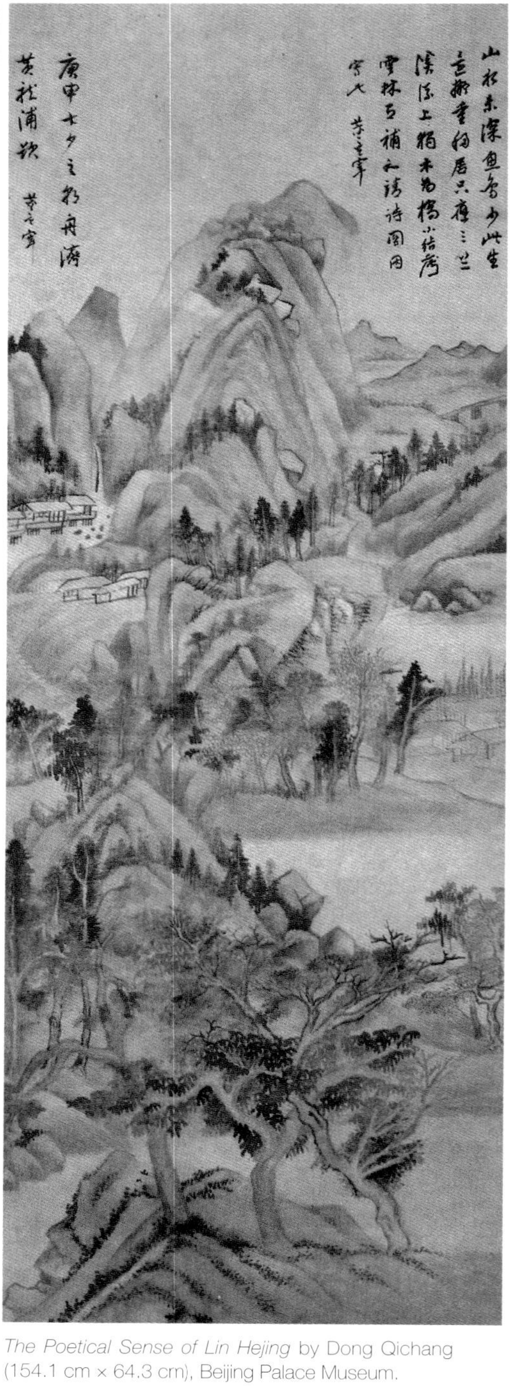

The Poetical Sense of Lin Hejing by Dong Qichang (154.1 cm × 64.3 cm), Beijing Palace Museum.

Paintings were divided into north and south schools, but the criteria were not based on where painters came from; they only related to the style of painting. The north school started from the imperial artist Li Sixun and his son in the Tang Dynasty and passed to Ma Yuan and Xia Gui of the Imperial Art Academy in the Song Dynasty. The south school can be traced back to Wang Wei, a poet and artist of the Tang Dynasty, passing to Dong Yuan of the Five Dynasties, Mi Fu of the Song Dynasty, and Huang Gongwang of the Yuan Dynasty.

Mo Shilong was a close friend and a role model for Dong Qichang, and they often exchanged views and shared many ideas. Dong elaborated the development of scholar painting:

"Scholar painting was started by Wang Youcheng (Wang Wei) and was followed and developed by Dong Yuan, Seng Juran, Li Cheng, and Fan Kuan. Li Longmian, Wang Jinqin (Wang Xian), Mi Nangong, and Hu Er (Mi Fu and his son Mi Youren) learned from Dong and Ju, and then the tradition was passed on to the 'Four Masters of Yuan Dynasty' of Huang Zijiu, Wang Shuming (Wang Meng), Ni Yuanzhen (Ni Zan), and Wu Zhonggui (Wu Zhen). Wen Zhengming and Shen Zhou of this dynasty inherited the style and the practice. However, painters such as Ma Yuan, Xia Gui, Li Tang, and Liu Songnian followed the style of General Li and were different from ours."

Chen Jiru, another native from the same town as Dong Qichang continued:

"Li school (Li Sixun and the north school) was characterized with fine, thin brushwork and did not follow the fashion of the scholars while the school of Wang (Wang Wei and his south school) had the features of Hui Neng and could not be followed by Shen Xiu."

The theory of south and north painting schools spread widely because of Dong Qichang's influence, and it controlled the development of scholar painting in the Ming and Qing Dynasties. It provided for the first time a theoretic system for classifying

Chinese paintings, similar to that of Italian and Dutch art during the Renaissance in Europe. While it appeared to be objective, Dong's preference for the southern school was clear. For him, it equated to scholar painting, with a sudden awaking, scholarly spirit and leisurely tranquility as associated virtues.

The "Four Wangs" and the "Four Monks"

From the reign of Emperor Shun Zhi (1644–1661) to the early period of Emperor Kang Xi (1662–1722) of the Qing Dynasty, scholar paintings reached the peak of its popularity and developed two distinct directions. While the "Four Wangs" were the orthodox school which followed Dong Qichang's painting style, and were favored by the imperial court, the "Four Monks" and the Eight Masters of Jinling and Xin'an consisted of many painters of the Ming Dynasty who had escaped to the South. They explored spirit and innovation and used their landscapes to express their personal feelings and political views.

The "Four Monks" were Zhu Da, Shi Tao, Shi Xi, and Hongren. At the end of the Ming Dynasty, the Manchu entered Beijing and established a (unified) Qing Dynasty, a repetition of the South Song Dynasty and the Yuan Dynasty. Zhu Da and Shi Tao were descendants of the Ming royalty, and Shi Xi, and Hon Gren considered they were the loyal subjects of that dynasty. With a strong sense of nationalism, the four used their brushes to express their personal feelings and their loyalty to the fallen Ming Dynasty. In art they insisted on innovation with continuity and rejected imitation that lacked reason. They stressed the importance of life experiences and paid special attention to individual inspiration. They finally broke through the (virtual) fence of copying and created a new era with a bold new style, which influenced the painters of future generations. Zhu Da and Shi Tao made the most important contributions.

Zhu Da (1626–1705), also known as Bada Shanren, was a descendant of the Ming imperial family and was brought up in a literary family. After the fall of the dynasty, he became a Buddhist monk and later a Taoist, and he gave himself many vivid names, among them were Bada Shanren, Xue Ge, Ge Shan, Yige Shan, Liang Yue, and Dao Lang. He expressed his emotions through symbolism, implication, and exaggeration. He often painted odd subjects to express his cynical feelings and his sadness about the fall of the Ming Dynasty. He used simple but bold brushwork with simple patterns, dangerous images, and cool tones. His landscape originated with Dong Yuan and was modeled on Dong Qichang's pithy and elegant style with wet brushwork. Influenced by Lin Liang and Xu Wei of the Ming Dynasty, his flower-and-bird paintings had a unique style: on each piece of paper, he painted just one bird, one fish, or one flower to create a sense of mystery. Bada Shanren incorporated his calligraphy skill into his brushwork, and also in the outline of the whole image. Thus, his painting pattern was based on his control of abstract thinking. He used ink to express virtually everything in nature. It seemed that to his eye, birds, flowers, and mountains were all black and white. He refused to use color, which lent a kind of disturbance to his work. The strong symbolization of his paintings indicated his extreme feelings, including his curses, his avoidance of reality, and his condolences to the Ming Dynasty.

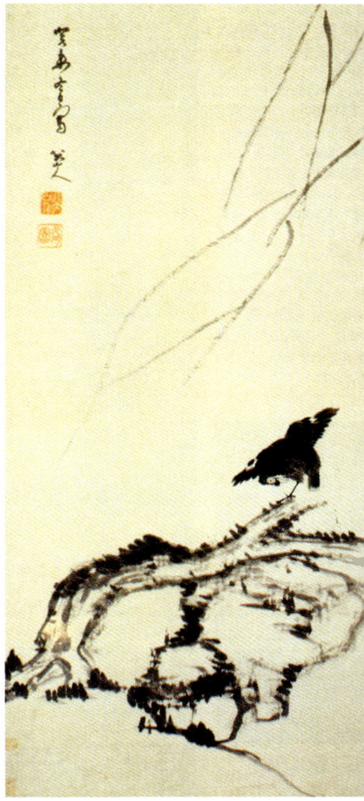

Withered Wood and an Ichthyornis, scroll, by Shi Tao (149.5 cm × 70 cm), Beijing Palace Museum.

Shi Tao (1642–1707), originally surnamed Zhu, was given the title Yuan Ji after he became a monk; he was also known as Shi Tao, Kugua Heshang, and Dadizi. He too was a descendant of the Ming imperial family. He had frequent exchanges of letters with Zhu Da, and they

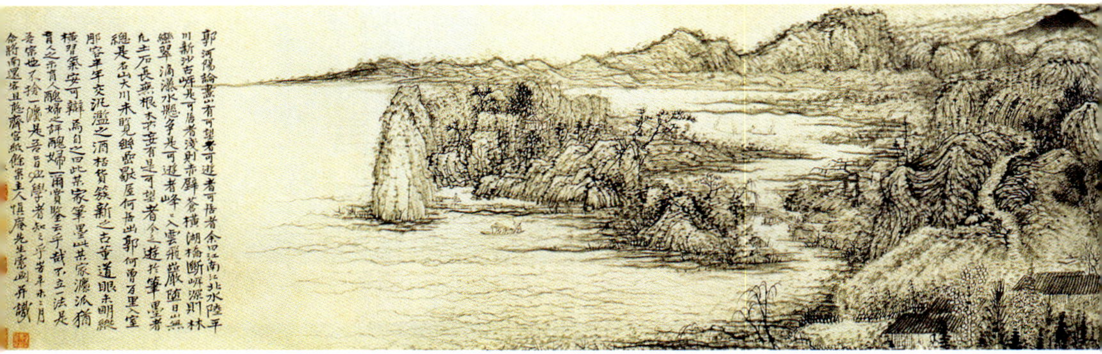

Draft painting *After Visiting Various Fantastic Mountains*, scroll, by Shi Tao (42.8 cm × 258.5 cm), Beijing Palace Museum.

cooperated in paintings but never met; they appreciated each other's work. Shi's sufferings brought by the fall of the Ming Dynasty and his tragic personal experiences always occupied the main position in his heart, and he could only express his emotions through painting. His landscapes were modeled on various painters but had his own unique style of vibrant, refreshing images, and a new bold composition. His brushwork changed frequently in extreme but elegant pictures. His experience of traveling greatly contributed to his paintings, as he recreated all the mountains he visited in them. His paintings, the clouds in the Huangshan Mountain, the river town in the South, the willows in the autumn, the pine trees along steep mountains, the images of Lushan Mountain, and the scenery of Huanyin, Yangzhou, and Changshan, were all artistic recreations of nature: he rarely painted from nature. Many of Shi Tao's works survive, including *Voice of the Mountains and Waters* (*Shanshui Qingyin*), *Xiyuan Elegant Paintings Album* (*Xiyuan Yatu Ji*), *Autumn of Huaiyin and Yangzhou* (*Huaiyang Jieqiu Tu*), *Album of the Eight Wonders in Huangshan Mountain* (*Huangshan Basheng Ce*), *Paintings of Visiting Lushan Mountain* (*Lushan Youlan Tu*), and *Watching Mountains in Yuhang* (*Yuhang Kanshan Tu*).

Shi Xi (dates unknown; religious name Kun Can) and Hong Ren (1610–1661; religious name Jianjiang Heshang) were known as "painter monks." They too considered themselves subjects of the Ming Dynasty, but had less resentment and a more detached

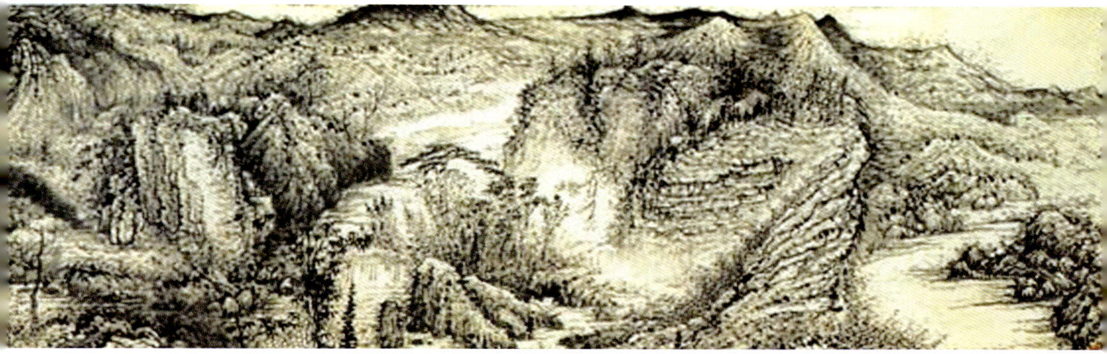

attitude compared to Zhu Da and Shi Tao. Shi Xi's landscape paintings were modeled on the paintings of Wang Meng and Huang Gongwang, but were made by copying the real scenery. Painted using texture methods, his works were generous but not rigid, with a vast scale. Hong Ren followed Ni Zan's painting style in landscapes. He often painted famous mountains, especially Huangshan, and was a representative of the "Xin'an Family."

Just like the "Four Masters of the Yuan Dynasty," who were universally respected in the Ming and Qing Dynasties, the "Four Monks" of the late Ming and the early Qing Dynasties and their painting styles are highly appreciated by painters and collectors now. The historian of fine art Wang Bomin commented on Four Monks' paintings,

"Their paintings consist of the thick atmosphere of Buddhism and Taoism thinking. They often combined different emotions such as sadness and resentment together in their paintings. In general, their paintings were simple. In history, the Confucians valued a simple style and preferred tranquility and simplicity, just as in the old saying, 'White jade without carving and polishing is valueless.' In the matter of their specific differnces in paintings, Hong Ren won for his elegance and unconventionally free brushwork; Kun Can for his honesty in painting style and steady brushwork; Bada Shanren (Zhu Da) for his romantic charm and simple brushwork;

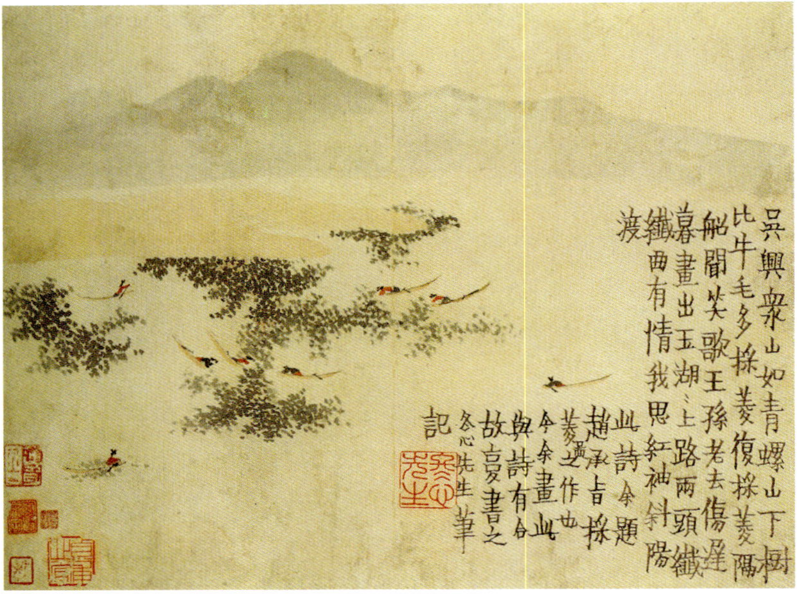

Picture Album of Plucking Water Chestnuts by Jin Nong, Beijing Palace Museum.

and Shi Tao for his boldness and unrestrained brushwork. During a period when most painters intended to copy ancient paintings, they broke the mold and demonstrated their unique paintings to the world. This is very unusual in the history of Chinese art."

The "Four Wangs" refers to Wang Shimin (1592–1680, artist name Xun Zhi, also called Yan Ke and Luxi Laoren) born in Taicang, Jiangsu Province; Wang Jian (1598–1677, also called Xiang Bi and Ranxiang Anzhu), also born in Taicang; Wang Hui (1632–1717, artist name Shigu, also called Ken Yan Shang Ren) born in Changshu, Jiangsu Province; and Wang Yuanqi (1642–1715, artist name Mao Jing, also called Lu Tai). Together with Wu Li and Yun Ge (1633–1690, artist name Shou Ping, also called Nan Tian), who was born in Changzhou Jiangsu, they were collectively known as the "Four Wangs and Wu and Yun" or the "Six Masters of the Early Qing Dynasty." They all accepted Dong Qichang's theory of art as infallible law and devoted themselves to copying ancient paintings. They stressed brushwork skills and sought a gentle style. The "Four Wangs" came to have outstanding social positions, traveled extensively, and had large numbers of students with great influence among the officials. Their paintings were appreciated by the imperial court and thus were regarded as the orthodox school and were influential until the modern age.

The most common comments on "Four Wangs" are that they had a solid foundation in brushwork and developed a unique painting composition and rhythm. However, since they neglected both the observation of nature and the personal experience of nature, most of their paintings are monotonous and lethargic, and lack new concepts and direction, which prevented them from making greater achievements. Actually, what the "Four Wangs" achieved was to elevate the academic study of ancient paintings to an unprecedented level. What interested them were Dong Yuan and Juran of the Five Dynasties, Li Cheng, Fan Kuan, Guo Xi, Mi Fu and his son, Zhao Boju and Wang Shen of the Northern Song, and Zhao Mengfu and the "Four Masters of the Yuan Dynasty," all of whom belonged to the southern school as denoted by Dong Qichang. Wang Bomin has pointed out that the studies of the "Four Wangs" on the paintings of southern school lasted for more than a century, and it was their pious attitude alone that deserved respect. Just as Chinese scholars treasured the teachings of wise ancestors, Chinese painters also believed that the true essence of landscapes had been illustrated with equally perfect language. Often painters of the Ming and Qing periods would claim to have copied ancient works, just to reflect their modesty and show their respect of the general fashion of the time, but they did not really blindly follow ancient painters. A typical example is that even Shi Tao and Bada Shanren, painters with strong personal styles, sometimes would say they were just copying some ancient painters, which no one now believes.

The End of Scholar Paintings and Famous Chinese Painters of Modern Times

The "Yangzhou Eight Eccentrics" of the mid-Qing Dynasty are considered the last masters of Chinese scholar paintings. From the reign of Jia Qing (1796–1820) of the Qing Dynasty to the early twentieth century, traditional society gradually declined, and as a result of the social transformation, the cultural environment that traditional scholars lived in also disappeared. Western influence advanced with a vengeance and to an extent and with a speed which was never experienced before, and inevitably changed painting. Scholar painting and imperial painting gradually declined. Shanghai and Guangzhou, two trading ports, became the new centers of painting with the "Hai School" and the "Lingnan School" as the representatives of the new era (Hai means overseas in Chinese). The "Hai School" combined traditional Chinese styles with the newly arrived Western painting skills.

The "Yangzhou Eight Eccentrics," or "Yangzhou Painting School," refers to a group of scholar painters in Yangzhou in the middle eighteenth century, including Jin Nong, Huang Shen, Zhen Xie, Li Shan, Li Fangying, Luo Pin, Hua Yan, Gao Fenghan, Min Zhen, Bian Shoumin, and several others. The "Yangzhou Eight Eccentrics" all showed strong personality in their paintings. Their attitudes towards painting traditions were in clear contrast to that of "Four Wangs and Wu and Yun," as they seldom copied paintings of the so-called south school. Instead, they followed the style of Shi Tao and regarded Xu Wei and Bada Shanren as

Seals in Painting and Calligraphic Works

Since the Ming and Qing Dynasties, seals have been an integral part of painting and calligraphic works. A well-rounded painter is expected to be well-versed in painting and calligraphic theories, and have a thorough knowledge of and be highly skilled in painting, calligraphic, and carving techniques. Most famous painters are also good at carving seals that complement and form a unity with their paintings. Seals in paintings and calligraphic works are mostly carved by the painters and calligraphers themselves, or are seals of the prefacers, the collectors, and appraisers. Seals typically feature birth names, courtesy names, verses, auspicious words, mottos, and collection and appraisal marks.

their artistic guardians. The "Yangzhou Eight Eccentrics" were not good at painting landscapes, but specialized in birds, flowers, plum blossoms, and bamboo. They often considered themselves to be blossoming plum, orchid, bamboo, and chrysanthemum. During the reign of Qianlong (1736–95) of the Qing Dynasty, Yangzhou was a prosperous consumer city with strong trading activity, so many of these scholars made a living by selling their paintings and calligraphy. Flower-and-bird paintings were suitable to illustrate the beauty of freehand brushwork, and painters could use fewer and simpler strokes to radiate the elegance of Chinese characters.

Of the "Yangzhou Eight Eccentrics," Jin Nong (1687–1764, also called Dongxin Xiansheng) and Zheng Xie (Zheng Banqiao) were considered to possess the most typical scholarly characteristics. Jin Nong lived in poverty and was very cynical about society. He liked traveling and had been to many famous mountains. It was said that he only started to learn painting in his fifties, and started with the style of Wen Tong of the Song Dynasty and Wang Mian of the Yuan Dynasty and gradually developed his signature style of simplicity, which was called the "Jin Nong Style." He often painted flowers with light ink, and plum blossoms with tilted branches. Occasionally, he also painted landscape and people with his own rhythm and their own personalities. Zheng Banqiao served as a low-ranking official. He alienated the authorities when he insisted on applying for emergency relief for people after a natural disaster, so he resigned and went to Yangzhou where he made a living by selling his paintings. Like Bada Shanren and Shi Tao, he used his work to express his personal resentment and to illustrate his lofty social attitude and moral sanity against a background of corruption. He painted only with ink and his signature compositions were orchids and bamboo. His paintings have very strong visual effect, but, in the eyes of traditional scholars, lack inner grace.

Painters in China's trading port Shanghai were considered to belong collectively to the "Hai School," and some went beyond the traditional scholar paintings. Zhao Zhiqian (1829–84), Ren Bonian

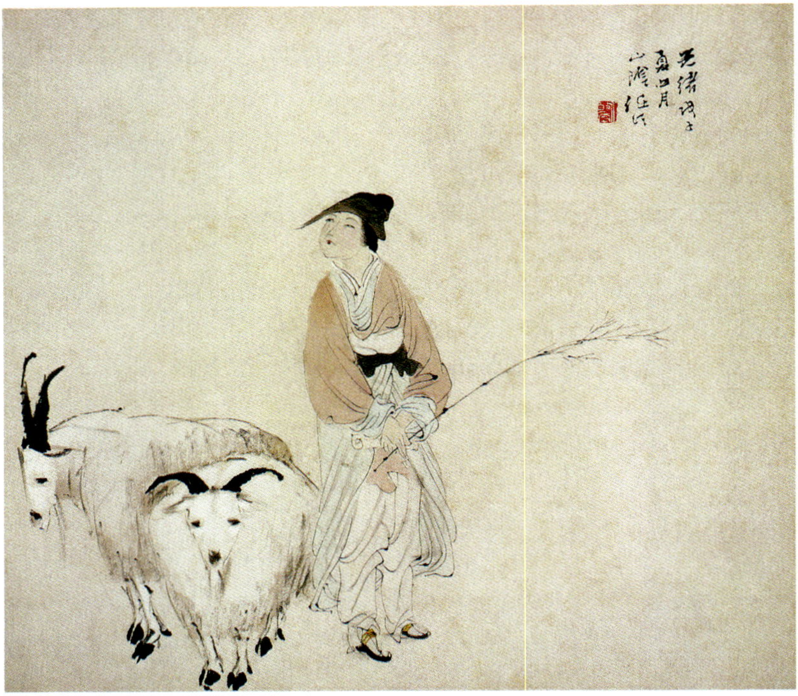

A Lady, color on paper, by Ren Bonian, Nanjing Museum.

(1840–96), Wu Youru (1840–93), and Wu Changshuo (1844–1927) are typical. During this period, scholars no longer had rich families to support them and did not enjoy their former high social status, so had become craftsmen or artisan painters. Zhao Zhiqian barely supported himself by selling his work. Thus, he could not spend time on ancient calligraphies and paintings as Dong Qichang did, for his flower-and-bird paintings had to meet the demands of his clients, but he still endeavored to continue the tradition and the scholarly standard of grace and elegance. Compared with his predecessors, Zhao's paintings were more meticulous and colorful and were enjoyed by both secular society and the scholarly circle.

Ren Bonian started as an apprentice in a fan-painting workshop and was recognized as a talented young artist. He was especially good as a portrait and a flower-and-bird painter. Ren Bonian painted with light and graceful ink strokes and went beyond most imperial court painters in his accuracy, meticulousness, and radiance and clarity. He painted carefully each bit of a single flower, grass, feather, insect, or fish. His portrait paintings were world class, and accurately and gracefully depicted the subjects.

Wu Youru was the first person to transform the traditional Chinese paintings into a modern industry. In the tenth year of the reign of Guang Xu (1884), he was employed as the editor-in-chief and chief painter of *Dianshizhai Huabao* (*Painting Supplement*) for *Shenbao* (*Shanghai News*). Over a decade he published more than 4,000 paintings in this newspaper: he reported news with articles illustrated with the traditional line-drawings, painted pictures of foreign lands and subjects, such as trains, buildings, ships, gunboats, and, of course, people, which were welcomed by ordinary people.

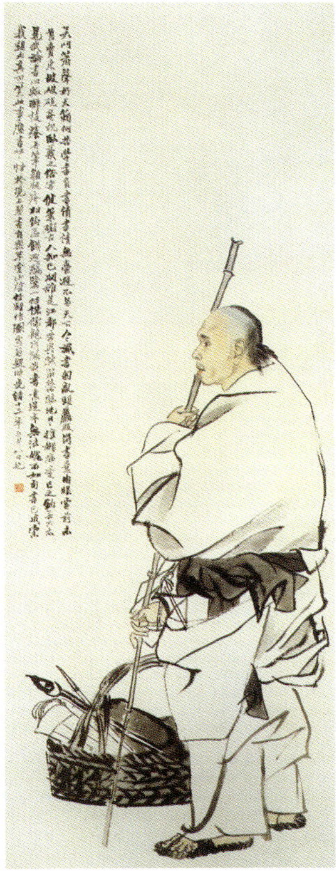

Portrait of Painter Gao Yi by Ren Bonian (130.9 cm × 48.5 cm), Shanghai Museum.

Like Ren Bonian, Wu Changshuo was also a career painter, but with a literary background. He had served as the first president of Xileng Yinshe, a famous art society in Hangzhou. While Wu was a student of Ren, his painting style was influenced to a great extent by Zhao Zhiqian and Chen Chun, Xu Wei, Badashan Ren, Shi Tao, and the "Yangzhou Eight Eccentrics." Wu was good at a different style of calligraphy using soft brush pens made of sheep's hair and he was inspired to paint subjects with a unique type of brush stroke for each. He included the strength and elasticity of Lishu (an official script style of calligraphy developed in the Han Dynasty) and Zhuanshu (a style often used on seals) in painting branches and limbs, and the vibrancy and enthusiasm of Xingshu and *caoshu* (a running hand and cursive script in Chinese calligraphy) in painting chrysanthemums and grapes. He went beyond Zhao Zhiqian in using color. He studied and adopted many techniques in Chinese folk and Western paintings. He constantly mixed red, yellow, and green into reddish brown to seek a sense of harmony in conflict.

What happened to the "Hai School" and other painters of the late Qing Dynasty demonstrates clearly a changing society and its associated view of art. The scholar era had definitely ended. With the abolishing of the imperial examination system, traditional scholars did not have any chance of becoming officials and in theory they would be common people. However, the aesthetic standard of the scholar paintings developed over thousands of years was part of the nation and still had a place in society. So their legacy lived on through the paper and the brush strokes which once served their purposes. Their paintings were closely connected with the emotions of the Chinese people and of how they experienced nature and the world. To a foreigner "Chinese painting" refers to all the paintings in China while a Chinese person knows that it covers only those who follow the style of ancient paintings and those done by traditional scholar painters. For the sake of historical continuity, "Chinese painting," comprises the characteristics of traditional aesthetics and ways of expressing them.

Many painters in the twentieth century still practiced the traditional painting style, and many have become great masters and celebrities. However, modern society is very different, so that although society in general still accepts the notion that "Chinese styles are the fundamental structures, Western skills are for practical uses," the traditional painters still have to face many challenges from increasingly influential Western culture and its associated values. They need to readjust to meet the new roles they will play in a society where the traditional Chinese values have gradually been eroded from their dominant position. Some painters have tried to create new techniques and to look for inspiration from other Chinese art heritages, such as the Dunhuang murals and the folk arts, but these have failed to become mainstream. The concept

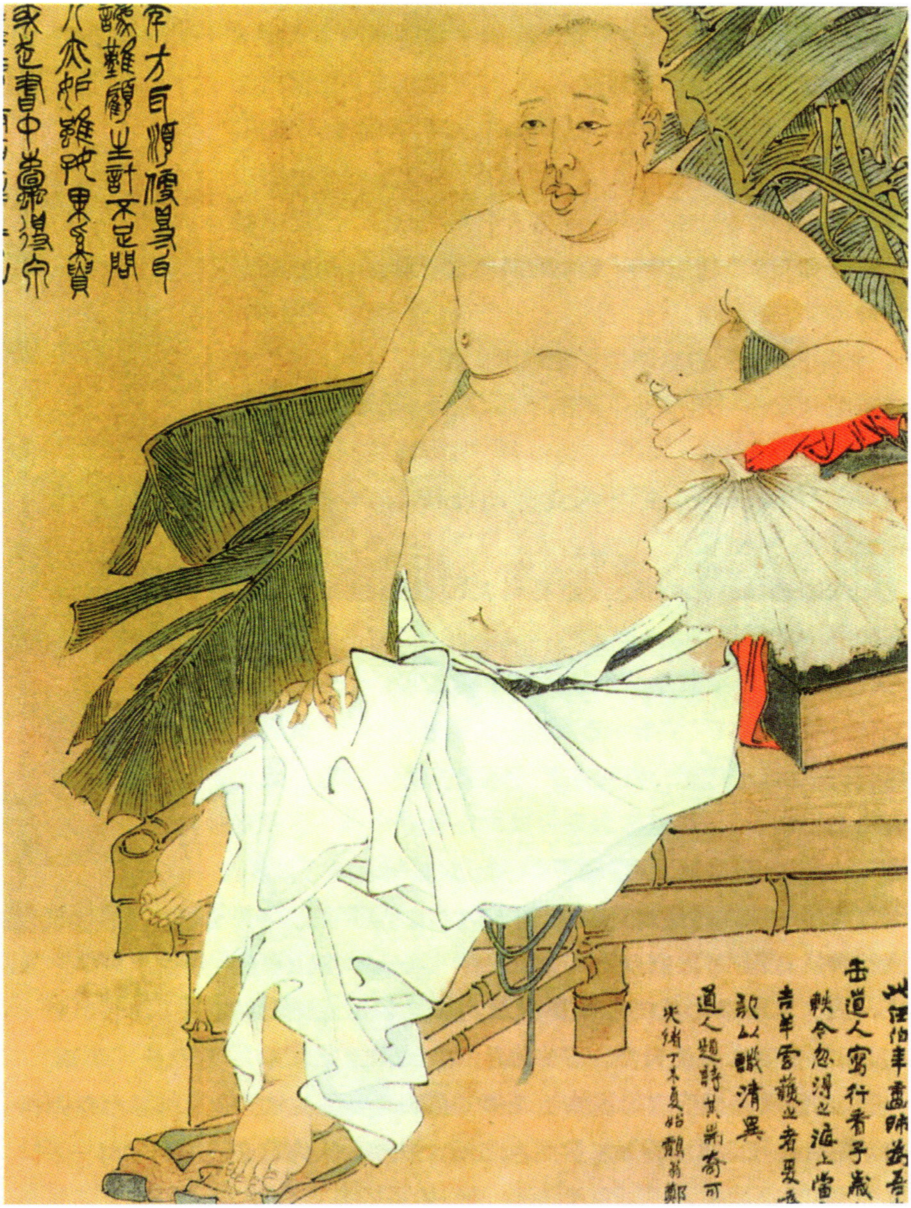

Enjoying the Coolness Under the Banana Trees, scroll, Wu Changshuo's portrait by Ren Bonia (detail), Nanjing Museum.

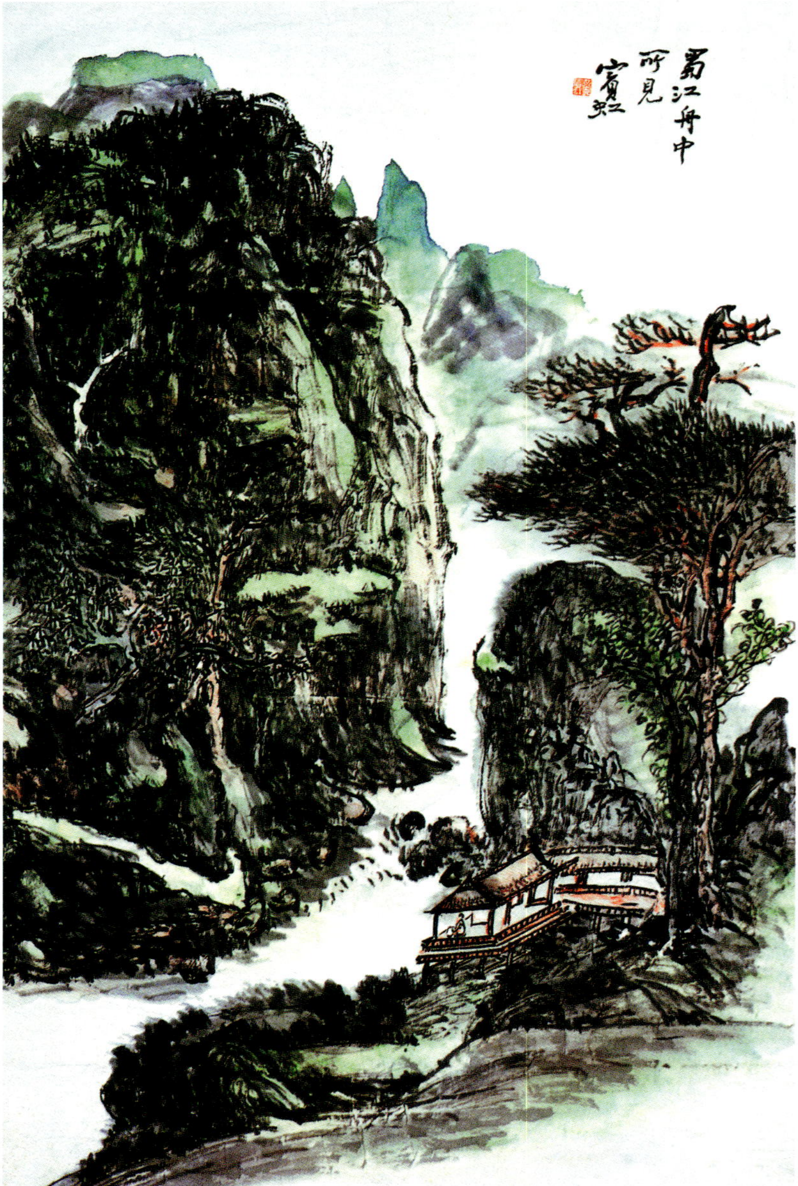

Sights from a Boat on Shujiang River by Huang Binhong (76.5 cm × 48 cm), Nanjing Museum.

and format of scholar painting actually have become an integrated part of the "Chinese national culture," along with the thoughts of Confucius, Mencius, Laozi, and Zhuangzi. It has even gained the title of "national painting," and its rise and fall are closely linked with the fortune of the "national culture."

In the first half of the twentieth century, China experienced the collapse of the last imperial dynasty, the civil wars of warlords, the establishment of the Republic of China, the war against the Japanese invasion, the civil war between the Communist Party and the Nationalist Party, the establishment of the People's Republic of China, and many political movements thereafter. In spite of all these major social, political, and cultural changes, a large number of great masters of Chinese painting emerged. They are profoundly conscious of the national cultural values, and their paintings keep a certain distance from modern thought and aesthetic concepts. They were inevitably influenced by modern society, but they responded spontaneously to transform traditional painting by combining it with modern reality. Their resolution and determination to face all the external challenges and to create a modern style of their own are inspirational.

Qi Baishi (1863–1957), from Hunan Province, reminds us of Wang Mian of the Yuan Dynasty and Jin Nong of the "Yangzhou Eight Eccentrics," whom he admired. Other favorite painters included Xu Wei, Shi Tao, Zhu Da, Li Chan of the "Yangzhou Eight Eccentrics," and Wu Changshuo of the "Hai School." He had worked as a carpenter, so his experience and inspiration as a folk artist is unique. Qi Baishi was a very diligent artist and lived a long life. Critics say he only completed the perfect combination of the aptitude of the rural poets and the style of scholar painting at the age of seventy. His paintings belonged to this tradition, but not entirely, for you can smell the fragrance of rural life in them, in a sharp contrast to the dusty scent of scholarly museums in a typical scholar painting. Qi Baishi's freehand brushwork in his late years was rustic rather than unrestrained, with the traces of innocence

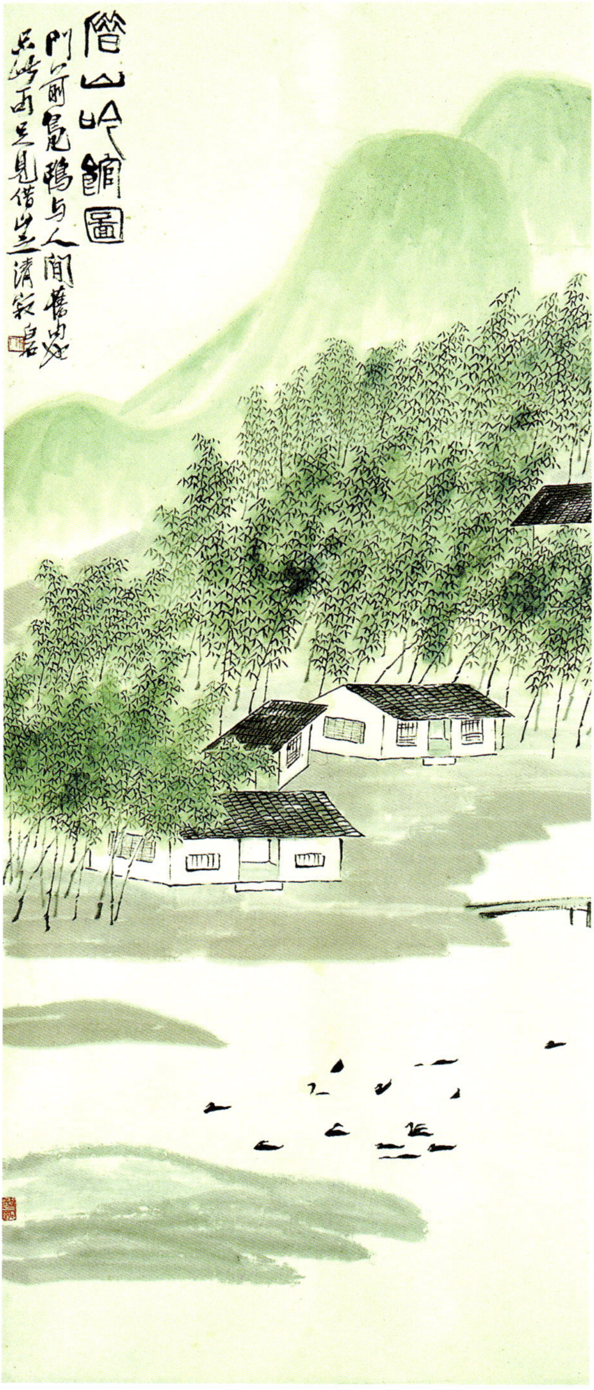

Picture of My Jieshan Yinguan Study (1932), color on paper, by Qi Baishi (128 cm x 62 cm), one of the mountains-and-waters scrolls), Chongqing Museum.

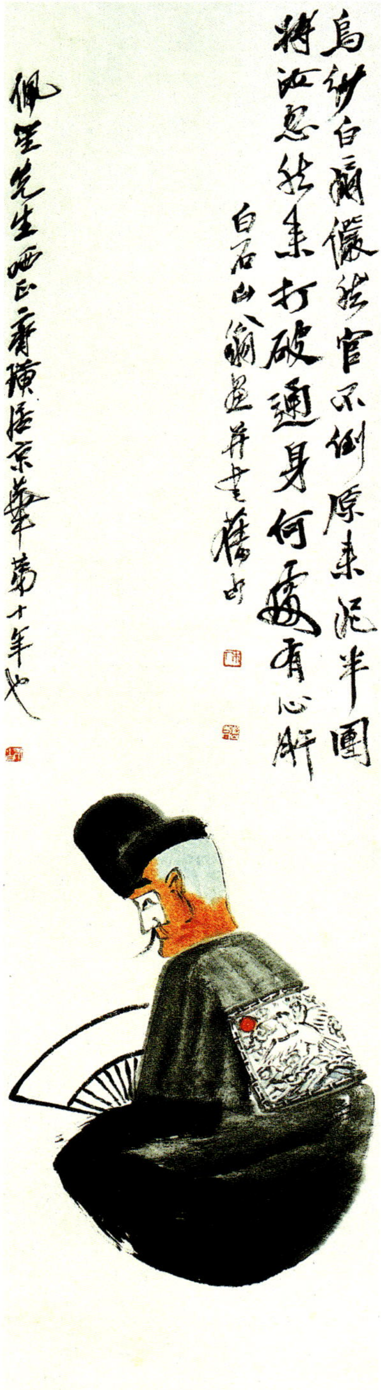

Tumbler (*Bu Dao Weng*) (1926), color on paper, by Qi Baishi (128 cm × 33 cm), China Art Gallery.

and vibrancy of a rural carpenter. His paintings are full of the sights and sounds of the rural life: frogs, cicadas, crops, chicks, locusts, and even daily family utensils were his subjects. His masterpieces include *Corns and Dragonflies* (*Yumi Qingting*), and *Loud Frog Croak* (*Washang Shili*). Traditionally, scholar painters would use pale color to depict a lofty grace, but Qi Baishi painted red flowers and dark green leaves with strong visual impact.

Huang Binhong (1865–1955) was a master painter who learned early but matured late. He was well educated and devoted his youth almost entirely to studying and imitating ancient paintings. Similar to the "Four Wangs," he inherited the tradition of the painters of the Song and Yuan Dynasties towards nature, and he visited many mountains and rivers in China. He completed the transformation of his brushwork at the age of eighty and became a great master of fine art.

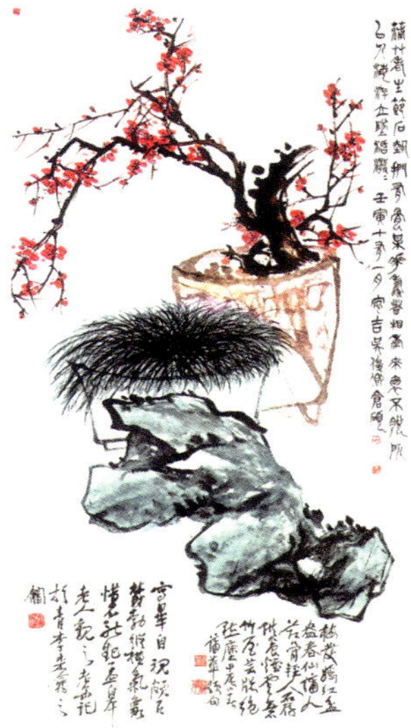

Plum Blossoms and Rocks (1902), by Wu Changshuo (127 cm × 67 cm), Hangzhou Xiling Publishing House

Pan Tianshou (1897–1971) and Fu Baoshi (1904–65) were geniuses of painting. Wang Bomin commented on Pan Tianshou's paintings:

"People usually use 'depth, weight and grandness' as the criteria to judge a painting since the start of the Republic. Pan Tianshou's paintings were perfect in meeting all these criteria, especially 'grandness.' Even when he painted small part of a sketch, you feel the grandness. The 'grandness' does not refer to the size of the paintings, but to his style of 'solid frames' or 'solid bones,' depicting the power and force of his brushwork."

"Strong bones and empty minds" is a tradition of Taoism, meaning a person should have strong bones to carry his duties but an empty mind so as to have no worries. Pan Tianshou had the honesty and simplicity of a common farmer and the culture and wisdom of

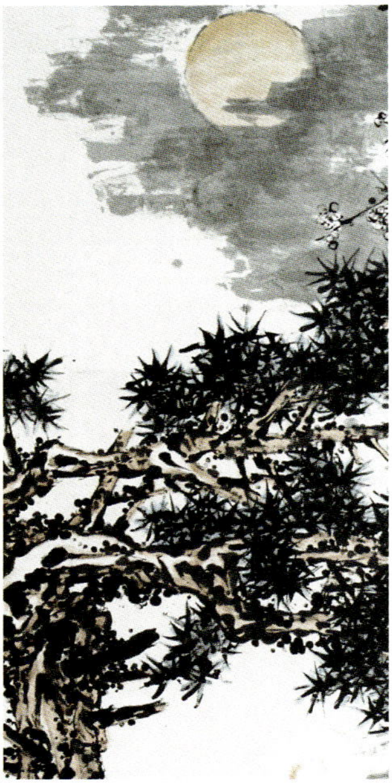

Picture of Pines, Rocks, Plum Blossom, and the Moon by Pan Tianshou (329 cm × 149 cm), Pan Tianshou Museum.

a well-educated scholar. He combined the painting styles of both the northern school and southern school, deviated from them to improve the gentle, exquisite approach of flower-and-bird paintings of the Ming and Qing Dynasties, and created a style of force and strength. Flower-and-bird, bamboo, and stone were the main subjects. His work had the structure and rigidness of sculpture, yet radiated the refreshing tranquility of morning mist. Fu Baoshi admired Shi Tao tremendously and even changed his name from Ruiling to Baoshi in his honor. He liked painting after drinking alcohol and was a romantic artist with poetic quality. He went to Japan to study Western paintings and was good at commanding the color palette. His landscapes are vibrant and full of expressiveness. His figure painting could be compared to the skill of Gu Kaizhi of the Eastern Jin Dynasty. His masterpieces include *Nine Songs* (*Jiu Ge*) and *Walking with Beauty* (*Liren Xing*). Although Pan Tianshou's and Fu Baoshi's paintings still belonged to scholar painting conceptually, they had paved a way for modern Chinese paintings to prosper.

Modern Chinese Paintings

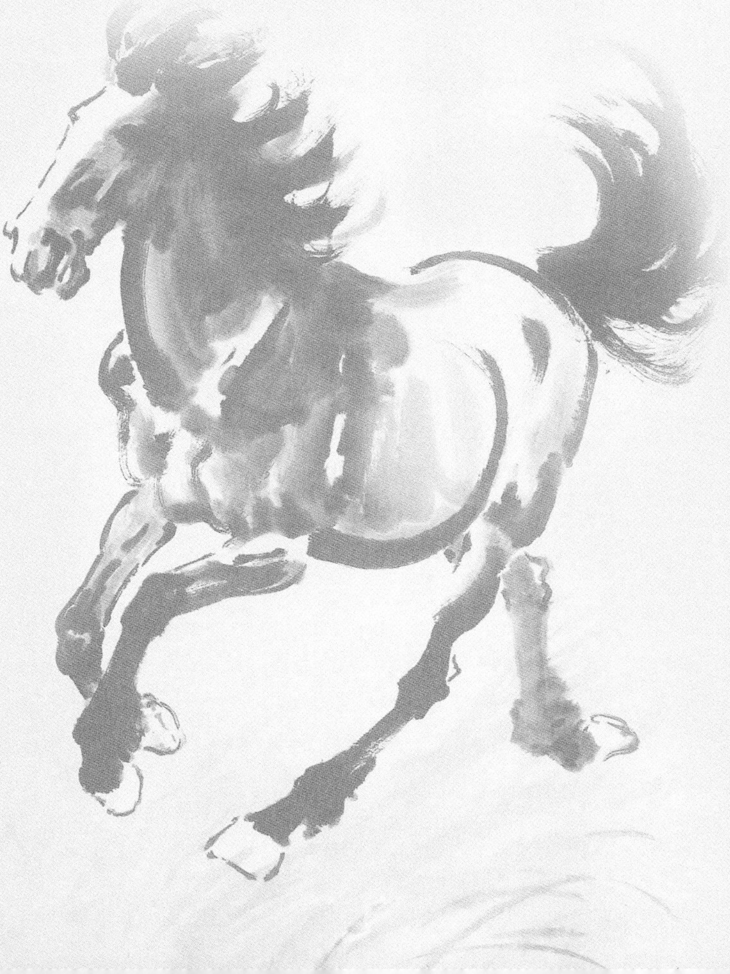

Painters Studying Abroad

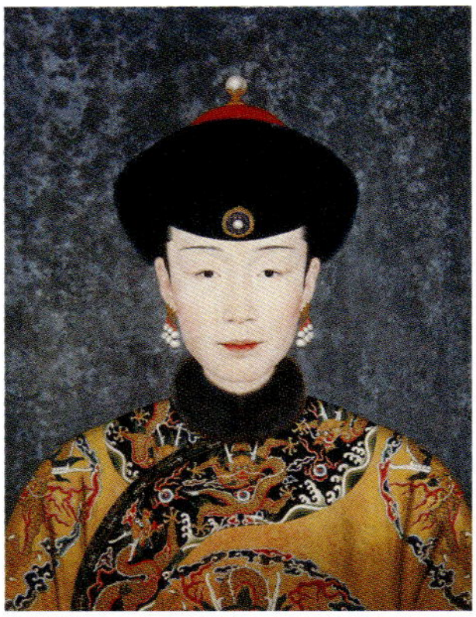

Portrait of a Bright and Virtuous High-Level Imperial Concubine, oil on paper, by Giuseppe Castiglione, Qing Dynasty, Beijing Palace Museum.

Traditional Prints in Folk Arts

The development of China's traditional prints is closely related to the engraving industry, and its centers in the Song and Yuan Dynasties were Jian'an in Fujian and Hangzhou in Zhejiang. They moved to Nanjing and Beijing in the Ming Dynasty. A new phase of development came with the rise of the Huizhou School of prints. As early as the fifteenth century, this school was noted for its printing and for its numerous, highly skilled artists, especially those from the Huang and Wang families. During the Ming and Qing Dynasties, the Huang family in Xin'an produced more than 200 volumes of prints;

In 1601, an Italian missionary Matteo Ricci came to China and brought with him some European paintings. His gifts for Emperor Shenzong of the Ming Dynasty (1573–1619) included oil paintings of the Christian God and the Madonna. While the Chinese painters were surprised at the vivid resemblance to real people, the portraits were not much appreciated, and they did not take up oil painting. In the early Qing Dynasty, many European missionaries came to China and many of them could paint in oil. They were the first group of foreign painters to serve at the imperial court, and were asked to do portraits; they included Italian artists Giuseppe Castiglione (1688–1766) and Joseph Panzi (1733–1812), and French painter Jean-Denis Attiret (1702–68). Emperor Qianlong chose several young servants to learn oil painting from them.

After the Opium War, China's exchanges with foreign countries became more frequent. More Western religious and commercial paintings arrived, exerting influence on traditional Chinese painting. But it was not until the late ninteenth century that China had painters who really mastered Western skills. During the reign of Tongzhi (1862–74), several French missionaries established an orphanage in Shanghai and taught oil painting, among other skills, which the orphans passed on to society. In the late Qing Dynasty and the early Republic of China, Zhou Xiang, Zhang Yuguang, and Xu Yongqing, all very active in Shanghai, were from this orphanage. Meanwhile, some Chinese scholars went to Europe to see and to study masterpieces with their own eyes. Xue Fucheng

(1838–94), who served as ambassador to Great Britain, France, Italy, and Belgium in the late Qing Dynasty, wrote the popular book *Visiting Oil Paintings* in Paris, describing his experiences visiting a waxwork museum and an art museum. The political activist and philosopher Kang Youwei (1858–1927) also wrote of his appreciation for the paintings of the Italian Renaissance in his article, "A Journey to Italy." Through these pieces, Chinese intellectuals understood for the first time another kind of painting, completely different from their own.

Many Chinese painters started to try painting in oil from books and magazines, and they explored various types of pigments, painting in the Chinese traditional style; this did not change until the young men who studied abroad returned. Li Tiefu (1869–1952) went to the United States in 1887 and was taught by J. S. Sargent (1856–1925). Li Shutong went to Japan and on his return in 1910, he taught in Tianjin, Hangzhou, and Nanjing. He initiated the practice of copying statues and drawing from human models. He also organized a painting society in the university to study Western painting.

After the Revolution of 1911, more Chinese went abroad to study, mainly in Europe, the United States, and Japan; they included Li Yishi, Feng Gangbai, Wu Fading, Li Chaoshi, Fang Junbi, Lin Fengmian, Xu Beihong, Pan Yuliang, Zhou Bichu, Pang Xunqin, Yan Wenliang, Chang Shuhong, Lv Sibai, Wu Zuoren, Tang Yihe, Zhou Fangbai, Wu Guanzhong, Wu Dayu, Zhao Wuji, and Zhu Dequn. When they first went to Western Europe, Impressionism and Post-Impressionism had become popular, and thus the influence of classical Western painting was gradually reduced. Li Yishi,

it had more than 100 members, who produced representative works such as *Cultivating Rectitude: Illustrated and Explained* and *The Legend of Ancient Women of Virtue*. While the Huizhou School was celebrated for its elegant and elaborate style, prints in Jinling (Nanjing), Wulin (Hangzhou), and Suzhou developed their own characteristics.

New Year Pictures in Folk Arts

New Year pictures printed on wood emerged in the late Ming Dynasty and expanded in the early Qing Dynasty, with a number of production centers springing up across the country, which printed many copies and marketed them across vast geographic regions. They featured prominent local characteristics, and among the most famous were Yangliuqing, Taohuawu, and Yangjiabu. New Year picture workshops emerged at Yangliuqing in the west of Tianjin during the reign of Emperor Wan Li of the Ming Dynasty and thrived under Emperor Qianlong of the Qing Dynasty; shortly afterwards, it became a major center for New Year pictures in northern China. Yangliuqing New Year pictures covered a wide range of subjects, including mythology, local customs, historical tales, operas, novels, babies, and beauties. They were strongly drawn and were brightly colored. Due to their elaborate workmanship and intense colors, they sold briskly in northern, northeastern,

Wu Fading, Li Chaoshi, Xu Beihong, Yan Wenliang, and Chang Shuhong who had all studied in Europe promoted realism in painting. In Japan, a new painting movement, represented by Kuroda Seiki (1866–1924), introduced Impressionism and changed fine art education there. Wang Yuezhi, Chen Baoyi, Hu Gentian, Yu Jifan, Feng Zikai, Chen Zhifo, Fu Baoshi, Wang Jiyuan, Guan Liang, Xu Xingzhi, Ni Yide, Wei Tianlin, and Wang Shikuo all went to Japan. Since Japan did not have a long-lived tradition of painting in oil, the Chinese students tended to follow Impressionism, and on their return to China, they often taught painting and its associated concepts in schools.

Xu Beihong (1895–1953), Liu Haisu (1896–1994), and Lin Fengmian (1900–90) studied abroad and became famous as oil painters as well as masters of Chinese painting, and had a profound influence on the formation and development of China's modern painting. In 1912 at the age of seventeen, Liu Haisu established the Shanghai Academy of Drawing and Art. In 1919, it was renamed the Shanghai School of Fine Art. This was the first institution of higher education in formal art education; in the 1920s China's first national art school, National Beijing School of Art, China's first art university college, Hangzhou National University College of Art and Department of Fine Art, Nanjing Central University, and Suzhou School of Fine Art, were also established. Xu Beihong, Liu Haisu, Lin Fengmian, and Yan Wenliang (1893–1988) taught in these institutions and contributed their unique artistic understanding.

Xu Beihong was trained in the tradition of academism in Paris and was a realist, who insisted

and northwestern China. Taohuawu was home to the largest cluster of arts and crafts businesses in northern Suzhou. Its New Year pictures can be dated back to the Ming Dynasty, and workshops emerged during the Qing Dynasty in the reigns of Emperor Kangxi, and Emperors Yongzheng and Qianlong. Taohuawu's New Year pictures mostly illustrated tales, and depicted cityscapes and the lives of city dwellers. They were made with chromatic wood-carving methods, and used a shading technique developed during Emperor Qianlong's time. They were realistic and brightly colored.

Yangjiabu, located in the northeast of Shandong's Wei County, saw rapidly expanding New Year picture production in the reign of Emperor Qianlong and then flourished in the reign of Emperor Tongzhi of the Qing Dynasty. Its New Year pictures mostly illustrated myths, but also included a wide variety of subjects. They are printed primarily with separate color sheet-works. The pictures were dramatic in design, had detailed and ornamental backgrounds, strongly contrasting colors, and were simple and vivid in style.

Zhuxian Town in Henan, Fengxiang in Shaanxi, Mianzhu in Sichuan, Quanzhou in Fujian, and Foshan in Guangdong also produced New Year pictures of local styles. The pictures declined in the late Qing Dynasty with the spread of Western lithography to China.

on the benefits of sketching and of accuracy in perspective. He strongly believed that the main objective of art was realism and that real life was the source of art. His other major contribution was his effort to improve Chinese traditional painting by integrating it with Western classical realism. On the other hand, he also tried to use the personal emotions from Chinese paintings in his oil works. As with Li Shutong (1880–1942), a master of poetry, calligraphy, and painting, Xu Beihong's oils had many Chinese characteristics although he used Western painting techniques; both artists were faithful to Chinese painting. For example, *Yugong Moves Mountains* and *Jiu Fang Gao* were painted with ink on Xuan paper, but Xu used real persons as models and Western techniques; both paintings inspired a tremendous interest in art after so many years of scholar painting. His paintings of galloping horses, so different from the pet horses in Han Gan's paintings, make the animals muscular and active – he was a master of anatomy.

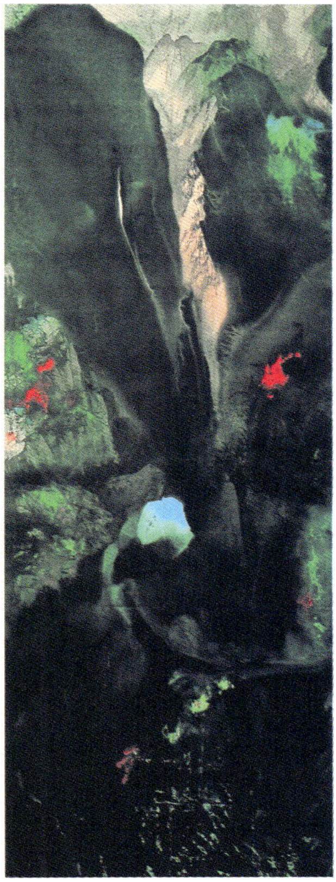

Silent Valley (1965), by Zhang Daqian (269 cm × 90 cm).

Liu Haisu went to France in the 1930s and was most interested in the Romantics and Post-Impressionists. He enthusiastically imitated Titian, Rembrandt, Delacroix, van Gogh, and Cezanne. But he embraced different schools in his later paintings and teaching. The paintings Liu Haisu did after he returned are considered masterpieces in Chinese oil painting. His splash-ink and splash-color works were the final expression of his sensitivity to painting trends and his bravery in daring to be first.

Lin Fengmian studied in fine art schools in Dijon and Paris, where he was influenced by academism, Impressionism, and Fauvism. He devoted all his life to finding a way to integrate Chinese and Western

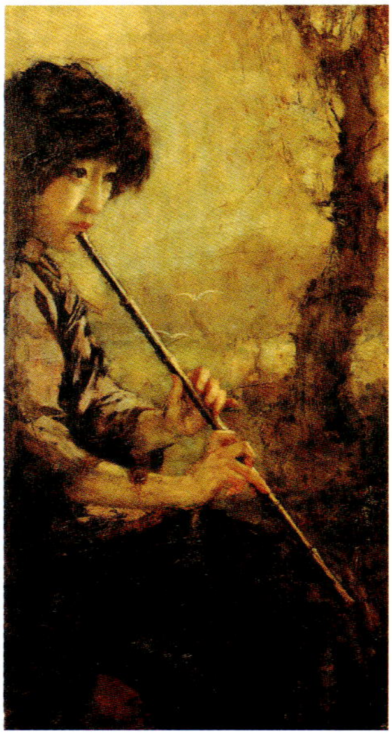

Music on a Vertical Bamboo Flute (1926), oil painting, by Xu Beihong (48 cm × 35 cm).

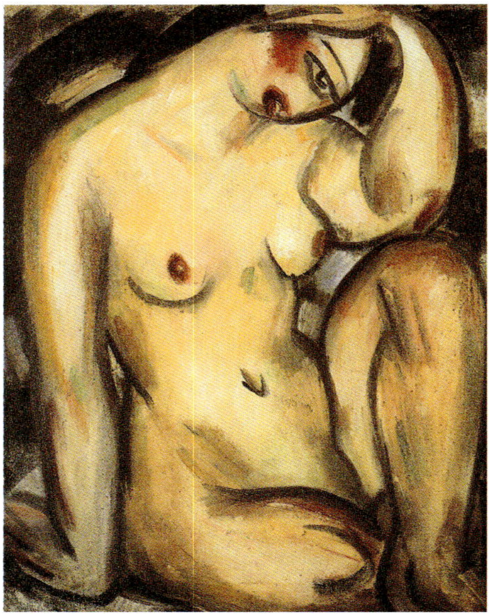

Naked Woman (1934), oil painting, by Lin Fengmian.

painting, and all his paintings could be regarded as his experiments in this regard. While most of his work in his middle and later years were painted on Xuan paper, color and form had become the theme with his paintings and elements of Western skills playing supporting roles. Almost all of his paintings used characteristic elements of Chinese paintings, such as maids from the imperial palace, characters from drama, landscape, and flowers-and-bird, the final results were an organic blend of Chinese calligraphic lines and Western formalism.

Revolutionary Realism

In 1920s and 1930s, many Chinese painters who shared a common interest formed art groups and launched various activities. Pang Xunqin (1906–1985) established the Jue Lan Society in 1932, to introduce and promote Western modern painting to the general public, and the China Independent Fine Art Association was established by Chinese students trained in Japan to promote Neorealist painting. However, both failed to make any significant impact as they were only active for a limited time and only in Shanghai. During the first national fine art exhibition in early 1929, the argument between Xu Beihong and Xu Zhimo on the assessment of Western modern painting indicated the disagreements: the former denounced Impressionism and Fauvism, calling the work of Renoir, Cezanne, and Matisse shameless, while the latter argued strongly in their favor. Judging from oil painting from that time, more painters chose to follow Impressionism, and few studied classical oil painting, and even fewer really mastered it.

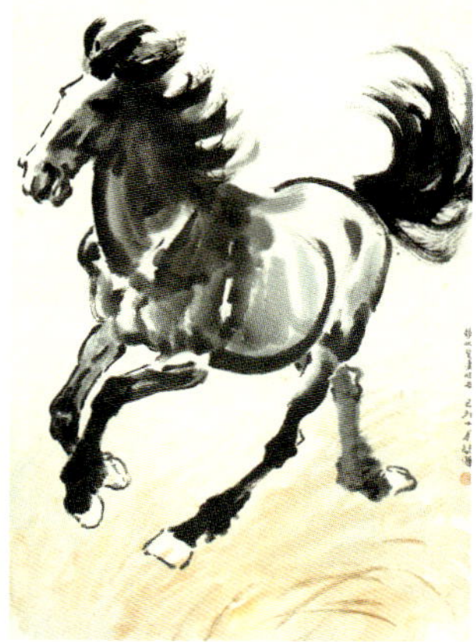

Galloping Horse (1939), ink and wash on paper, by Xu Beihong (95 cm × 68 cm), Xu Beihong Museum.

After the Japanese invasion, Chinese painters took up painting as weapons to assist the war effort, and put their artistic differences aside. The painters, like many ordinary people, often lost their homes and became refugees, going to remote areas in northwest and southwest China that were still governed by the Nationalists. Their new experiences and lifestyles inspired them to express new emotional dimensions in their work. They were accumulating ideas and experimented with new forms and movements of fine art. Many painters changed their style in order to draw propaganda in a realistic style. Xu Beihong wrote that the war against Japanese aggression promoted China's Realistic painting, and he was happy that many of the new painting movements disappeared. After Japan was defeated, Modernism emerged again. In 1945, Lin Fengmian, Ni Yide, Guan Liang, Li Zhongsheng, Yu Feng, Zhao Wuji, and Yu Yanyong held the first exhibition of the Independent Fine Art Association (but

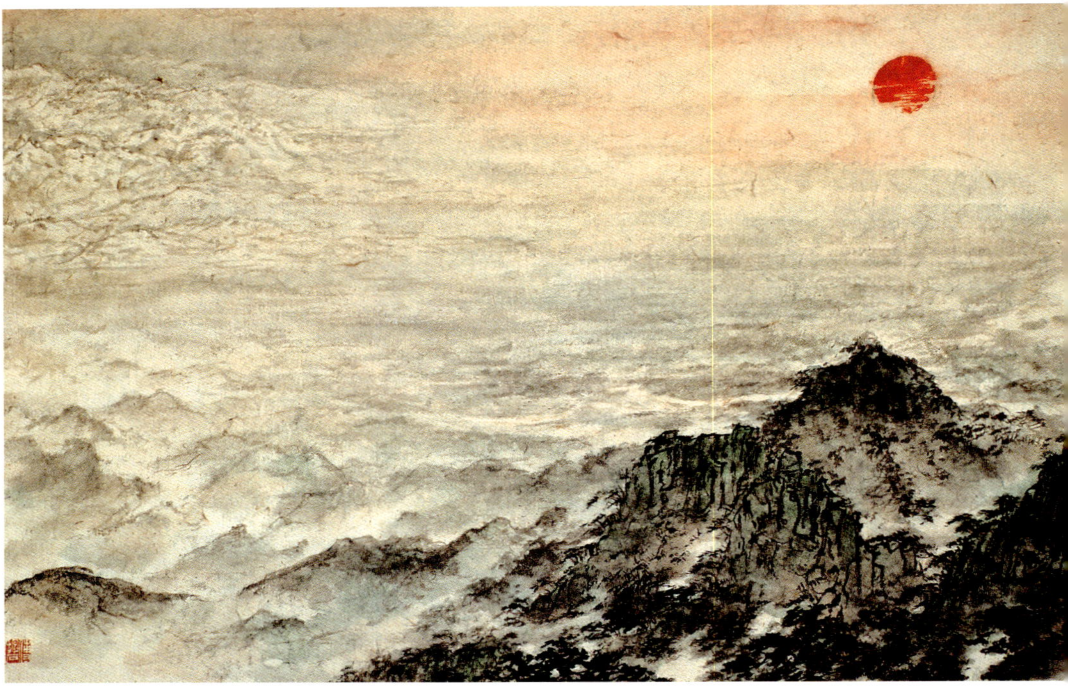

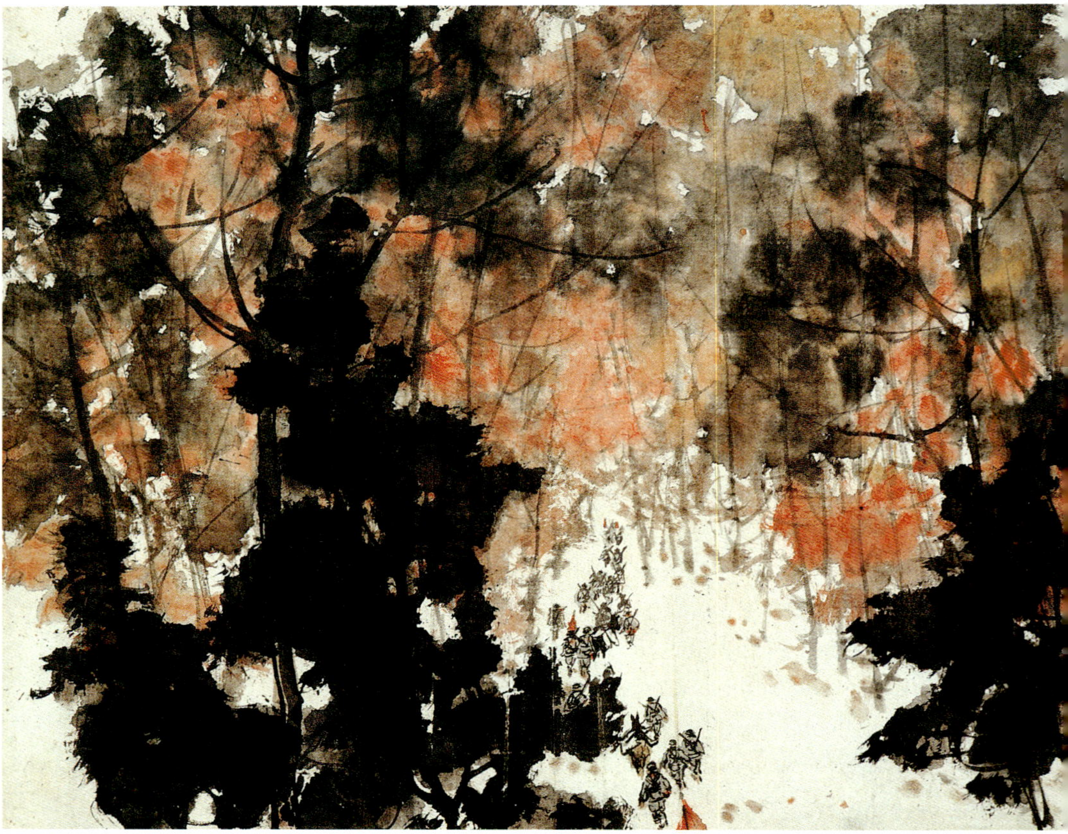

their activities stopped in 1949). Although Realism and the Taoist concept of using art to promote *Dao* had dominated the field of art, neither the traditional scholar paintings nor the Western classical style seemed to be appropriate in a time of war.

Wood engraving, which was easy to work and made for clear presentations was very popular in China from the 1920s to the 1940s. The greatest novelist and art critic in the twentieth century, Lu Xun (1881–1936) promoted it actively, and under his influence, many bright young artists gathered in Shanghai, then the cultural and artistic center of China, and devoted themselves to the New Culture Movement. The Shanghai wood engravings of the 1930s followed the Western style because of the German Expressionism promoted by Lu Xun. To many angry young Chinese painters, the paintings of the German artist Kathe Kollwitz (1867–1945) represented the voices and images of the international proletarians and revolutionists. The early works of Li Hua (1907–44), Jiang Feng (1910–82), and Huang Xinbo (1916–80) demonstrated their efforts to find an internationally and mutually understandable language. On June 2, 1932, Chundi Fine Art Institute, established by the members of Fine Artist Left-wing Alliance, held a wood-engraving exhibition in Shanghai, and German engravings collected by Lu Xun were included.

In 1942, the Chinese Communist Party leader, Mao Zedong, published his famous article, "A Lecture Note in Yan'an on Literature and Art." He proposed that literature and art should serve politics, revolution, and the war effort, and workers, peasants, and soldiers, and that literature and art were to be subject to revolutionary requirements as stipulated by the Communist Party at that time. Mao Zedong's talk exerted great influence, and spread nationwide through various channels. During the war against the Japanese invasion, many progressive intellectuals, including the left-wing wood-engraving artists in Shanghai, gathered in Yan'an. Chinese traditional painting had lost its popularity, and only a few painters painted in oil in the arduous environment of the Shaanxi Gansu Ningxia Region, which

< up *Such a Beautiful Landscape* (1959), by Fu Baoshi (65 cm × 30.2 cm), private collection.
< down *Poetical Sense of Mao Zedong* (1962), by Fu Baoshi (46.3 cm × 58.4 cm), Nanjing Museum.

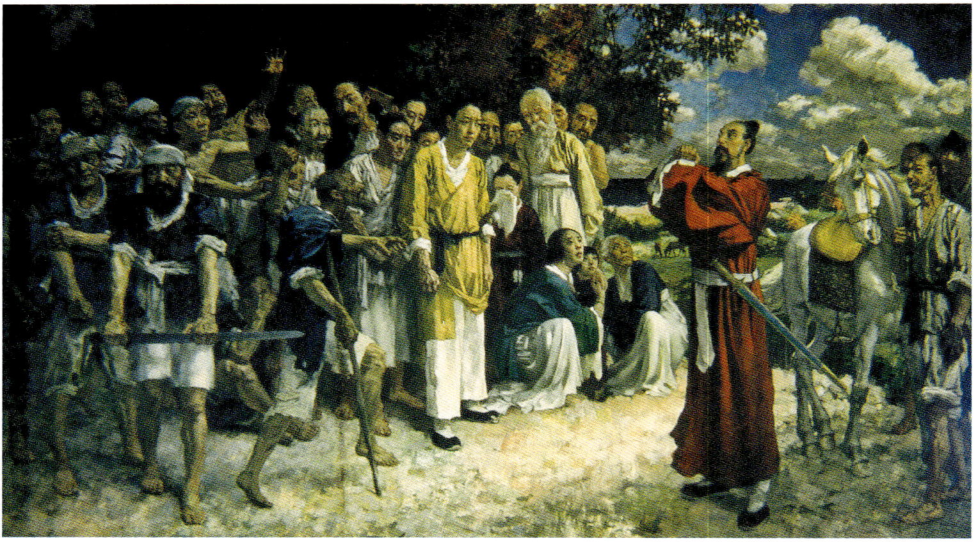

Tian Heng and Five Hundred Rebels (1928-30), oil on canvas (198 cm × 355 cm), Xu Beihong Museum.

was under the control of the Communist Party. Most painters adopted the more popular art forms that were suitable for political purposes, especially wood engravings. The artistic and political views of Lu Xun, and the Realism of Xu Beihong and his belief that "the sketch is the basis of all forms of modeling arts," were in line with Mao Zedong's art theory and became the mainstream view of arts in Yan'an. Though wood engraving became the only accepted medium, these artists believed that the past traditions and the foreign arts should serve the need of the present. Compared with the wood engravings in Shanghai in 1930s, their works were both nationalistic and more realistic.

After the war and the foundation of the People's Republic of China, painters had to deal with new issues: the relationship between art and politics; how to serve the needs of the workers, peasants, and soldiers; and how to express the lives of the common people. Realism in paintings, with an expression of idealism for depicting the themes of the new era, were very popular with painters, and the oil paintings of 1950s reflect revolutionary history and the effort to build a new China. The government selected students to go to the then Soviet

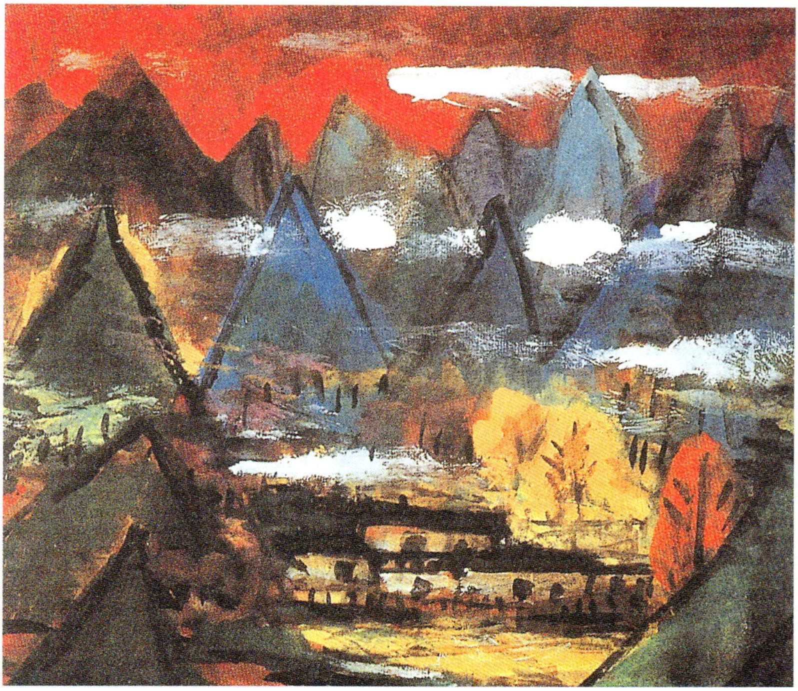

Huangshan Mountain (1980s), oil painting, by Lin Fengmian.

Union and East European socialist countries to learn painting, and also invited painters from the Soviet Union and Romania to teach at the national fine art institutes in Beijing and Hangzhou. So Chinese students learned oil-painting skills, and also accepted the painting methods of Socialist Realism, which are now seen as extreme art concepts by some, but there was an urgent need then to reform the stagnant field of art. The new society and the Chinese people had experienced great changes, and needed new visual images, and Socialist Realism successfully fufilled these needs. Artists used the optimistic and exaggerated styles of folk arts, as well as traditional art forms. This style, which was entitled "Revolutionary Romanticism," was a mixture of the heroism of a new era, Utopian intention, and petty bourgeois interest. The paintings radiated confidence, and were full of the new and traditional national characteristics.

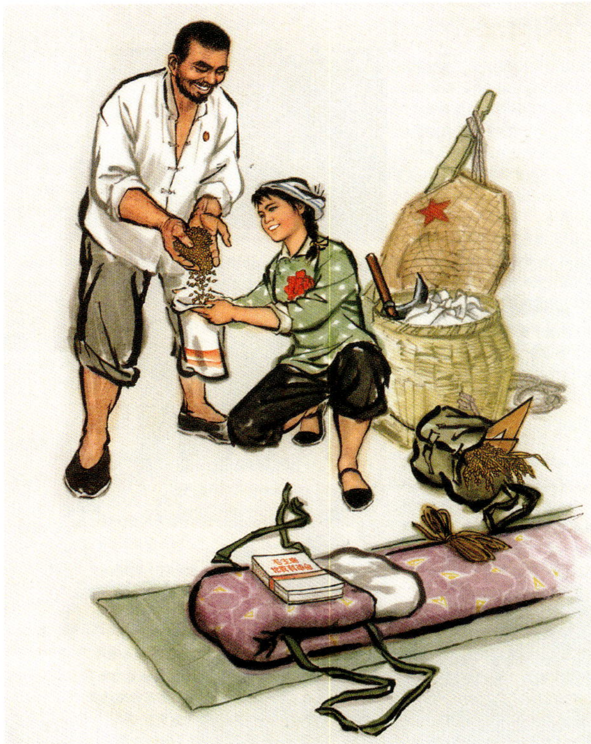

Before Going to the University (1970s), by Wen Chengzhi.

The Cultural Revolution (1966–1976) pushed the new art movement to its very limits. From the end of 1960s, eight newly adapted Peking Operas with revolutionary realism themes were imposed on society and had to be used as models not only for drama but for all other art works. This led to many paintings appearing to be similar to the stage settings of and scenes from the eight operas; in retrospect it is easy to criticize these paintings as pretentious, exaggerated, and extremely political, but still they remain art. Leaving aside the political elements, the paintings during the Cultural Revolution featured "redness, glory, and light," and constructed a new, powerful visual system, which required new skills and artistic ability. It was a unique combination of Modernism and Nationalism and can be called Socialist Realism art with

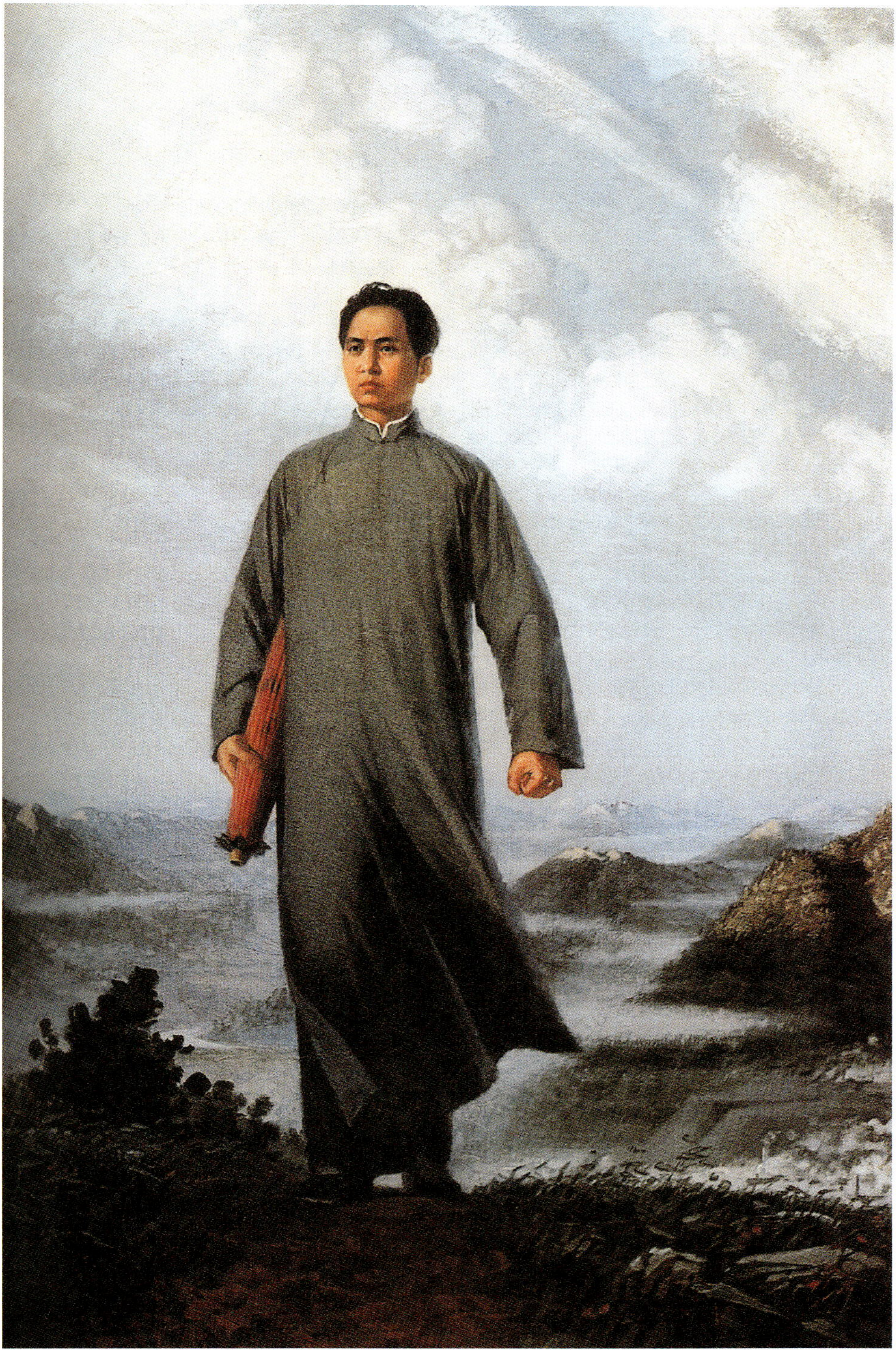

Chairman Mao's Trip to Anyuan (1967), by Liu Chunhua.

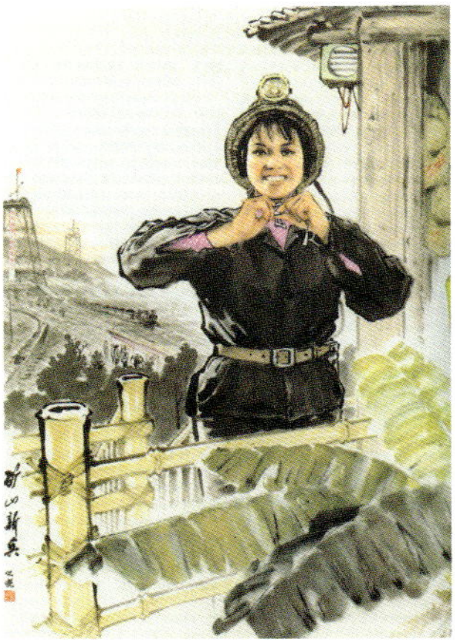
New Soldiers at the Mine (early 1970s), by Yang Zhiguang.

Chinese characteristics. The sincerity and courage the artists showed in their pursuit of art during this very difficult time are admirable.

We will examine four representative works. Dong Xiwen's oil *The Founding Ceremony of the People's Republic of China* (*Kaiguo Dadian*), Luo Gongliu's oil *Tunnel Warfare* (*Didao Zhan*), Kang Zuotian's Chinese traditional painting *Red Sun's Radiance Warms Ten Thousand Generations* (*Hongtaiyang Guanghui Nuan Wandai*), and Chen Yanning's oil *Chairman Mao Inspects Rural Areas in Guangdong* (*Maozhuxi Shicha Guangdong Nongcun*). The first two were painted in 1950s while the latter two were products of 1971 during the Cultural Revolution. *The Founding Ceremony* reproduces the scene on the Tiananmen Gate on the day when the Republic was declared. Dong was one of best painters in China and an expert on Dunhuang murals. The artist combined the realism of West paintings with the flat coloring technique of Chinese artists. *Tunnel Warfare* depicts the courage and wisdom of the Chinese people during the war against the Japanese invasion. Luo was a specialist from the era of Luxun Art School in Yan'an, and he merged revolutionist determination with Western classical oil techniques. The theme of *Red Sun's Radiance* is the contrast between past miseries and present joys. While not a traditional scholar painting, it uses Chinese traditional painting materials of Xuan paper, ink, and color. The figures are vigorous and bright, and Kang skillfully portrays life-like objects in bright sunshine, the symbol of the new society. *Chairman Mao Inspects Rural Areas in Guangdong*, of course, focuses on the chairman, but most impressive is its image of "new socialism in the countryside," especially the farmers of South China who are

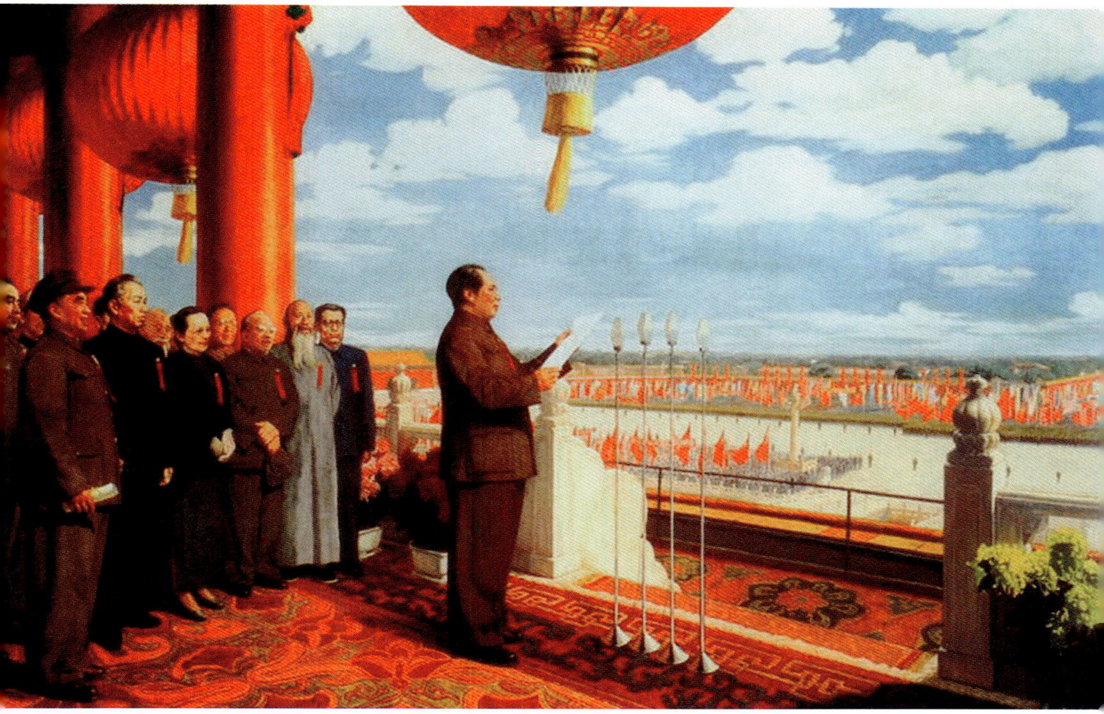

The Founding Ceremony of the People's Republic of China (1953), oil on canvas, by Dong Xi Wen (310 cm × 176 cm).

depicted. These paintings, as with all artistic products, are a part of the society to which they belong, but on the other hand, they reflect the history and development of the individual. Once completed, the art work's relationship or relevance to specific facts and the social environment is not that important, and thus, its artistic value is far more treasured than its past social contribution.

"Modern" and "Post-Modern"

In 1979, the Communist Party of China, in its Third Plenary Session of the 11th Central Committee, adopted an open-door policy and embarked on the task of leading China in the Four Modernizations, and with that China entered a new era. Its

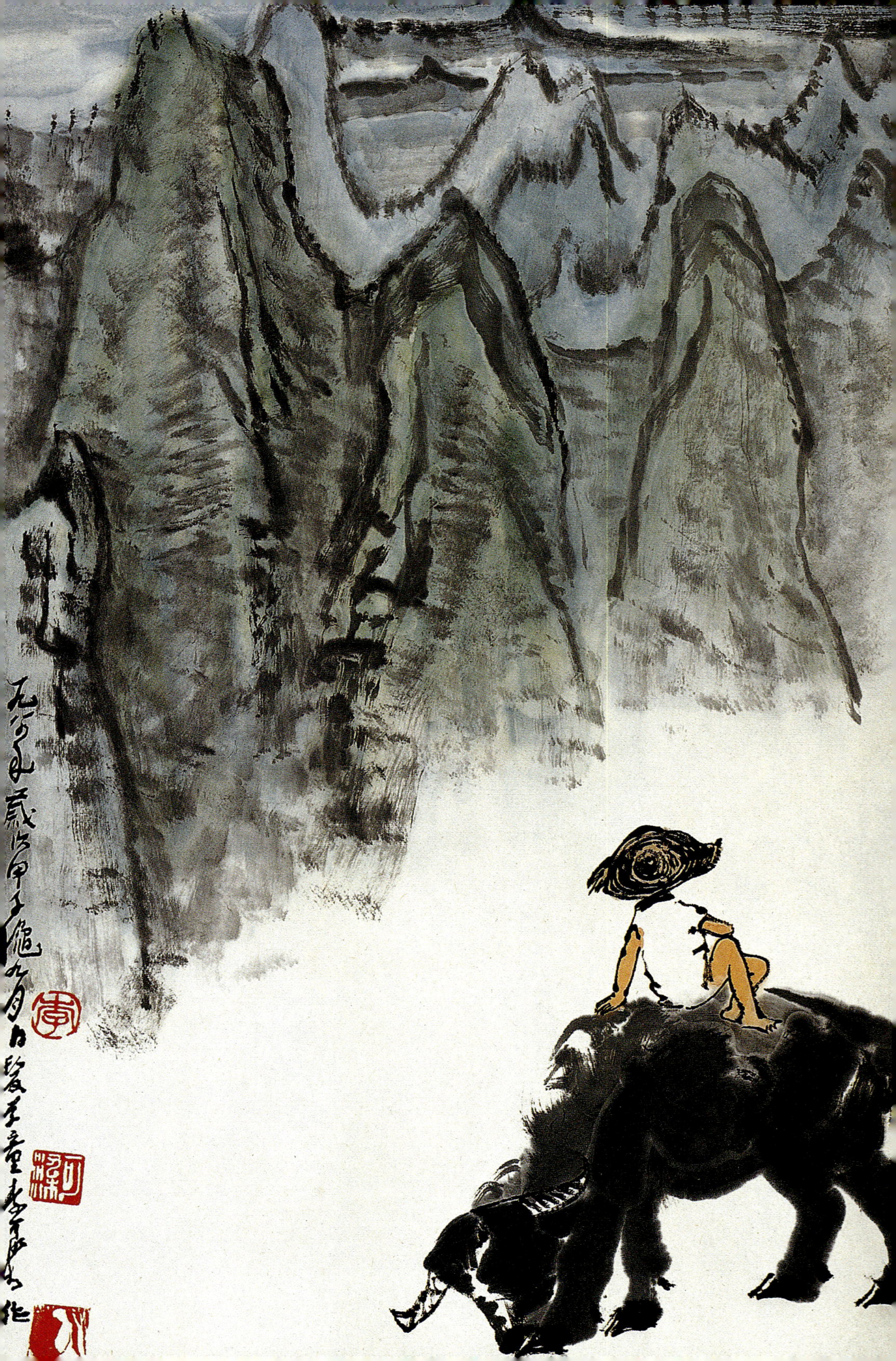

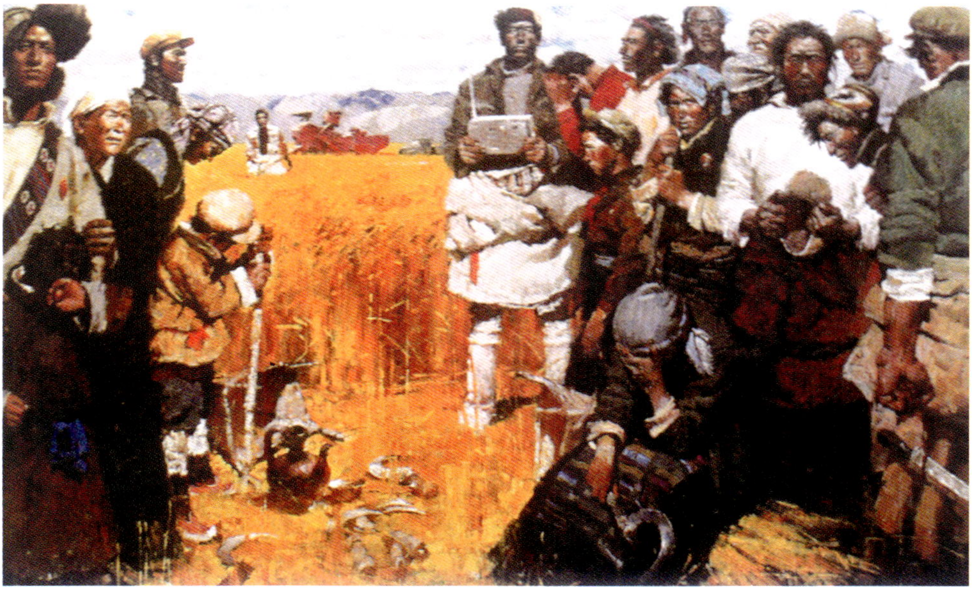

Shedding Tears over the Bumper Harvest (1976), by Chen Danqing (154 cm × 235 cm).

intellectuals and artists experienced the most relaxed academic and artistic environment since 1949. They reflected on the past and, where they had experienced social tribulation and spiritual destitution, looked beyond the borders, eager to make up for lost time and enthusiastic to find out about developments in art around the world.

The art of the new era still carried the marks of the period just ended. Familiar Realism paintings still attracted the attention of society; in particular, a group of students of the Fine Art Institute of Sichuan exhibited paintings in the early 1980s, and they caused a sensation because the work showed the Cultural Revolution as a tragedy. Though their painting skills were considered rather primitive, they modeled their work on the Exhibitionist style of Russian painters in the ninteenth century, and their narrative expressions echoed the sentiments of the public. Gao Xiaohua's painting *Snow on a Certain Day* (*Mounian Mouri Xue*) reminded people of Vasili I. Surikov's *The Morning of the Execution of the*

< *Scenery on the Mountains* (1984), by Li Keran (68.4 cm × 45.6 cm).

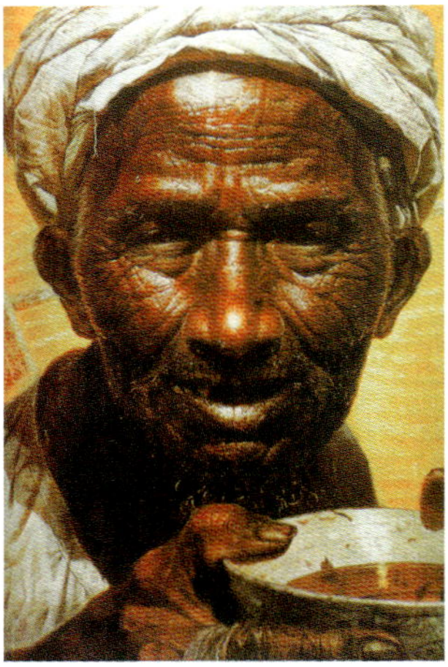

Father (1980), oil painting, by Luo Zhongli (222 cm × 115 cm), China Art Gallery.

Streltsy: only the Russian noble has been changed, to a Chinese Red Guardsman. Luo Zhongli attempted to paint a portrait of a common worker similar to that of Dong's Mao Zedong. His masterpiece *Father* (*Fuqin*) achieved great success mainly because of his innovative idea, as he stated he had been enlightened by the photographic realism popular in the United States. *Pictures of Tibet* (*Xizang Zutu*) painted by Chen Danqing of the Beijing Central Academy of Fine Art received recognition from many of his colleagues. He spent his childhood in Shanghai, once the only city in China where Western influence was accessible to ordinary people. The style of *Pictures of Tibet* can be traced back to France's Jean Franqois Millet (1814–1875) and Gustave Courbet (1819–1877). The painter was very loyal to the sketches he had made in Tibet and did not add unnecessary touches or refinements as many Chinese painters would have done.

In the following decade, innovation was a major theme. Though the Westernized modern art almost died in the 1970s and the so-called openness and creativeness were no longer big topics, China developed radical art with tremendous energy. According to the art critic Gao Minglu, social background dictated the development of art, and there was a perception that pioneering art equaled elite art. The artists completed their new Long March within a short period of time, for they experimented with the different schools of Western art and then confidently developed a style of their own. Around 1985, "Modern" art exhibitions appeared like mushrooms. Every exhibition and every artist issued a definition of Modernism, but fortunately there was no middle class to flood them with money, so they

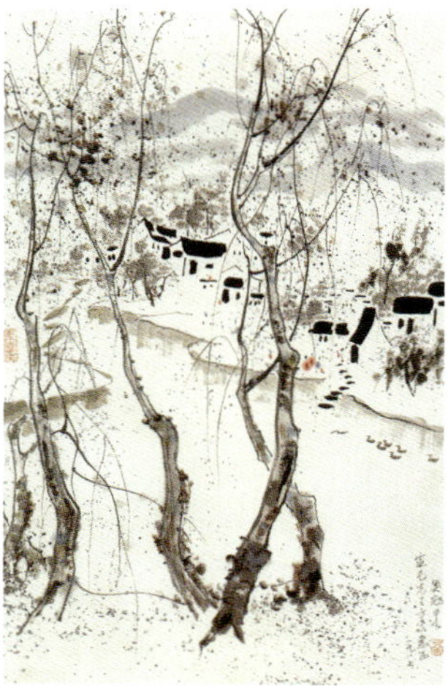

Spring South of the Yangtze River (1987), ink and wash on paper, by Wu Guanzhong (68 cm × 43 cm).

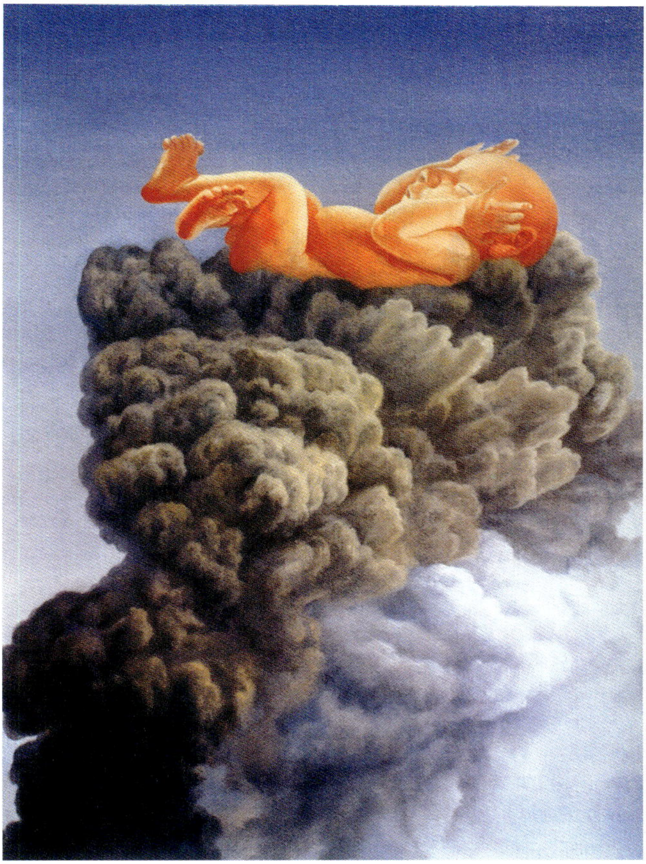

November 1, 2005 (2005), oil on canvas, by Fang Lijun.

maintained their innocent purity in art. The first All China Modern Art Exhibition held in 1989 in Beijing did not have the usual cynical atmosphere associated with "Modern" art. Even artists whose work was grotesque always claimed to be behaving responsibly and mentioned "destiny"; they were still idealists and moved from deconstruction to reconstruction.

To some artists' surprise, the symbols that highlight modern Chinese art and that can compete with both the Western and the ancient Chinese art were actually created during the Cultural Revolution. This was supported by the Venice Biennial sponsor's trip to China in 1990. Wang Guangyi's painting depicting the mass denouncement held by workers, peasants, and soldiers during the Cultural Revolution was placed together with the trademarks of Coca-Cola. Thus the visual symbols of the Mao Zedong era, including Mao's own image, became part of modern Chinese art. The Italian group took many such paintings to Venice where they were first shown to the Western world.

With the progress of China's reform and open door policy, more Chinese painters have to recognize and deal with markets and their temptation. They have compromised by continuing to use Chinese traditional painting mediums, realizing that real modern Chinese art is not a matter only of declarations and slogans, and have abandoned their efforts to look for inspiration from Modernism as a way to influence society; they work to meet the demand of the market. Their efforts to find a non-Western, pioneering art is itself a continuation of the balancing act between the West and China, modernity and tradition, and elite and popular. It is a continuing compromise.

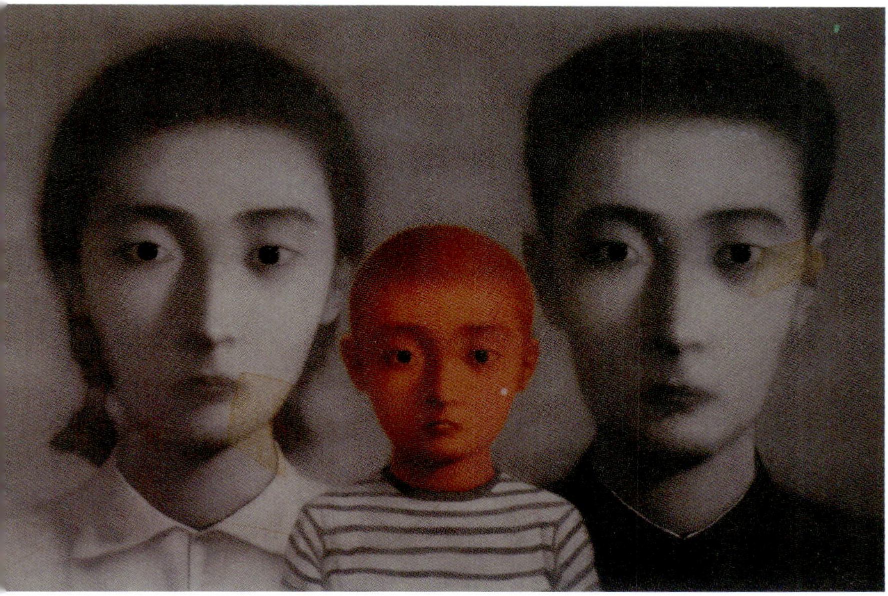

No. 1 Big Family (2001), by Zhang Xiaogang (200 cm × 300 cm).

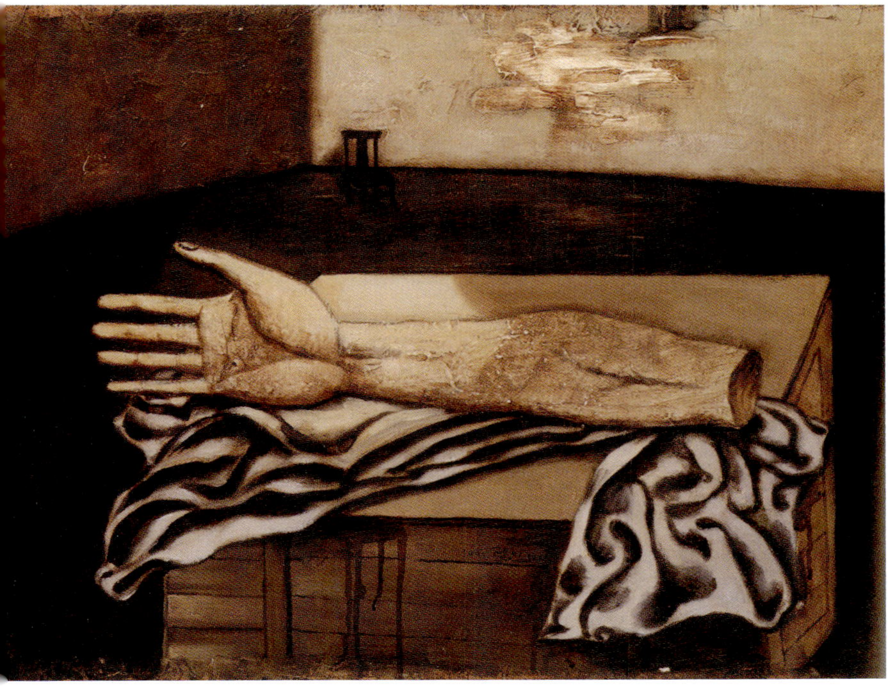

Hand, (1991), oil on canvas, by Yang Qian, (50 cm × 70 cm).

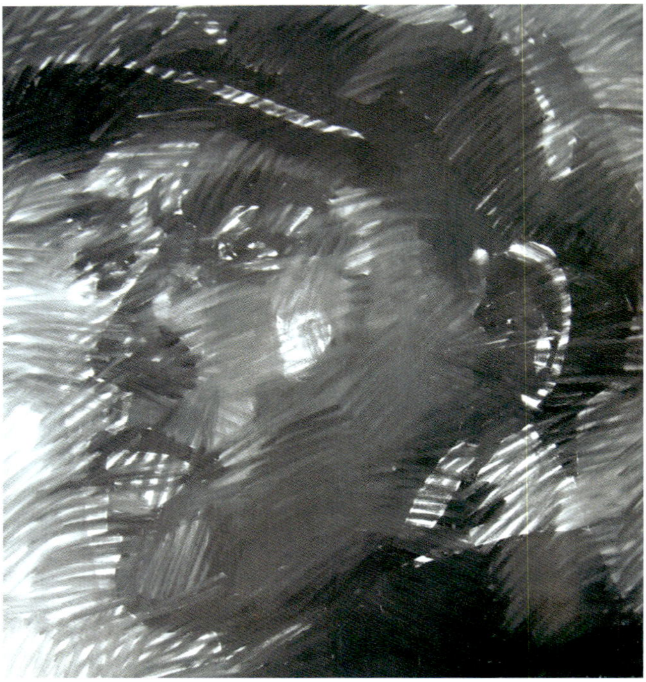

Revolutionist (2000), by Yue Minjun (75 cm × 57 cm).

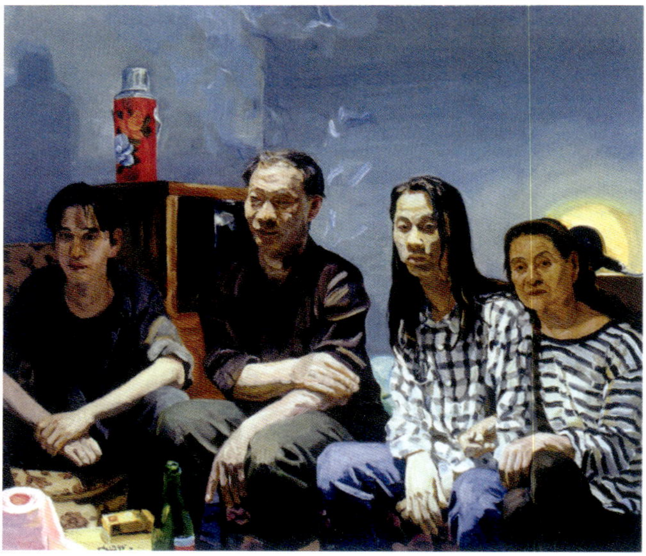

Son (1995), by Liu Xiaodong.

Appendix:
Chronological Table of the Chinese Dynasties

The Paleolithic Period	c.1,700,000–10,000 years ago
The Neolithic Period	c. 10,000–4,000 years ago
Xia Dynasty	2070–1600 BC
Shang Dynasty	1600–1046 BC
Western Zhou Dynasty	1046–771 BC
Spring and Autumn Period	770–476 BC
Warring States Period	475–221 BC
Qin Dynasty	221–206 BC
Western Han Dynasty	206 BC–AD 25
Eastern Han Dynasty	25–220
Three Kingdoms	220–280
Western Jin Dynasty	265–317
Eastern Jin Dynasty	317–420
Northern and Southern Dynasties	420–589
Sui Dynasty	581–618
Tang Dynasty	618–907
Five Dynasties	907–960
Northern Song Dynasty	960–1127
Southern Song Dynasty	1127–1276
Yuan Dynasty	1276–1368
Ming Dynasty	1368–1644
Qing Dynasty	1644–1911
Republic of China	1912–1949
People's Republic of China	Founded in 1949